Moral Issues in Special Education

Moral Issues in Special Education

An Inquiry into the Basic Rights, Responsibilities, and Ideals

Robert F. Ladenson

ROWMAN & LITTLEFIELD
Lanham • Boulder • New York • London

Published by Rowman & Littlefield
An imprint of The Rowman & Littlefield Publishing Group, Inc.
4501 Forbes Boulevard, Suite 200, Lanham, Maryland 20706
www.rowman.com

6 Tinworth Street, London SE11 5AL, United Kingdom

Copyright © 2020 by Robert F. Ladenson

All rights reserved. No part of this book may be reproduced in any form or by any electronic or mechanical means, including information storage and retrieval systems, without written permission from the publisher, except by a reviewer who may quote passages in a review.

British Library Cataloguing in Publication Information Available

Library of Congress Cataloging-in-Publication Data

Names: Ladenson, Robert F, author.
Title: Moral issues in special education : an inquiry into the basic rights, responsibilities, and ideals / Robert F. Ladenson.
Description: Lanham : Rowman & Littlefield, [2020] | Includes bibliographical references and index.
Identifiers: LCCN 2020008405 (print) | LCCN 2020008406 (ebook) | ISBN 9781475855333 (cloth) | ISBN 9781475855340 (paperback) | ISBN 9781475855357 (epub)
Subjects: LCSH: Special education—Moral and ethical aspects.
Classification: LCC LC3969 .L33 2020 (print) | LCC LC3969 (ebook) | DDC 371.9—dc23
LC record available at https://lccn.loc.gov/2020008405
LC ebook record available at https://lccn.loc.gov/2020008406

For Joanne—again and always

Contents

Preface		ix
1	Basic Moral Questions: The Need for Philosophical Analysis	1
2	The Moral Right of American Children to Receive an Appropriate K–12 Education	19
3	The Zero-Reject Policy	49
4	Inclusion, Community, and Justice	81
5	K–12 Public School Suspensions and Expulsions	107
6	Special Education Due Process Review: A Hearing Officer's Moral Responsibility	129
7	Appropriate K–12 Education for Children with Disabilites: Whose Moral Responsibility?	155
Acknowledgments		185
Index		189
About the Author		195

Preface

This book identifies and analyzes important yet insufficiently explored basic moral questions concerning K–12 special education. It represents my best efforts to think through carefully and thoroughly questions I have pondered and, in some cases, struggled with, for many years.

Special education in American K–12 public schools is shaped largely in terms of both its organization and implementation by the Individuals with Disabilities Education Act (IDEA), which is a federal statute enacted in 1975. Intense disputes have been ongoing since the IDEA was enacted that concern matters such as decisions about the content of educational programs for diverse particular children with disabilities, educational methods to address different kinds of educational disabilities, and resource allocations for K–12 special education.

My primary aim in this book is to help readers gain clearer and deeper *moral* understanding of these disputes. The chapters focus upon different issues, elucidating why difficulties in resolving them are not solely a consequence of their factual or legal complexity. To the contrary the issues also implicate in essential ways moral questions that call for interpretive reflection and judgment about the application of concepts such as happiness and unhappiness, fairness, human dignity, and freedom.

My book aims to achieve a successful combination of experience and theory. The experience comes from twenty years during which I was a special education due process hearing officer. I heard and decided cases in this position involving disputes between parents of children with disabilities and K–12 public school districts under federal and state special education laws. Each of the basic moral questions I consider in this book figured importantly in one or more of the most significant among the cases I was called upon to adjudicate.

The theory comes from the forty-three years I taught and did academic writing in the subjects of moral, political, legal, and educational philosophy as a professor of philosophy. Throughout the book I draw upon major writings, both contemporary and historical, in moral, political, legal, and educational philosophy as conceptual resources. I consider such writings invaluable for framing morally crucial questions about an issue, especially when one experiences discomfort caused by a sense that the issue may be morally problematic, and yet finds it hard to articulate the crux of the problem.

Moral understanding of controversial issues, about which disputing parties all have strong convictions and feelings, does not consist in awareness of the "morally correct" way to think about the issues. It requires instead the following two kinds of understanding. First, it calls for clear articulation of the reasons that one believes morally justify one's own viewpoint.

Second, it involves understanding from the inside viewpoints different from one's own. Such includes not only awareness of arguments advanced to support the contrary viewpoints but also understanding of why some morally conscientious and thoughtful individuals find the arguments persuasive, which in turn entails appreciating their force, at least to some extent.

Greater moral understanding in regard to intensely disputed issues in American K–12 special education could help disputing parties apprehend each other's positions more clearly (e.g., key arguments the other side presents and fundamental concerns motivating the arguments). As a corollary it also could help disputing parties understand better their own positions—both their strongest and their less than strongest arguments, from a moral standpoint, and the core moral considerations implicit in the strongest arguments.

Throughout this book I have tried to write in language that readers unfamiliar with the terminology and discourse style of academic philosophy can understand, and always to make it apparent why and how particular philosophical points bear upon basic moral questions in American K–12 special education. I have not attempted coverage of every controversy in American K–12 special education with significant moral dimensions. My aim instead is to help readers gain a heightened awareness of the relevance, depth, and complexities of basic moral issues that underlie the most important and longest standing of these controversies.

Throughout this book I have often stated or implied my own conclusions or viewpoints. In every such instance, however, my objective has been to open or to further discussion rather than to close it. I hope that sharing the results of these efforts with thoughtful readers will further moral understanding in regard to the ongoing intensely disputed issues in American K–12 special education.

Chapter 1

Basic Moral Questions
The Need for Philosophical Analysis

Nearly six and one-half million children receive special education in American K–12 public schools, as estimated by the U.S. Department of Education.[1] Their educational programs are shaped, to a great extent, by the provisions of a federal statute, the Individuals with Disabilities Education Act (IDEA), which was enacted in 1975 and went into effect in 1978.[2]

Congress enacted the IDEA to address the inadequacy of educational services for children with special educational needs. The congressional findings section prefacing the IDEA states that prior to its enactment "the educational needs of millions of children with disabilities were not being fully met because the children did not receive appropriate educational resources . . . were excluded entirely from public school and from being educated with their peers . . . [or] undisclosed disabilities prevented them from having a successful educational experience."[3]

Under the IDEA states may receive federal financial support for K–12 public school special education programs provided that a free appropriate public education (FAPE), implemented "to the maximum extent appropriate" in the "least restrictive environment," is made available to every child eligible for services.[4] The IDEA sets forth a comprehensive and detailed legal framework of rules and regulations concerning education in K–12 public schools for children with disabilities, which a state receiving IDEA funds must assure are complied with by school districts. All fifty states have opted for IDEA funding.

In the early twentieth century—when special education programs were initiated in American K–12 public schools—and for more than a half-century afterward, the inclination to stigmatize, shun, and/or marginalize children with disabilities was both widely prevalent and strong throughout American society.[5]

In this social environment parents frequently placed their children with disabilities in institutions; there, with only a small number of exceptions, a child at best received custodial care with no effort made to educate him or her and at worst suffered grave abuse and/or severe neglect.[6]

Throughout the first half of the twentieth century, special education programs grew and developed in American K–12 public schools. Many of the educators involved viewed themselves as participating in an effort to create a vastly preferable alternative, both educationally and morally, to "putting away" children with disabilities.[7]

Many consider enactment of the IDEA in 1975 a major moral achievement.[8] However, as with the similarly regarded 1964 Civil Rights Act (to which the IDEA is at times compared), controversial, complex, and difficult-to-resolve issues have emerged since the IDEA's provisions went into effect in 1978. The IDEA has severe critics who contend that these issues indicate grave moral flaws at the IDEA's core and crucial ways in which special education in American K–12 public schools has gone irretrievably off the rails under the IDEA framework.

Unsurprisingly, advocates for children with disabilities and their families reject the above viewpoint unequivocally. Among these advocates are several spokespersons for organizations that played a key role in moving Congress to enact the IDEA. Such advocates affirm with great force and conviction that, to the contrary, American children with disabilities have a moral right to receive special education in K–12 public schools, and that the IDEA has played an indispensable role in effectuating this right.

The first section of this introductory chapter summarizes important provisions of the IDEA which give rise to the principal disputed issues between severe critics of K–12 special education under the IDEA (hereinafter, "the severe critics") and advocates for children with disabilities and their families (hereinafter, "the advocates"). The second section identifies the principal disputed issues and summarizes the respective positions of the severe critics and the advocates with regard to these issues.

The third section sets forth six morally basic questions for special education in American K–12 public schools. Without addressing these questions, it is impossible to frame a non-question-begging, let alone plausible, position on any of the key points of disagreement between the severe critics and the advocates regarding K–12 special education for children with disabilities under the IDEA.

The fourth section provides a summary of the topics to be considered in the chapters that follow (chapters 2 through 7). Each chapter focuses on one of the six morally basic questions identified in the third section. The discussions in each chapter apply concepts drawn from major works of moral, political, legal, and educational philosophy.

THE IDEA

As noted above, under the IDEA states receive financial support for special education programs provided they assure that every student eligible for services receives a FAPE, implemented "to the maximum extent appropriate" in the "least restrictive environment."

The IDEA, as also noted above, outlines extensive procedures that states accepting funds under the Act must assure are followed by school districts. For example, school districts must initiate efforts to identify every child among those they serve who may have special educational needs. Having identified such students, school districts must then decide in each case whether to conduct a full-scale evaluation to determine that child's eligibility for services.

The IDEA provides an extensive range of parents' rights with regard to the evaluation process when a school district decides to conduct a full-scale evaluation. If an evaluated child is found eligible to receive special education, then a school district must develop an Individualized Educational Plan (IEP) through conference meetings of teachers and school staff who will implement the student's plan. The IDEA requires that an eligible student's parents be invited to participate in the IEP conference meeting.

Under the IDEA, states that accept funds must establish an administrative review process which enables parents to challenge any decision of a school district where they disagree concerning "identification, evaluation, or educational placement of the child or provision of a free appropriate public education to [the] child."[9] The parents' challenge takes place before an impartial hearing officer in a proceeding referred to in the IDEA as an "impartial due process hearing." The IDEA gives parents (and school districts as well) a right to appeal a due process hearing officer's decision in federal or state court.

The IDEA sets forth extensive rights, both substantive and procedural, for children with disabilities with regard to school discipline; the most important of these concern long-term suspensions and expulsions.[10]

If a child with a disability has been suspended for ten days in the course of a school year, the district must conduct a special meeting before any further day of suspension may be imposed. This meeting will determine whether or not the infraction giving rise to the contemplated next (eleventh) day of suspension was a manifestation of the child's disability.

If decided in the affirmative, then a functional analysis (an inquiry into the circumstances tending to trigger the child's unacceptable behavior) must be done and a behavioral intervention plan put in place if one has not already been developed and implemented. When a child already has a behavioral intervention plan, it must be modified appropriately or replaced if necessary.

If a child is determined to be a danger to himself or others, he may be placed in an interim alternative educational setting for up to forty-five days before returning to his prior educational placement or to a new placement decided upon for him. Parents who want to challenge a school district's decision concerning removal of their child to an interim alternative educational setting have a right to a hearing presided over by an impartial hearing officer. The hearing officer's decision may be appealed in either federal or state court.

The passage by Congress of the IDEA in 1975 was preceded in 1972 by two landmark court cases: *Pennsylvania Association for Retarded Children v. Commonwealth of Pennsylvania (PARC)* and *Mills v. Board of Education of the District of Columbia (Mills)*.[11] *PARC* involved a statute allowing the Commonwealth of Pennsylvania to deny educational services to mentally retarded children. In *Mills* the Board of Education of the District of Columbia claimed that owing to lack of funds it had a right to exclude from public schooling a broad class of students, including children with behavioral problems, emotional disturbances, and hyperactivity.

In *PARC* and *Mills* the respective courts found the denials of services to the students at issue violated the students' equal protection and due process rights under the Fourteenth Amendment of the U.S. Constitution. The defendants in both cases (the Commonwealth of Pennsylvania in *PARC* and the Board of Education of the District of Columbia in *Mills*) signed consent decrees giving every child within the disability categories involved the right to a free, appropriate public education; these consent decrees also established a range of due process protections.

Judicial decisions following enactment of the IDEA have established firmly that the severity of a child's disability does not qualify as a legally justified basis for denying the child coverage under the IDEA. In another landmark case, *Timothy H. v. Rochester, New Hampshire, School District*, a school district argued that a student's disabilities were so severe that he could not benefit from an education and therefore the school district was not required under the IDEA to provide a special education program for him.[12]

In rejecting the school district's position, the U.S. Court of Appeals for the First Circuit stated emphatically that "[t]he language of the Act in its entirety makes clear that *a 'zero-reject' policy is at the core of the Act*" (emphasis added).[13]

The most critical issue for legal interpretation of the IDEA concerns how to understand what the word "appropriate" means in the context of a special needs student's right to a FAPE. This question was addressed in the following words of the U.S. Supreme Court in the case of *Board of Education of the Hendrik Hudson School District v. Rowley (Rowley)*:

> Insofar as a State is required to provide a handicapped child with a "free appropriate public education" we hold that it satisfies this requirement by providing personalized instruction with sufficient supporting services to permit the child

to benefit educationally from that instruction. Such instruction and services must be provided at public expense, must meet the State's educational standards, must approximate the grade levels used in regular education and must comport with the child's IEP. In addition, the IEP, and therefore the personalized instruction should be formulated in accordance with the requirements of the Act and if the child is being educated in the regular classroom of the public education system, should be reasonably calculated to enable the child to achieve passing marks and advance from grade to grade.[14]

The Supreme Court did not set forth any specific standards in *Rowley* for deciding whether the education a child with disabilities receives permits him or her to "benefit educationally." The Court made it clear, however, that a school district need only satisfy a distinctly limited standard for the educational services it provides a student. In this regard the Court said,

> By passing the [IDEA], Congress sought primarily to make public education available to handicapped children. But in seeking to provide such access to public education, Congress did not impose any greater substantive standard than would be necessary to make such access meaningful. Indeed, Congress expressly recognized that in many instances the process of providing special education and related services is not guaranteed to produce any particular outcome. Thus, the intent of the [IDEA] was more to open the door to public education to handicapped children on appropriate terms than to guarantee any level of education once inside.[15]

As for the "least-restrictive-environment" (LRE) requirement of the IDEA, the Act expressly mandates that "special classes, separate schooling, or other removal from the regular education environment occur only when the nature or severity of the disability of a child is such that education in a regular classroom with the use of supplementary aids and services cannot be achieved satisfactorily."[16]

When disagreements arise about whether education of a child with disabilities "cannot be achieved satisfactorily" in the regular education environment, a crucial question remains: What are the proper legal standards to employ for resolving such disagreements? Although several circuits of the U.S. Court of Appeals have addressed this question, the U.S. Supreme Court has not done so.[17]

POSITIONS OF SEVERE CRITICS AND RESPONSES OF ADVOCATES

Special education, shaped closely in terms of its implementation framework by rules and regulations of the IDEA, has come to occupy an important place over the past several decades in American K–12 public schools. Despite this fact, special education has severe critics who condemn it as (1) unfair, (2) educationally ineffective, and (3) the principal cause of divisive and dysfunctional relationships between families of children with disabilities and public school districts.

Apropos the charge of unfairness, severe critics identify two concerns as most troubling. First, educational progress of children with disabilities is often limited as compared with other students and also, in some cases, can be extremely expensive. For example, educating a child with severe intellectual disabilities requires, in most cases, (1) a special education teacher, (2) a one-on-one aide, (3) the services of an inclusion specialist to help incorporate regular education inclusion into the child's educational program "to the maximum extent appropriate," and (4) diverse related services personnel as needed (e.g., a speech and language therapist, an occupational or physical therapist).

Furthermore, in the case of any child with a disability, if the child's disabilities pose significant educational issues the school district is not able to address, then it must bear the often-costly expense of an out-of-district placement.

Does not fairness thus require, ask the severe critics, redistributing public expenditures for K–12 public education so that much of the portion now devoted to educating children with severe intellectual disabilities would go to help other students with great educational needs, but also greater likelihood of benefiting from the expenditures? An obvious group to target in this regard, say the severe critics, would be low-achieving regular education children in poverty.[18]

The second problem area related to unfairness for the severe critics concerns the extensive provisions of the IDEA, summarized in section I, regarding discipline. The IDEA imposes significant limitations of both a procedural and substantive nature upon school discipline of children with disabilities which do not apply to regular education students.[19] Attempting to apply disciplinary measures in compliance with these limitations, the severe critics object, is both time consuming and—in some instances—expensive.

Given the unavoidably frequent subjective judgments involved when deciding whether the limitations are applicable in specific cases, say the severe critics, differential disciplinary treatment for students with disabilities can generate strong feelings of resentment on the part of nondisabled students and their families about disruptive classroom behavior.[20]

To this point, severe critic Mark Kelman writes, "[T]here are many cases in which emotionally and behaviorally disordered children have proven disruptive, even when mainstream teachers are tolerant, supportive, and adequately assisted by special education aides. . . . [A] high level of integration may well improve the educational experience of disabled children, but harm nondisabled children."[21]

Apropos (2) in the list of criticisms above—that special education often is ineffective—the severe critics direct their most intense attention to the least-restrictive-environment mandate of the IDEA. This mandate calls for education of children with disabilities in the regular education classroom "to the maximum extent appropriate." The following words of severe critic Miriam Kurtzig Freedman express a common stance of the severe critics in this connection:

> The [IDEA] promotes inclusion as a civil right, in spite of weak data supporting it as an educational "best practice" for many SWD [students with disabilities] for improved educational results in many situations. . . . To make inclusion work schools often provide paraprofessionals (or one to one aides), accommodations or modifications, co-teaching, and other approaches to maintain the child in a classroom. Such procedures are often provided even when there is scant or nonexistent evidence that they actually improve learning for SWD and are not detrimental to other students.[22]

Another severe critic, Robert Worth, puts the above point bluntly, saying, "Parents of severely disabled kids . . . regularly try to shoehorn them into mainstream classes, even when it would do little good for the child and plenty of harm to the rest of the class."[23]

As for point (3) in their critique, the severe critics object that the IDEA's mandated procedural safeguards have fostered an adversarial climate in which parents feel compelled to advocate for their children against their schools. In this climate, say the severe critics, educators focus more on process compliance than on improving educational performance of children.[24] The IDEA's procedural safeguards, in the severe critics' opinion, have resulted in an educational system "built upon mistrust between parents and schools [which] is unwise and not sustainable."[25]

Given their witheringly negative assessments of special education in American K–12 public schools on the combined grounds of unfairness, ineffectiveness, and divisiveness, many severe critics would agree that, in the words of Miriam Kurtzig Freedman, the time has come "to consider ending the entitlement status of IDEA."[26]

IDEA advocates dissent emphatically from the calls of the severe critics to end the entitlement status of the Act, rejecting the position of the severe critics thoroughly and unequivocally. With regard to the charge of unfairness summarized above, the following two replies could address, respectively, the severe critics' complaints of excessive expense and excessively protective procedural safeguards for children with disabilities.

First, the greatest per pupil expenditures generally involve children with severe intellectual disabilities and/or severe physical disabilities with adverse effects upon the ability to learn. High expenditure levels are often needed in such cases for the children to have any meaningful education at all. The sole alternative is custodial care, and not education.

Second, apropos the extensive procedural safeguards related to school discipline of children with disabilities, one needs to acknowledge the high correlation between long-term school expulsions, on the one hand (followed by motivation-destroying academic failure), and/or rejection by peers, on the other hand. Further, such situations often lead to dropping out of school, social isolation, and/or depression, resulting in tragically diminished life chances.

In response to the complaint of ineffectiveness, the advocates would say the severe critics' disparagement of inclusion completely misses the most important point in its favor. Inclusion, they would say, aims to avoid, or prevent, grievous harms of exclusion, which the severe critics either ignore or badly underestimate. The advocates might cite as illustrative in this regard the following recollections offered by Jonathan Mooney. (He is looking back in young adulthood at the impact upon him, in third grade, of removal from his regular education class for reading instruction in a resource room):

> Even Mr. R. (Mooney's 3rd grade regular classroom teacher) couldn't stop the snide embarrassing looks my classmates gave me every time I left to go to the resource room.... Sometimes for cruel fun kids would ask me what room I was going to even though they knew.... They wouldn't wait for an answer but just laughed and called me stupid.[27]

The advocates would say they could cite many more examples similar to the above. But they would insist that doing so is unnecessary to underscore the irreparable damage that exclusionary educational practices can often cause to a child's self-confidence, sense of self-esteem, and motivation to learn. The same kinds of damage, the advocates would acknowledge, result inevitably when children with disabilities are placed without appropriate support into regular education classes. That is why, the advocates would point out, the IDEA's least-restrictive-environment mandate calls for provision of "appropriate" "supplementary aids and services."

Furthermore, the advocates maintain that when such are provided, inclusion of children with disabilities in regular education classrooms need not diminish the education of nondisabled students and even has the potential to enrich it in transformative ways. Apropos the latter, strong commitment to regular classroom inclusion by K–12 public school districts throughout the United States, say the advocates, could catalyze far-reaching, lifelong changes in prevailing attitudes and behavior of nondisabled persons toward individuals with disabilities. Such attitudinal change, the advocates insist, would make American society both more just and more kind.

Finally, the advocates would disagree categorically with the severe critics' view that the right for parents of a child with a disability to challenge educational decisions concerning their child at a due process hearing (under the IDEA) has resulted in a system based upon mistrust between parents and school districts. The advocates would counter this view by noting that trust in the system requires the confidence of everyone involved that the system is fair. In this regard, the advocates would contend, the IDEA's procedural safeguard of a right to due process is indispensable to uphold the moral right of American children with disabilities to receive an appropriate K–12 public education—a right they possess no less than do nondisabled students.

THE MORALLY BASIC QUESTIONS

The attitudes of many—if not most—people about special education in American K–12 public schools tend to lie uneasily between the polar opposite positions of the severe critics and the advocates as summarized above. On the one hand, the widespread stigmatizing and shunning that faced children with disabilities and their families well into the twentieth century has been substantially replaced—compared with years past—by empathetic awareness of the immense problems they confront. Many, though by no means all, people agree that those children with disabilities have a moral right, like all other children, to receive an appropriate K–12 education.[28]

On the other hand, there also is widespread recognition of the following points: The costs of educating children with disabilities, in some instances, can be very high and the educational progress of the children, compared with nondisabled peers, in many cases is small. Furthermore, the presence of children with disabilities in a regular education class often poses difficult issues with regard to allocation of educational resources, especially teacher time. As with all American K–12 public schooling, taxpayers must cover all the costs.

For the above reasons, many people don't fully and clearly understand the rationales for practices, methods, and goals central to special education and incorporated in the IDEA. Prime examples in this connection are the zero-reject policy, the least-restrictive-environment mandate, the strict requirements and limitations regarding discipline of children with disabilities, and the IDEA's extensive procedural safeguards (especially the right of parents to challenge a school district's placement decision in a due process hearing).

Six morally basic questions raised by the disagreement between the severe critics of special education in American K–12 public schools and advocates for children with disabilities and their families are set forth below. No one—whether severe critic, advocate, or anyone else—has articulated all these questions clearly. And no one has analyzed them carefully and deeply enough for an adequate exploration.

(1) Do all American children, including children with disabilities, have a moral right to receive an appropriate K–12 education?
   (a) If the answer is "yes" then what are the justifying reasons?
   (b) If the answer is that no American child with a disability has a moral right to receive an appropriate K–12 education, then what are the reasons that justify this conclusion?
   (c) If the answer is that some, but not all, American children with disabilities have such a moral right then which children have it, which do not, and, in both cases, why?
(2) Is the zero-reject policy (under which a child with a disability is assured a free appropriate K–12 education under the IDEA regardless of the nature or extent of her/his disability) morally justified? If so, why? If not, why not?
(3) Do American children with disabilities have a moral right to inclusion in K–12 regular education classes and school activities?
   (a) If so, then (i) why?, (ii) does this moral right have limits?, (iii) if so, then what is their nature and moral justification?
   (b) If American children with disabilities do not have a moral right to K–12 regular education inclusion, then why not?
(4) Are the IDEA's procedural safeguards regarding school discipline of children with disabilities morally justified? If so, why? If not, why not?
(5) Are the IDEA's due process review procedures morally justified?
   (a) If so, then (i) why? and (ii) what is the basic moral responsibility of a special education due process hearing officer?
   (b) If not, then why not?
(6) What are the basic moral responsibilities relative to K–12 special education of American children with disabilities of (a) lawmakers, (b) K–12 public school educators, and (c) parents of children with disabilities?

One cannot set aside the above six questions on the ground that they concern abstract, theoretical matters of interest only to philosophers of education and moral philosophers. To the contrary, all six questions require clear and, to the extent possible, precise answers if one construes the dispute between the severe critics and the advocates as, at bottom, about *moral* issues.

Costly expenditures for the K–12 public education of a given child with a disability are morally justified if (a) they are essential for providing the kind of K–12 education to which the child has a moral right and (b) such expenditures do not prevent other students (both nondisabled and children with disabilities) from receiving the kind of K–12 education to which they have a moral right.

Doubts about the educational effectiveness of particular instructional methods in special education (e.g., inclusion of children with disabilities in regular education classrooms) raise *morally relevant* concerns only if the effectiveness in doubt relates to attainment of goals entailed by the *moral right* of children with disabilities to receive an appropriate K–12 education. The IDEA's extensive limitations and restrictions upon school discipline of children with disabilities are *morally unjustified* only if not essential for upholding the children's *moral right* to receive an appropriate K–12 education.

If the procedural safeguards of the IDEA have resulted in divisiveness, such is *morally objectionable* only if it could have been avoided in a *morally justified* way. Such divisiveness would not be *morally objectionable* if it resulted unavoidably from parents' efforts to claim the *moral rights* of their children with disabilities to receive an appropriate K–12 education. The respective moral responsibilities of lawmakers, K–12 public school educators, and parents of children with disabilities apropos the children's K–12 education encompass diverse kinds of effort—which are all essential for providing the kind of education to which these children have a moral right.

None of the issues in dispute between the severe critics and the advocates is easily separable from the six basic moral questions identified above concerning special education in American K–12 public schools. Nonetheless, both the severe critics and the advocates seldom address the questions explicitly (or even implicitly), and rarely at the level of depth required.

Severe critics, for example, frequently dismiss assertions of the advocates that key entitlements under the IDEA are indispensable for giving legal effect to the moral rights of children with disabilities concerning K–12 public education. They view these assertions as badly misplaced civil libertarian rhetoric. In the same vein, however, advocates often brush aside the concerns of the severe critics about expense, unfairness, educational ineffectiveness, and divisiveness as failures to take seriously the moral right of children with disabilities to receive an appropriate K–12 education.

Characteristically absent on either side is an adequate analysis of the six basic moral questions identified above. Each side would need to set forth such an analysis in order to justify its thoroughgoing rejection of the other side's stance.

However, the absence does not appear to stem entirely or even primarily from either obstinate refusal or failure to consider, in the heat of impassioned disagreement, the basic moral questions. A serious effort to address these questions leads quickly to complex and philosophically deep issues; these involve interpretive controversy over understanding and application of such concepts as happiness/unhappiness, justice, human dignity, and freedom relative to education of children with disabilities.

Ordinarily, neither diverse professionals in special education nor parents of children with disabilities and their advocates are well attuned to these issues, so despite their moral centrality the issues hover in the background unaddressed. The chapters that follow, summarized briefly below, thus deal with the basic moral questions for special education in American K–12 public schools in a focused, sustained, and philosophically informed way.

OVERVIEW OF CHAPTERS 2 THROUGH 7

Chapter 2 has two principal components. First, it sets forth an analysis of an appropriate K–12 education which applies to a group referred to in the chapter as "Group A." Group A consists of the following members: (1) all American children who are nondisabled and (2) all American children who are eligible for special education under the IDEA definition of a "child with a disability," except for children with severe or profound intellectual disabilities (referred to in chapter 2 as "Group B").

Under this analysis an appropriate K–12 education for children in Group A has two prongs. It must be reasonably calculated to help children acquire knowledge and develop abilities required (1) to exercise rights, fulfill responsibilities, and exemplify ideals of membership in the American democratic body politic and (2) to have a reasonable chance for success in seeking the basic human good of self-fulfillment.

The second principal component of chapter 2 is an account that seeks to justify the conclusion that children in Group A have a moral right to receive an appropriate K–12 education, understood in terms of the above two-pronged analysis. The account consists of four arguments for this conclusion, each proceeding from the standpoint of a different major philosophical theory; each major theory differs from the other three in the concept it takes as central to the idea of social justice. The four theories, paired with the respective concepts they take as central to the idea of social justice, are as follows:

1. utilitarianism—happiness and avoidance of unhappiness;
2. Rawlsian Justice as fairness—fairness;
3. capabilities account of social justice—human dignity; and
4. moderate libertarianism—liberty (freedom).

All four of the arguments developed are highly plausible. That is to say, each argument could be found persuasive by a large group of reasonable and thoughtful persons. A persuasive argument need not establish its conclusion beyond a reasonable doubt. Instead, it sets forth considerations that call for careful reflection; this shifts the burden of persuasion to the other side of the issue by requiring a thoughtful, considered response.

To summarize, the application of different major philosophical theories of social justice, with differing conceptual cores, produces an overlapping consensus. Such consensus, accordingly, provides a persuasive justification of the judgment that American children in Group A have a moral right to receive an appropriate K–12 education, understood in terms of the two-pronged analysis.

Chapter 3 first sets forth an analysis of an appropriate K–12 education for children in Group B—that is, for children with severe or profound intellectual disabilities. According to that analysis, a K–12 education for a child with a severe or profound intellectual disability condition is appropriate if and only if it is reasonably calculated to foster significant development of central human capabilities relevant in the child's case, given the particular aspects of his/her disability condition.

Chapter 3 then develops a justification of the judgment that all children in Group B have a moral right to receive an appropriate K–12 education in the sense specified immediately above. The justification follows the same strategy of argument utilized in chapter 2. Four arguments are presented to support the judgment, from the respective standpoints of utilitarianism, Rawlsian Justice as fairness, the capabilities account of social justice, and moderate libertarianism.

On first impression none of these theories seems to provide an adequate basis for a moral justification of the judgment. On deeper analysis, however, each theory can be interpreted in a way that lays the groundwork for a well-reasoned justification of such a judgment. This enables the framing of plausible responses to challenges that even some disability rights advocates find difficult to answer.[29] The analysis in chapter 3 thus, in effect, morally justifies the zero-reject policy at the core of American special education law.

Chapter 4 focuses upon the inclusion of children with disabilities in regular education classrooms, school activities, and school functions. The chapter opens with a brief summary of a special education due process case in which the author was the hearing officer. The case serves well as a point of departure for the discussion that follows. The brief case description provided illustrates strikingly the intense and deep controversy surrounding the idea of inclusion in the context of American K–12 special education.

Chapter 4 focuses upon two conceptions, both of which are indispensable elements of any reasonable interpretation of the idea of inclusion. The first conception—the ideal of an inclusive educational community—concerns aspirations that embody moral ideals for K–12 education of children with disabilities, whether in Group A or Group B. The second conception—the principle of equal educational concern and respect—concerns morally basic required responsibilities of K–12 public school districts. (This is in contrast to ideals that from a moral standpoint are worthy of aspiration, rather than being basic moral requirements.)

Chapter 4 sets forth accounts of both conceptions and analyzes why, in some difficult cases, the two conceptions, although not inherently opposed, nonetheless tend to pull in opposed directions.

Chapter 5 opens with two case vignettes involving K–12 public school disciplinary decisions. The first vignette summarizes the factual background of a special education case the author adjudicated as a due process hearing officer. The second vignette concerns a situation involving expulsion of six regular education students, which gave rise to immense public controversy at the time it occurred. The two vignettes are considered carefully in connection with the IDEA's requirements concerning out-of-school suspensions and expulsions of children with disabilities.

Moral questions about school discipline apropos children with disabilities, whether of a general nature or relative to disciplinary decisions concerning specific children, cannot be separated from a troubling broader moral issue. Out-of-school suspensions and expulsions withhold educational services from children. The idea, however, that children have a moral right to receive an appropriate K–12 education is central to the moral justification of K–12 public education as understood by most Americans. Correlatively, the idea that government, acting in the name of the public, has a moral responsibility to provide it is also central to such justification.

Prima facie tension thus exists between using out-of-school suspensions and expulsions as disciplinary measures and the idea that every child in the United States has a moral right to receive an appropriate K–12 public education. Chapter 5 identifies and justifies five conditions for deciding in specific cases whether or not an out-of-school suspension or expulsion violates a student's right to receive an appropriate K–12 education.

When a school district's policies and practices concerning out-of-school suspensions and expulsions satisfy these five conditions, any reasonable concerns regarding the fairness to nondisabled students (specifically with regard to the IDEA's procedural and substantive due process requirements for suspensions and expulsions) are addressed adequately.

Chapter 6 concerns the right of due process review, which the IDEA provides when parents of a child with a disability want to contest the appropriateness of K–12 educational decisions made by school district personnel concerning their child. The discussion in chapter 6 identifies and evaluates the morally relevant considerations with respect to the IDEA's mandated special education due process review system. It then analyzes the controversy between the severe critics and the advocates about whether this mandate is morally justified and arrives at the following two conclusions.

First, the system has a morally indispensable function—it upholds the moral right of children with disabilities to receive an appropriate K–12 education. This system provides a method with the force of law behind it to meaningfully effectuate the right in diverse, hard-to-resolve cases. Second, the morally justified response to diverse, valid criticisms of the way the system operates in practice is not to eliminate the system. It is instead to try to remedy its shortcomings and address major background problems which affect American K–12 special education, such as racism and economic deprivation. Neither revising the IDEA nor making changes in how it is implemented alone can solve such problems.[30]

Chapter 6 also considers the hearing officer's duty of fidelity to the rule of law. This is an indispensable element of any plausible conception of morally justified due process review procedures for American K–12 special education, yet it has not been analyzed in sufficient depth. The examination includes an account of the duty's moral basis, degree of stringency, and limits. These are brought into focus through close analysis of immensely difficult and emotionally wrenching moral issues raised by the first of the two case vignettes in chapter 5.

Chapter 7 sets forth a general account of the respective moral responsibilities of lawmakers, K–12 public school educators, and parents of children with disabilities in regard to provision of an appropriate K–12 public education for American children with disabilities. The account draws heavily upon the arguments and analyses developed in chapters 2 through 6.

Chapter 7 concludes with a brief discussion that returns to the key points of disagreement between the severe critics of American K–12 special education and the advocates for children with disabilities and their families (as summarized at the beginning of this first chapter). The concluding discussion utilizes the arguments and analyses developed in chapters 2 through 7 as conceptual resources.

SUMMARY

The discussion in this chapter has identified six morally basic questions for K–12 special education in America. The chapters that follow will each focus upon one of these six questions in turn. They will show why and how that question is important to the moral dimensions of the significant policy issues under consideration—issues related to special education or to planning and implementation of educational programs for children with disabilities. The analyses and discussions in chapters 2 through 7 will seek to make it apparent that careful consideration of the six morally basic questions is essential to thoughtful deliberation regarding American K–12 special education.

NOTES

1. National Center for Educational Statistics, U.S. Department of Education, Digest of Educational Statistics, 2011, Table 18, Number and percentage of Students served under Individuals with Disabilities Education Act Part B by age and State jurisdiction, Selected years 1990–1991 through 2009–2010.

2. 20 U.S.C. 1400 et seq. The original name of the IDEA upon enactment in 1975 was the Education for all Handicapped Children Act (EAHCA).When Congress reauthorized the Act in 1997 it changed the Act's name to the Individuals with Disabilities Education Act (IDEA). In the 2004 reauthorization the Act was again given a new name—this time the Individuals with Disabilities Education Improvement Act (IDEIA). Most practitioners in the field of special education, however, continue to refer to the Act as the IDEA.

3. 20 U.S.C. 1400 (c) (2) (A)–(D).

4. 20 U.S.C. 1412 (a) (1); (5) (A).

5. Robert L. Osgood, *The History of Special Education: A Struggle for Equality in American Public Schools* (Westport, Conn: Praeger, 2008), 44–45, 94.

6. Osgood, *The History of Special Education*, 31–36, 80–84.

7. Osgood, *The History of Special Education*, 50–54, 80–84.

8. eg., Martha Nussbaum, *Frontiers of Justice* (Cambridge, MA: Harvard University Press, 2006), 210.

9. 20 U.S.C. 1415 (b) (6) (A).

10. 20 U.S.C. 1415 (k).

11. 343 F. Supp. 279 (1972), 348 F. Supp. 866 (1972).

12. 855 F.2d 954 (1st Cir.) (1989), cert denied 973 U.S. 982 (1989).

13. *Timothy H. v. Rochester, New Hampshire School District*, 960.

14. 458 U.S. 176, 203–04 (1982).

In *Rowley* the Supreme Court did not consider the essential requirements of an appropriate K–12 educational program for children with disabilities who are educated in other placements than a regular education classroom. In the recent case of *Andrew F. v. Douglas County S.D. RE 1* (580 U.S. ____ 2017), however, the Supreme Court, in an (extremely rare) 8–0 decision, supplemented its ruling in *Rowley* with the following statement:

> While *Rowley* declined to articulate an overarching standard to evaluate the adequacy of the education provided under the [IDEA] the decision and statutory language point to a general approach. To meet its substantive obligation under the IDEA a school must offer an IEP reasonably calculated to enable a child to make progress in light of the child's circumstances.
>
> *Rowley* had no need to provide concrete guidance with respect to a child not fully integrated in the regular classroom and not able to achieve grade level. That case concerned

a young girl who was progressing smoothly through the regular curriculum. If that is not a reasonable prospect for a child his IEP need not aim for grade level advancement. But his educational program must be appropriately ambitious in the circumstances, just as advancement from grade to grade is appropriately ambitious for most children in the regular classroom.

The goals may differ, but every child should have a chance to meet challenging objectives. (pp. 13–14)

As the unanimous agreement of the Justices of the Supreme Court suggests, the Court's opinion and ruling in *Endrew F* follows directly in terms of both logic and common sense from the standard the Court set forth in *Rowley* for an appropriate K–12 education in the case of a child with a disability who is educated in the regular education classroom.

15. *Board of Education of the Hendrik Hudson School District v. Rowley*, 192.
16. 20 U.S.C. 1412 (a) (5) (A).
17. E.g. *Roncker v. Walther* 700 F.2d 1056 (6th Cir. 1983), *Daniel R.R. v. State Board of Education* 874 F.2d 876 (4th Cir. 1989), *Sacramento City School District v. Rachel Holland* 14 F. 3d 1298 (9th Cir. 1994), *Harman v. Loudoun County Board of Education* 118 D. 3d 990 (4th Cir. 1997).
18. Robert Worth, "The Scandal of Special Education," *The Washington Monthly* 31 (June 1999): 272–81.
19. Mark Kelman, "The Moral Foundations of Special Education Law," in *Rethinking Special Education in a New Century*, ed. Chester E. Finn Jr., et al. (Washington, DC: Thomas B. Fordham Foundation, 2001), 78.
20. Kelman, "The Moral Foundations of Special Education Law," 78.
21. Kelman, "The Moral Foundations of Special Education," 80.
22. Miriam Kurtzig Freedman, "Special Education: Its Ethical Dilemmas, Entitlement Status, and Suggested System Reforms," *University of Chicago Law Review* 79, no. 1 (2012): 12–13.
23. Worth, "The Scandal of Special Education," 276.
24. Freedman, "Special Education," 18.
25. Freedman, "Special Education," 21.
26. Freedman, "Special Education," 22.
27. Jonathan Mooney and David Cole, *Learning Outside the Lines* (Simon and Schuster: New York, 2000), 35.
28. See, e.g., Al Baker, "Working to Combat the Stigma of Autism," *New York Times*, July 1, 2013, A 18.
29. E.g., Michael Berube, father of a child with Down's syndrome named Jamie wrote,

> Jamie came into the world asking us a fundamental question. . . . Assuming that we can even imagine a form of social organization in which citizens like Jamie are nourished, supported, and encouraged to reach their full human potential why might we seek to create it at all? There's no self-evident reason why we should. (*Life as We Know It* [New York: Random House, 1996, 226)

30. See appendix I of chapter 7.

Chapter 2

The Moral Right of American Children to Receive an Appropriate K–12 Education

Do all American children have a moral right to receive an appropriate K–12 education? If so, then for what reasons? If not, then why not? If the answer is that only some American children—either with disability conditions or nondisabled—have this moral right, then which children have it, which do not, and why?

As noted in chapter 1, crucial issues exist concerning how one answers these complex, yet morally basic, questions. They hover unaddressed in the background of most major controversies between severe critics of special education under the IDEA framework and advocates for children with disabilities and their families.

Chapter 2 sets forth a justification of the idea that American children have a moral right to receive an appropriate K–12 education. The justification applies to all nondisabled children; it also applies to most, *but not to all*, children with disability conditions enumerated in the IDEA. The justification to be developed applies only in part to children with mild or moderate intellectual disability conditions, and not at all to children with severe or profound intellectual disabilities.

Every American child, whether nondisabled or with a disability, has a moral right to receive an appropriate K–12 education. However, the justification of this belief for children with severe or profound intellectual disability conditions raises large issues requiring further discussion in a separate dedicated chapter. Such will be provided in chapter 3, which focuses on justification of the zero-reject policy underlying American special education law.

Chapters 2 and 3, considered together, are intended to justify the judgment that *all* American children have a moral right to receive an appropriate K–12 education. The justification developed over these two chapters will address the following two principal questions:

(1) What is the essential content of an appropriate K–12 education (i.e., the kind of K–12 education to which every American child has a moral right) for the following two groups of children, considered respectively in chapters 2 and 3:

   Group A, consisting of both American children who are not disabled and American children who have disability conditions enumerated in the IDEA *other than severe or profound intellectual disability* and

   Group B, consisting of American children who have severe or profound intellectual disability conditions?

(2) What reasons justify the judgment that all American children (i.e., both Group A and Group B) have a moral right to receive an appropriate K–12 education containing such essential content?

THE RIGHT TO AN APPROPRIATE K–12 EDUCATION: ITS ESSENTIAL CONTENT AND MORAL JUSTIFICATION

Tennis great Andre Agassi recounts in his autobiography the time he spent at the Bollettieri Tennis Academy. His father, consumed by the desire that Agassi become the top-ranked professional tennis player in the world, sent him there when he was thirteen years old.[1] Nick Bollettieri, the owner and director of the academy, founded it to provide live-in training for tennis prodigies, and intended to develop them into professional-level tennis players.

Agassi paints a bleak picture of the school (the Bradenton Academy), where he and the other prodigies were bused on weekdays for their high school education; he concludes with the following assessment:

> Bradenton Academy exists because the Bollettieri Academy keeps sending it a bus full of paying customers every semester. The teachers know . . . they can't flunk us and we cherish our special status. *We feel a lordly sense of entitlement, never realizing that the thing to which we're most entitled is the thing we're not getting—an education.* (emphasis added)[2]

These words of Agassi reflect a firm conviction, shared widely and felt deeply throughout the American democratic body politic, that American children have a moral right to receive an appropriate K–12 education. This right is ordinarily understood as what philosophers of law term a claim-right.[3] In the case of every claim-right there is a claimant—that is, a right holder—and a correlative responsibility bearer—that is, someone responsible for providing whatever the claimant is entitled to.

In the case of the right to an appropriate K–12 education, American children are the right holders. The correlative responsibility to provide such an education is shared. The fulfillment of this responsibility poses complex, multidimensional issues, which no one organization or single person could adequately address. Accordingly, the co-bearers of this shared responsibility are lawmakers (elected legislators and judges), K–12 educators (school administrators, teachers, and other educational staff members), and parents of K–12 school-aged children.

Articulating the *moral* justification of the above view of American children's *moral* right and of the correlative shared responsibility of lawmakers, educators, and parents to provide such an education raises fundamental questions of moral justification. These are addressed immediately below.

The widespread acceptance and strong affirmation of the judgment that American children in Group A have a moral right to receive an appropriate K–12 education do not in themselves *morally justify* the judgment. Gravely unjustified judgments from a moral standpoint have been (and, sadly, continue to be) shared widely and affirmed strongly in various social groups, even large ones. Entire nations have judged that slavery, racism, religious persecution, subordination of women, or discrimination against LGBT persons is morally permissible.

An adequate moral justification of the judgment that children in Group A have a moral claim-right to receive an appropriate K–12 education must specifically address the crucial issues, identified below, related to the concept of deprivation of freedom.

Anyone with even a minimal understanding of morality considers it wrong to deprive a person of freedom. This does not mean that he or she regards the rule "Do not deprive of freedom" as an absolute. It means instead that he or she considers the rule morally basic in the sense that, along with other basic moral rules such as "Do not kill," "Do not cause pain," "Do not cheat," "Keep your promises," and so forth, violating the rule "Do not deprive of freedom" always calls for a moral justification.[4]

The vast majority of American children in Group A receive their K–12 education in public schools financed by taxation. Thus a moral justification is needed for governmental efforts to assure that children in the United States are provided an appropriate K–12 education, as such efforts unavoidably deprive some individuals (i.e., taxpayers) of freedom (e.g., the freedom to decline making tax payments used for operation of K–12 public schools).

The widespread acceptance and strong affirmation of the moral judgment that Group A children have a moral right to receive an appropriate K–12 education reflects general underlying agreement with three points, to be enumerated immediately below and then discussed in depth. The three points concern, respectively, (1) the essential objective of an appropriate K–12 education for children in Group A, (2) what it means to be an educationally deprived person in contemporary America, and (3) the moral responsibility of American government to prevent and to remedy educational deprivation.

When analyzed adequately and understood in relation to one another, the three points respond persuasively to the concern raised above regarding deprivation of freedom.

The points will be discussed individually in the following subsections:

(1) An appropriate K–12 education for American children in Group A has a two-pronged objective. It must be reasonably calculated to help children acquire knowledge and develop abilities central to the following:
   (a) exercising the rights, fulfilling the responsibilities, and exemplifying the ideals of membership in the American democratic body politic and
   (b) having a reasonable chance for success in seeking the basic human good of self-fulfillment.
(2) In contemporary America any child in Group A not provided an appropriate K–12 education is an educationally deprived person.
(3) Government in the United States has a moral responsibility to take steps reasonably calculated to prevent educational deprivation; the most important step relative to American children in Group A is to assure that they are provided an appropriate K–12 education.

The Two-Pronged Objective of an Appropriate K–12 Education for Children in Group A

For purposes of clarifying the first prong of the essential objective given in (1), some additional words are needed again concerning terminology. Throughout this chapter the phrase "American democratic body politic" will be used to refer to everyone protected by the Bill of Rights and the Fourteenth Amendment equal protection and due process clauses of the U.S. Constitution. This group encompasses many more persons than either all eligible voters in the United States or all U.S. citizens. It also includes, for instance, children, individuals with the legal status of permanent residency, and artificial persons (i.e., diverse kinds of organizations).

The *rights* of membership in the American democratic body politic are grounded in the U.S. Constitution.[5] The *responsibilities* concern standards of conduct to which members of the American democratic body politic must adhere widely in order for American government to function at all. The members of the American democratic body politic must also significantly exemplify the *ideals* if democracy in America is to flourish.[6] The preceding points will be elucidated below.

The jurisprudential scholar Robert Cover defines a "nomos" as a "normative world . . . of right and wrong, lawful and unlawful, and valid and void" that persons in a human society "create and maintain"—a world whose apprehension is inseparable from the sense of oneself as a social being.[7] "To inhabit a nomos," says Cover, "[means] to know how to live in it."[8]

Knowledge and abilities underpin the exercise of rights, exemplification of ideals, and fulfillment of responsibilities required for membership in the American democratic body politic. They are indispensable for identifying, understanding, and taking part in discussion of public issues, and for acting upon them. This is especially true in regard to the moral dimensions of public issues. Knowing how to live in the nomos of contemporary America requires such knowledge and abilities.

With regard to self-fulfillment, the subject of the second prong of (1), the following words of philosopher Alan Gewirth express its core elements:

> [S]elf-fulfillment consists in carrying to fruition one's deepest desires or one's worthiest capacities. It is a bringing of oneself to flourishing completion, an unfolding of what is best in oneself so that it represents the successful culmination of one's aspirations or potentialities. In this way self-fulfillment betokens a life well lived, a life that is deeply satisfying, fruitful, and worthwhile. . . . To seek a good human life is to seek for self-fulfillment.[9]

Given the integral relationship between self-fulfillment and a good human life, helping children acquire knowledge and develop abilities central to seeking self-fulfillment is surely an essential objective of an appropriate K–12 public education.

The discussion below addresses a critical question concerning the two prongs of the essential educational objective for children in Group A (as set out above in [1]): Which knowledge and abilities *that an appropriate K–12 public education may reasonably be considered able to provide* are essential for (a) participating in the American democratic body politic and for (b) having a reasonable chance for success in seeking the basic human good of self-fulfillment?

(a) Rights, Responsibilities, and Ideals of Membership in the American Democratic Body Politic

Political theorists Amy Gutmann and Dennis Thompson place the concept of democratic deliberation at the moral core of American democracy.[10] As they understand this concept, it sets forth an ideal of democratic deliberation unrealizable in bargaining among parties motivated solely by self-interest, whether individuals, groups, or organizations. Democratic deliberators, in the ideal sense, may seek to advance their self-interest. However, they would also recognize their responsibility to justify the proposals they advance from the standpoint of the public interest.

Such a responsibility would apply, in their view of the concept of deliberative democracy, to anyone who engages in democratic deliberation. Thus in contemporary democratic societies this would include lawmakers, other public officials, and candidates for public office; journalists, mass media figures, and internet bloggers; business, public interest, or religious organizations; and members of the general public when discussing public matters with one another.

The principles and values underlying the conception of the public interest—held widely by democratic deliberators—often run deep, sometimes to the point of willingness to die in their defense. The deep commitment of such deliberators, however, would coexist along with the realization that any reasonable person affirms diverse principles and values. Among these no value is ultimate and no principle is absolute (except, possibly, as a matter of philosophical or theological theory, rather than as a practical guide to decision).

Democratic deliberators thus understand that new factual information, or arguments one had not considered previously, can change a person's mind concerning *which* deeply held values or principles have priority in a particular situation. They regard the depth and intensity of their commitments to the values and principles they affirm as entailing a responsibility to consider carefully the opinions of those with whom they disagree on public issues. Only by doing so, they realize, is it possible to achieve understanding of how their own affirmed values and principles apply with respect to the issues.

The distinctive attitude of democratic deliberators toward discourse on public matters can be referred to appropriately as the attitude intrinsic to democratic deliberation. Such an attitude consists of the following four elements:

(1) conception of themselves as holders of rights essential to the moral justification of American democracy; these include, but are not limited to, the following rights, which the philosopher John Rawls refers to as "the system of basic liberty": "political liberty . . . freedom of speech and assembly, liberty of conscience, freedom of thought, freedom of the person, along with the right to hold personal property, and freedom from arbitrary arrest and seizure, as defined by the rule of law";[11]
(2) recognition that reasonable people often disagree about interpretation of the grounding values and principles as well as about how the morally central rights apply with respect to diverse pressing issues;
(3) realization that, for practical purposes, no value is ultimate and no principle is absolute;
(4) in light of (1), (2), and (3), conception of themselves as bearers of the following responsibilities:

(a) willingness to listen to expressions of viewpoints with which one disagrees;
(b) careful consideration of all viewpoints, including both one's own and those with which one disagrees strongly;
(c) exercise of restraint in the context of disagreements over controversial, contentiously disputed, highly viewpoint-dependent, and difficult-to-resolve matters;
(d) readiness to defend others from violation of their rights as members of the American democratic body politic.

The notion of an American democratic body politic whose members share widely and deeply the attitude intrinsic to democratic deliberation corresponds with actual fact (either at this time or at any other time throughout American history), only to a very limited extent. The notion, however, denotes an aspirational ideal—the best attitude that the members could exemplify, as contrasted with an attitude beyond the realm of human capability.

When the attitude intrinsic to democratic deliberation is shared widely and deeply, American democratic government approaches more closely to the ideal of self-government or, in the words of Abraham Lincoln's Gettysburg Address, "government of the people by the people, and for the people."[12]

Exercising rights, fulfilling responsibilities, and exemplifying ideals as a member of the American democratic body politic in ways that express the attitude intrinsic to democratic deliberation do not require an expert grasp of public issues. It does, however, include the following five key abilities and kinds of knowledge and awareness:

- knowledge concerning fundamental aspects of the constitutional structure of American government and basic facts of American history;
- understanding of the reasons that justify the rights and responsibilities of membership in the American democratic body politic, especially the strong right of free expression essential to democratic deliberation;
- recognition, in light of such justifying reasons, of the great extent to which reasonable persons interpret differently the rights and responsibilities of members of the American democratic body politic;
- ability to follow lines of reasoning in arguments concerning public affairs, and, especially, to recognize logical gaps and inconsistencies; and
- ability to recognize whether factual evidence does or does not clearly support a particular conclusion, and readiness to exercise this ability regardless of the conclusions that may ensue.

The knowledge and abilities embodied in the above five elements are not possessed only by experts. Nonetheless, they seldom emerge naturally in the cognitive and social development of individuals. Rather, they require cultivation, for which in most cases an appropriate K–12 education is indispensable. Without an appropriate K–12 education, most people would lack the opportunity to acquire the knowledge and abilities necessary to exercise the rights and fulfill the responsibilities of members of the American democratic body politic in ways that exemplify the attitude intrinsic to democratic deliberation.

(b) Self-Fulfillment

Self-fulfillment, viewed as integral to a person's seeking a good life, has two dimensions—aspiration fulfillment and capacity fulfillment. Apropos aspiration fulfillment, the term "aspiration" refers to a person's deep desires—those she is willing to exert great effort and make considerable sacrifices to fulfill. Having such aspirations is essential for pursuing a self-defined good life with coherent focus and direction.

Aspirations are not cast in stone. Over the course of a typical human life a person modifies, eliminates, and/or forms additional aspirations in response to factors such as developmental life-stage changes, assessments and reassessments of one's own capabilities, and estimations of one's available resources. A wide array of factors could influence a person's various aspirations (e.g., background, cultural and social values, diverse personal experiences, or even chance events).

In the final analysis, however, a person chooses her own aspirations. In Alan Gewirth's words, "[A]spirations are themselves chosen, not merely undergone. Even if what you aspire to reflects your upbringing, including your cultural milieu, you can take effective cognizance of your aspirations, and decide whether to maintain them or to seek others."[13]

The concept of choice thus enters into the idea of the relationship between self-fulfillment and a good human life at two points relative to aspirations. The aspirations fulfilled when a person has a good life are (i) chosen by that person and (ii) fulfilled mostly by her voluntary efforts, which reflect her choices of action.

The second dimension of self-fulfillment concerns capacities, rather than aspirations. The relationship between capacity fulfillment and a good human life is well stated in the following words of Joel Feinberg:

> Self-fulfillment is variously described, but it surely involves as necessary elements the development of one's chief aptitudes into genuine talents in a life that gives them scope, an unfolding of all basic tendencies and inclinations, both those of the species and those that are peculiar to the individual, and an active realization of the universal propensities to plan, design, and make order.[14]

Autonomous, self-determined choices, while not sufficient, nonetheless are as essential for fulfillment of capacities as they are for aspiration fulfillment. Capacity fulfillment results primarily from a person's choices concerning those of her capacities to which she attaches the greatest importance, her decisions to endeavor developing them, and her diverse choices concerning how best she can do so. Furthermore, aspects and qualities of choice crucial for seeking capacity fulfillment are themselves developed most effectively through, and exemplified in, the making of choices. John Stuart Mill states the above point clearly and persuasively in the following passage from his classic essay "On Liberty":

> He who chooses his plan of life for himself employs all his faculties. He must use observation to see, reasoning and judgment to foresee, activity to gather materials for decision, discrimination to decide, and when he has decided, firmness and self-control to hold to his deliberate decision. And these qualities he requires and exercises exactly in proportion to the part of his conduct which he determines according to his own judgment and feelings is a large one.[15]

Crucial relationships between receipt of an appropriate K–12 education and meaningful development of the abilities Mill identifies in the above passage are clear and relevant to life as lived in the United States.

Acquiring greater knowledge throughout the years of K–12 schooling, for instance, enhances an individual's observational powers, thereby increasing the range of objects, whether natural or social, he can identify and observe. Developing the abilities to analyze, abstract, hypothesize, and interpret through study of such subjects as mathematics, the sciences, history, and literature (even at the K–12 level) vastly augments a person's reasoning powers, acumen in making judgments, and discrimination to decide.

Advancements in literacy and communication skills resulting from an appropriate K–12 education tend both to stimulate and to increase the frequency of successful outcomes in gathering materials for decision. Intellectual self-confidence gained from efforts put forth in successful learning experiences during the K–12 years (e.g., working one's way through challenging assignments) supports the resolve needed to follow through and act upon decisions one has made.

The above mentioned abilities, with respect to which an appropriate K–12 education is reasonably calculated to facilitate development, qualify a person to take advantage of potentially valuable opportunities she otherwise would not have had in virtually every significant area of her life. Especially important, such knowledge and abilities foster self-discovery by vastly increasing the likelihood a person will find interests that broaden, deepen to become abiding, and point her toward choices which, in Feinberg's words, develop her "chief aptitudes into genuine talents in a life that gives them scope."[16]

The Meaning of "Educational Deprivation" in Contemporary American Society

A deprived person lacks resources needed for a reasonable chance to attain success in seeking a good life. In contemporary America an appropriate K–12 education is such a needed resource. Without it, a person is unlikely to gain knowledge and develop abilities needed for deliberation that concerns (a) exercising the rights, fulfilling the responsibilities, and exemplifying the ideals of membership in the American democratic body politic and (b) having a reasonable chance for success in seeking the basic human good of self-fulfillment; both of these are essential for seeking a good life.

To reiterate the reasons, first, in regard to (a), a person lacking the above-mentioned knowledge and abilities cannot understand American democracy in moral terms from either a practical or a theoretical standpoint. Insofar as moral concern, and hence moral understanding, is integral to a good life, then something immensely important is missing from the life of a person who can inhabit the nomos—that is, enter into the moral world—of his own society to only a limited extent at best.

Second, in regard to (b), as Alan Gewirth states, to seek a good human life is to seek for self-fulfillment. Correlatively, there is no deeper source of unhappiness for a person capable of development and growth than to realize that she faces a life without any reasonable prospects for success in seeking self-fulfillment. In the case of American children who have not received an appropriate K–12 education, such a realization tends strongly to result in feelings of futility and ultimate hopelessness. This has devastating consequences for development of the self-confidence and motivational energy that success in seeking a good life requires.

Self-fulfillment is a basic good from the standpoint of American society, but for that very reason, relative to the United States, a person who reasonably apprehends her life as utterly lacking prospects for success in seeking self-fulfillment is a deprived individual.

Justification of the Judgment That the U.S. Government Has a *Morally Required* Responsibility to Assure That Children in Group A Are Provided an Appropriate K–12 Education

Most people (other than philosophical anarchists) consider some kinds of activities morally required functions of governments and other kinds of activities as discretionary for a government to do, in the sense of being morally justified but not morally required governmental responsibilities. There are, however, some important cases where from a moral standpoint it is a matter of deep and intense controversy whether a given kind of activity is required, discretionary, or unjustified for a government to undertake.[17]

In such cases, reasoned disagreement of opinion leads quickly to questions at the core of systematic philosophical reflection upon the subject of morality, encompassing in a broad sense the domains of moral theory, political philosophy, legal philosophy, and practical and professional ethics. Unsurprisingly, no settled consensus exists among philosophers about the answers to these questions.

Many of the philosophical debates and discussions that have pursued the questions most fully and deeply, have largely concerned, either explicitly or implicitly, contrast and comparison among four theories, all of which have been developed to analyze the concept of social justice. Each theory views a different idea as central to the concept.[18] The following are the four theories paired respectively with the ideas they posit as central to the concept of social justice:

(1) utilitarianism—happiness/avoidance or minimizing of unhappiness;
(2) Rawlsian Justice as fairness—fairness;
(3) Nussbaum's capabilities account of social justice—human dignity; and
(4) moderate libertarianism—liberty (freedom).

The discussion immediately below thus proceeds in the following way. Four separate arguments are set forth for the conclusion that American children in Group A have a moral right to receive an appropriate K–12 education. Each argument proceeds from the standpoint of a different one of the above major philosophical theories of social justice.

As with all philosophy, none of the four arguments closes the question at issue for once and for all. Each argument, however, has strong prima facie plausibility in the following respect. It is reasonable to believe that all of the arguments would be acknowledged by a substantial number of qualified persons in fields such as moral theory, political philosophy, legal philosophy, and philosophy of education as deserving careful and considered responses.

The fact that the conclusions of four arguments—each of which is grounded in a different major philosophical theory of justice—reach an overlapping consensus provides a strong justification of the judgment that American children in Group A have a moral right to receive an appropriate K–12 education.

Utilitarianism

According to utilitarianism, developed in its classic form by John Stuart Mill, the idea of well-being, understood to encompass both happiness and the absence of unhappiness, is essential to morality. Mill regarded assessment of human actions in terms of the extent to which they promote happiness and/or avoid, prevent, or minimize unhappiness for the greatest number of individuals as critical to understanding and applying all moral concepts.

In *Principles of Political Economy* Mill distinguished between "necessary" and "optional" governmental functions but did not identify a standard to apply for drawing the distinction in specific instances.[19] His general discussion of the distinction, however, suggests that Mill would have held that necessary functions are those a government has a moral responsibility to fulfill. Furthermore, to preserve consistency with his utilitarian moral theory, Mill would have considered a given function necessarily *governmental* if the following conditions apply:

(a) Carrying out the function is essential to avoid, prevent, or reduce grave conditions productive of unhappiness for a large number of individuals with respect to whom the government has responsibilities.
(b) There are strong reasons to doubt the function could be fulfilled adequately without governmental action.

In regard to (a) above, from a utilitarian perspective, appropriate K–12 education is crucial in two key respects. First, an appropriate K–12 education is indispensable for widespread development of abilities and attitudes intrinsic to the kinds of deliberation that must be common throughout the American body politic for democratic government in the United States to flourish. Availability of an appropriate K–12 education thus fosters intelligent and well-informed respect, support, participation, and commitment on the part of the persons over whom U.S. governments at all levels—federal, state, and local—claim legitimate governmental authority.

Second, for virtually every child in Group A, appropriate K–12 education is likewise indispensable for a reasonable chance of success in seeking the basic human good of self-fulfillment. Not having had an appropriate K–12 education tends to result in deep-seated feelings of inadequacy, alienation, and/or hopelessness—feelings that place persons on a trajectory that often includes prolonged unemployment, reliance upon public assistance, drug abuse, alcoholism, and/or criminal incarceration.

Apropos (b), the idea that American children in Group A could be assured an appropriate K–12 education without any governmental action at all presupposes assumptions that many would say are highly unrealistic; these assumptions concern how the total cost could be covered if financed solely by tuition payments of parents and private philanthropy.

Utilitarianism in its pure form (i.e., unmodified by combining it with a nonutilitarian approach) calls for moral judgments to be based solely upon comparative assessment of benefits (considerations productive of happiness) and harms (considerations productive of unhappiness). It is reasonable to conclude that such a harm-benefit assessment overwhelmingly supports providing an appropriate K–12 education, as understood in terms of the two-pronged analysis set forth in this chapter, for every American child in Group A. This conclusion becomes apparent when one considers the totality of harms likely to result from not doing so, specifically:

- the causes of unhappiness enumerated above that tend to result for educationally deprived individuals in American society and
- the sense of deeply bitter resentment, with all its unsettling social consequences, generated among the members of a large segment of the population—people who consider themselves, their families, and their friends as having been deprived of a reasonable opportunity for self-fulfillment in their lives.

One is hard pressed to think of realistically likely benefits that, from a utilitarian standpoint, could outweigh the above harms.

Rawlsian Justice as Fairness

John Rawls presented his theory of justice as fairness in *A Theory of Justice*—a book that became, by far, the most influential work in political philosophy among academic philosophers within the past half-century.[20] Rawls proposed two principles of justice (in an essay written subsequently to *A Theory of Justice*), which he set forth as follows:

(1) Each person has an equal right to a fully adequate scheme of equal basic liberties, which scheme is compatible with a similar scheme for all.
(2) Social and economic inequalities are to satisfy two conditions:
    First, they must be attached to offices and positions open to all under conditions of fair equality of opportunity.
    Second, they must be to the greatest benefit of the least-advantaged members of society.[21]

In regard to the first principle, the liberties that comprise the system of basic liberties are those enumerated above in the summary of attitudes intrinsic to democratic deliberation. These include "political liberty (the right to vote and to be eligible for public office) together with freedom of speech and assembly, liberty of conscience and freedom of thought, freedom of the person along with freedom from arbitrary arrest and seizure as defined by the rule of law."[22]

As for the second principle, its second part, which Rawls terms "the difference principle," concerns the distribution of income and wealth in society. The principle specifies that while such distributions may include inequalities, the distributions must, on balance, be to the greatest benefit of the least-advantaged members of society, in the sense that their position would be worse off if the inequalities were eliminated.[23]

The difference principle is, however, constrained by what Rawls terms "the priority of liberty." This means that any attempt to eradicate unjust inequality must not violate any of the equal liberties that make up the system of equal basic liberty referred to in the first principle.[24]

As Rawls conceives of government in a just society, lawmakers have a moral responsibility to regard the two principles of justice as paramount when deliberating about proposals for legislative enactment.[25] From this standpoint, it seems apparent that legislation directed at assuring that American children receive an appropriate K–12 education is a morally required governmental responsibility for the following reasons related respectively to Rawls's first and second principles of justice.

First, an appropriate K–12 education is designed to provide knowledge and develop abilities central to meaningful participation in American democratic deliberation, which requires understanding (both theoretical and practical) of the rights that make up the system of basic liberty in Rawls's first principle of justice.

Second, for the United States the vast preponderance of inequalities referred to in Rawls's second principle of justice concern the distribution of income and wealth. These inequalities result from a complex combination of deeply embedded economic, political, and cultural factors.

Major changes in all three of these domains would be needed even to approximate the requirements of Rawls's difference principle. Nonetheless, in light of the strong correlation between educational advancement and economic opportunity, any serious effort to meet Rawls's requirements would have to include the assurance that American children in Group A receive an appropriate K–12 education.

The Capabilities Account of Social Justice

The capabilities account of social justice, as developed by its leading theorist, Martha Nussbaum, "begin[s] with a conception of the dignity of the human being, and of a life that is worthy of that dignity—a life that has available in it truly human functioning."[26] Nussbaum presents a list of ten central human capabilities, which she claims are "part of a minimum account of social justice," in the respect that "a society that does not guarantee these to all its citizens, at some appropriate threshold level, falls short of being a fully just society."[27]

The following are the ten central human capabilities Nussbaum lists:[28]

(1) Life—being able to live to the end of a human life of normal length; not dying prematurely (i.e., before one's life is so reduced as to be not worth living);
(2) Bodily health—being able to have good health, including reproductive health; to be adequately nourished; to have adequate shelter;
(3) Bodily integrity—being able to move freely from place to place; to be secure against violent assault, including sexual assault and domestic violence; having opportunities for sexual satisfaction and for choices in matters of reproduction;
(4) Senses, imagination, and thought—being able to use the senses to imagine, think, and reason—and do these things in a "truly human" way informed and cultivated by an adequate education;
(5) Emotions—being able to have attachments to things and people outside ourselves; to love those who love and care for us; to grieve; to experience longing, gratitude, and justified anger;
(6) Practical reason—being able to form a conception of the good and to engage in critical reflection about the planning of one's life;
(7) Affiliation—
    (a) being able to live with and toward others; to recognize and show concern for other human beings; to engage in various forms of social interaction, to be able to imagine the situation of another,
    (b) having the social bases of self-respect and nonhumiliation; being able to be treated as a dignified being whose worth is equal to that of others;
(8) Other species—being able to live with concern for, and in relation to, animals, plants, and the world of nature;
(9) Play—being able to laugh, to play, to enjoy recreational activities;
(10) Control over one's environment—
    (a) Political—being able to participate effectively in political choices that govern one's life,
        (i) having the right of political participation,
        (ii) protection of free speech and association;
    (b) Material—being able to hold property (both land and movable goods, and having property rights on an equal basis with others)
        (i) having the right to seek employment on an equal basis with others,
        (ii) having freedom from unwarranted search and seizure.

In the context of American society, an appropriate K–12 education—as understood in terms of the two-pronged analysis developed in this chapter—enhances all ten of Nussbaum's central human capabilities. Such education is an integral component of three of them: (4) senses, imagination, and thought; (6) practical reason; and (10) (a) control over one's political environment. Nussbaum maintains that her ten central human capabilities "give shape and content" to a conception of human dignity that could both "gather broad cross-cultural agreement" and ground a "minimum account of social justice."[29]

Given the wide range of Nussbaum's ten capabilities, there is room for substantial debate and discussion about their implications for the requirements of social justice in diverse nations that differ respectively in their overall levels of material resources (e.g., the United States and Bangladesh). But from the standpoint of the capabilities account of social justice, it is readily apparent that in American society, children in Group A have a moral right to be provided an appropriate K–12 education.[30]

Moderate Libertarianism

According to libertarianism the primary responsibility of government is to avoid violating the moral rights of individual persons.[31] For libertarians, the right to liberty (freedom) stands out as the most important concept for understanding a government's responsibility and the limits of morally legitimate governmental authority.[32]

The right to liberty, according to libertarianism, has overwhelming moral force; it entails a strong presumption against any interference with an individual's liberty by actions of other individuals and especially by actions of government. Governmentally imposed limitations upon liberty of individuals, for libertarians, carry an exceptionally high burden of moral justification.

Within a framework of agreement upon the above ideas, however, there is an array of different outlooks—philosophically and politically significant—among libertarians. Two outlooks within this array, which one may refer to respectively as "moderate" and "radical" libertarianism, disagree fundamentally over a crucial issue concerning application of the idea of a moral right to liberty (freedom) with respect to an appropriate K–12 education. This issue will be discussed immediately below.

Moderate libertarians believe that a small number of instances meet the (exceptionally heavy) burden of moral justification for government limitations upon liberty of individuals. Some moderate libertarians regard the following argument as cogent:[33]

(i) Individuals have a moral right to liberty, in large part for the reason that liberty is needed to have a reasonable chance for success in seeking self-fulfillment.[34]

(ii) There are other needed prerequisites, besides liberty, however, for an individual to have a reasonable chance for success in seeking self-fulfillment.
(iii) An example of another needed prerequisite besides liberty, relative to the United States, is an appropriate K–12 public education.
(iv) Therefore, American children have a moral right to receive an appropriate K–12 education.

By acknowledging the cogency of the above argument, a moderate libertarian does not thereby forfeit her libertarian bona fides, provided that she remains firmly committed to the principle that governmental limitation upon individual liberty carries a heavy burden of moral justification. However, she combines this basic libertarian commitment with realistic assessment of the prerequisites for a reasonable chance to achieve success in seeking self-fulfillment. And she tries to make reasonable judgments in regard to education and social policy accordingly.[35]

Radical libertarians, in contrast to moderate libertarians, reject the notion that any circumstances whatsoever justify governmental limitations upon individual liberty. Radical libertarians self-identify as (philosophical) anarchists, and as such they reject the idea that governments, even if democratic, have any morally legitimate, let alone morally required, functions.[36]

Against the idea that government in the United States has a moral responsibility to assure that children receive an appropriate education, radical libertarians maintain the following: if government ceased to exist, such assurance would be achieved entirely without governmental action through a combination of the workings of a (completely) free market economy and voluntary philanthropic contributions.[37]

As noted earlier in the discussion of utilitarianism, many would regard the above radical libertarian position as unrealistically optimistic about whether American children—even children in poverty and children with disabilities—could be assured an appropriate education if supporting governmental action were withdrawn entirely.

There is, however, another strong criticism. The radical libertarian stance is not, and in the nature of the case cannot be, grounded in well-confirmed observations of educational practices in societies organized on radical libertarian lines. (There aren't any.) Accordingly, one has to regard the stance as speculation about which radical libertarians have great confidence, while others (e.g., utilitarians, Rawlsians, capabilities theorists, and moderate libertarians) are highly dubious.

Imagine, however, that a radical libertarian society somehow came into existence but that the above speculation inarguably turned out wrong. Under this hypothesized circumstance radical libertarians would have only two alternatives. First, they could abandon their stance, and become moderate libertarians apropos education. Second, they could decline to do so and instead double down with an unqualified denial that American children have a moral right to receive an appropriate K–12 education.

With regard to the second of the above alternatives, radical libertarians might argue as follows: "It would be wonderful if, in the case of every American child, the child's parents or some other private party concerned with the child's well-being assured that the child receives an appropriate K–12 education. The idea, however, that government in the United States has the ultimate moral responsibility to do so is both badly misguided and morally unjustified."[38]

Taking the above stance is one thing, justifying it is another. How would radical libertarians respond, for example, to the moderate libertarian justification (set forth above) of American children's moral right to receive an appropriate education? Moderate libertarians would say the argument simply traces out logical implications of ideas highly cohesive with, if not central to, libertarianism—ideas about why individual liberty is so immensely valuable. From this standpoint, denial that American children have a moral right to receive an appropriate K–12 education conflicts with a moral judgment that any plausible version of libertarianism must acknowledge.[39]

Summary of the Analysis Thus Far

The analysis began by noting a crucial issue concerning the concept of deprivation of freedom that must be addressed by any justification of the judgment that children in Group A have a moral right to receive an appropriate education.

The analysis then proceeded with two steps to address this issue. The first step was development of a conception of an appropriate K–12 education for children in Group A; under this conception, such an education has two prongs. It must be reasonably calculated to impart knowledge and develop abilities needed to (1) deliberate meaningfully about exercising rights, fulfilling responsibilities, and exemplifying ideals of membership in the American democratic body politic and (2) have a reasonable chance for success in seeking the basic human good of self-fulfillment.

The second step in the analysis was to argue that the above conception is applicable—in its entirety—with respect to all children in Group A. The argument sought to show that such a conclusion is justified by an overlapping consensus of four major philosophical theories of social justice, each embodying a significantly different account of the idea of moral responsibility in relation to governmental action (i.e., Utilitarianism, Rawlsian Justice as fairness, the capabilities account of social justice, and moderate libertarianism).

Each of the four major theories considered has been developed, analyzed, discussed, and debated extensively by academic philosophers. Given the detail and philosophical depth with which all these theories have been articulated, debate and discussion among proponents of each theory will in all likelihood continue for a long time.

The analysis expresses no opinion about which theory is strongest. Instead, it provides, from each theory's perspective, plausible justifications of the judgment that children in Group A have a moral right to receive an appropriate education (as understood in terms of the two-pronged analysis).

Each theory, as reiterated below, has a different moral concept at its core:

- utilitarianism (happiness/avoidance of unhappiness);
- Rawlsian Justice as fairness (fairness);
- capabilities account of social justice (human dignity); and
- Moderate libertarianism (liberty [freedom]).

The two prongs of the essential objective of an appropriate education for children in Group A concern knowledge and abilities of utmost importance from the standpoints of all four core moral concepts. The preceding argument thus provides a persuasive response to the issues raised near the beginning of this chapter concerning deprivation of liberty.

Considerations of happiness/avoidance or prevention of unhappiness, fairness, human dignity, and liberty (freedom) all converge to justify the judgment that American children in Group A have a moral right to receive an appropriate K–12 education.

THE MINIMUM CONTENT ACCOUNT

The idea of the two-pronged essential objective of an appropriate K–12 education developed in this chapter is central to a justified conception of the kind of education American children in Group A have a moral right to receive. In this context the two-pronged objective, although difficult to realize, may be reasonably considered as achievable. Yet questions of how to do so raise difficult, complex, controversial, and at times hotly contested issues.

These issues concern primarily the (1) expenditure for providing K–12 education, which raises issues about allocation of resources between education and other vital areas; (2) appropriate distribution of social resources allocated to K–12 education for economically deprived students and students with disabilities; (3) development and implementation of educational programs (i.e., what and how students are taught); (4) attention to adequate educational progress of students from both individual and aggregative standpoints; (5) division of responsibility between lawmakers, K–12 public school educators, and parents of school-aged children for providing education for children with disabilities.

All the above kinds of issues have generated intense, ongoing controversies. For the reasons set forth in this chapter, however, the idea that children in Group A have a moral right to receive an appropriate education is not only shared widely among the vast majority of Americans but also grounded in a plausible justification from a moral standpoint.

This morally justified consensus reflects widespread agreement upon the two principles stated below, arguably the minimum content of the moral right of any child in Group A to receive an appropriate education. This content encapsulates the entitlements which all who acknowledge the right would agree are necessary elements of it, regardless of other disagreements they may have over how the right should be interpreted:

(1) The right to a reasonable educational program: American children in Group A have a moral right to receive a K–12 education reasonably calculated to achieve the two-pronged essential objective of an appropriate K–12 education.
(2) The right to equal educational concern: American children in Group A have a moral right to equal educational concern on the part of the public educational agencies which share the ultimate responsibility to provide appropriate educational programs for them.[40]

For (1) above, the term "reasonable" needs some explanatory words. In the context of the moral right of a child in Group A to receive an appropriate education, the term denotes something stronger than the default justification of mere nonarbitrariness and weaker than the strong standard of justification beyond a reasonable doubt. Reasonable K–12 educational programs all have plausible justifications grounded in points that merit careful attention. They shift the onus of justification to the other side(s) of the question, at least to the extent of deserving a considered response.

A justification can be plausible even if it neither identifies every relevant consideration nor treats in depth every significant issue in connection with the factors it identifies. Plausible justifications are those a substantial number of reasonable persons could find persuasive.

As for (2) above, the phrase "educational concern" refers to efforts by those responsible for providing an appropriate K–12 education to identify and address specific areas of educational need and benefit for students. Such efforts encompass not only working with individual students but also developing general policies and programmatic initiatives. From a minimum content standpoint, significant failures on the part of schools in this regard violate the second principle. The following are the three clear kinds of violations (with examples of each):

  i. unresponsiveness: failure to respond in a reasonable and timely way to parents' (or children's) questions or meeting requests;
 ii. indifference: failure to give heightened attention and to provide significant assistance to students in danger of failing courses;
iii. neglect: failure to address high dropout rates among certain categories of students through collecting and analyzing data and developing programs to address the problem.

The minimum content account set forth above inevitably raises an important question of practical ethics. Can it provide helpful guidance for decisions concerning complex, controversial, contentiously disputed, and difficult-to-resolve questions of educational practice and policy? The preceding discussion in this chapter of the two-pronged essential objective of an appropriate K–12 education for American children in Group A contains significant resources in this regard.

With respect to the first prong, the ideal objective of civic education on the K–12 level is to foster development of the attitude intrinsic to democratic deliberation. Such an attitude, as contended, must be widespread throughout the American body politic for democratic government in the United States to flourish. As emphasized earlier, a person need not have expert knowledge and awareness of public affairs as a prerequisite to exemplifying the attitude intrinsic to democratic deliberation. However, she must have the kinds of knowledge, awareness, and abilities that an appropriate education for children in Group A is reasonably calculated to impart.[41] Again, specifically, these are as follows:

- knowledge concerning fundamental aspects of the constitutional structure of American government and basic facts of American history;
- understanding of the reasons that justify the rights and responsibilities of membership in the American democratic body politic, especially the strong right of freedom of expression essential to democratic deliberation;
- recognition, in light of such justifying reasons, of the great extent to which the rights and responsibilities of members of the American democratic body politic are interpreted differently by reasonable persons;

- ability to follow lines of reasoning in arguments concerning public affairs and, especially, to recognize logical gaps and inconsistencies; and
- ability to recognize when factual evidence clearly supports, or does not clearly support, a particular conclusion and readiness to exercise the ability regardless of the factual conclusions that may ensue.

Turning to the second prong, and following Alan Gewirth, the idea of self-fulfillment has two key aspects—aspiration fulfillment and capacity fulfillment. The role of individual choice is integral to both of these aspects. An appropriate education for children in Group A, therefore, must aim to impart knowledge and develop abilities that foster growth with respect to particular faculties. These are the faculties which John Stuart Mill described in "On Liberty" both as crucial for "discerning or desiring what is best," and also as exercised only in making choices. Mill's examples, noted earlier, are "observation to see, reasoning and judgment to foresee, activity to gather materials for decision, discrimination to decide . . . and firmness and self-control to hold to one's deliberate decision."

Mill makes clear that the abovementioned faculties can be developed only through exercise in the context of making choices. But the developmental process is facilitated immensely and often indispensably when a choice maker can draw upon background resources of relevant knowledge and abilities. To provide such invaluable background resources, an appropriate education for children in Group A must contain, at a minimum, the following elements:

(1) principal academic focus in primary grades (K–5) upon developing to the greatest feasible extent competence in the basic cognitive skills of reading, writing, and numerical calculation as well as in basic computer literacy;
(2) significant exposure in subsequent grades (6–12) to diverse areas of enduring intellectual, artistic, and social interest and importance—for example, mathematics, science, literature, languages, history, civics (including contemporary moral and political issues), visual arts, and music;
(3) curricula and teaching methods in all academic grades (K–12) reasonably calculated to stimulate the engaged interest of students and to promote development of a wide range of important intellectual abilities;
(4) curricula and teaching methods which aim to develop all five of the first-prong elements apropos knowledge and abilities essential for meaningful deliberation as a member of the American democratic body politic (as enumerated above).

SIGNIFICANCE FROM THE STANDPOINT OF APPLIED ETHICS OF THE MINIMUM CONTENT ACCOUNT OF THE MORAL RIGHT OF CHILDREN IN GROUP A TO RECEIVE AN APPROPRIATE K–12 EDUCATION

"Applied ethics," as understood here, refers to an approach drawing extensively upon various fields of philosophy. These fields include moral theory, political philosophy, legal philosophy, and other relevant philosophical areas. They are used as conceptual resources to identify and examine concrete, specific (contrasted with abstract, general) ethical issues either for society as a whole or for individual persons about whom decisions must be made.[42]

As stated in chapter 1, such an approach is invaluable for (1) framing morally crucial questions about applied ethics issues, especially when one experiences a sense of discomfort in trying to address a question and yet finds it had to articulate the crux of the problem; (2) aiding in identification of morally relevant considerations with regard to the crucial questions; and (3) ruling out morally unacceptable answers to them.

The minimum content account of the moral right of children in Group A to receive an appropriate education could function as an important tool of applied ethics analysis. It is relevant to controversial, highly viewpoint-dependent, and hard-to-resolve issues concerning special education in the United States.

In disputes between parents of children with disabilities and public school district personnel, the parties often harbor attitudes, beliefs, and sentiments that prolong or exacerbate their conflict. For example, parents frequently believe or strongly suspect that the school district wishes to deal with the issues in connection with their child's special education program in the least costly and burdensome way.

At the same time, school district personnel often believe the following (although they rarely say so explicitly): the district personnel, in their opinion, have been compelled to expend large amounts of unproductive time and effort responding to the parents' extremely uninformed or unreasonable concerns, issues, and complaints.

An applied ethics analysis incorporating the minimum content analysis of the moral right of children in Group A to receive an appropriate K–12 education cannot itself settle the most intense disputes concerning education with respect to either programs for individual children or general policy matters. It provides a framework, however, which foregrounds the basic moral objectives of an appropriate education for Group A children.

Utilizing such a framework could facilitate reasonable and responsible compromises that each party considers principled. It could help disputants to understand and to appreciate the moral force of each other's position, their disagreement with the other's position notwithstanding (e.g. with respect to key arguments of the opposing side and basic concerns motivating them.)

As a corollary it could also help to provide each party a deeper moral understanding of its own position—of both its strongest and its less than strongest arguments—from a moral standpoint, and the core moral commitments implicit in the strongest arguments.

CRUCIAL DIFFERENCE BETWEEN GROUP A AND GROUP B CHILDREN FOR THE PURPOSE OF UNDERSTANDING WHAT AN APPROPRIATE K–12 EDUCATION MEANS

The IDEA enumerates diverse disability conditions entitling a child to receive special education and related services if such a condition adversely affects his or her educational performance. The following conditions are the ones currently covered under the IDEA: intellectual disabilities, hearing impairments (including deafness), speech or language impairments, visual impairments (including blindness), serious emotional disturbance, orthopedic impairments, autism, traumatic brain injury, other health impairment, and specific learning disabilities.[43] Each of the above disability conditions is defined explicitly in the IDEA's associated federal regulations.[44]

The analysis in this chapter applies fully to all nondisabled children and to all children with disability conditions enumerated in the IDEA, with the exception of intellectual disability. Nothing intrinsic to any of the IDEA's enumerated disability conditions, exclusive of intellectual disability, makes a child unable to derive meaningful benefit, with the aid of special education and related services, from receiving an appropriate K–12 education.

In regard to children with intellectual disability conditions, the analysis applies in a modified way, for reasons explained below, to children whose intellectual disability conditions are within the mild or moderate ranges. Intellectual disability has varying degrees of severity, which the *Diagnostic and Statistical Manual of Mental Disorders, Fifth Edition* (DSM-5) of the American Psychiatric Association divides into four categories—mild, moderate, severe, and profound.[45]

The two-pronged objective of an appropriate K–12 education for American children applies only partially with respect to children with intellectual disability in the mild or moderate range; it does not apply at all to children whose intellectual disability conditions are in the severe or the profound range.

Persons with intellectual disability conditions in the DSM 5's mild or moderate ranges can, with support, make personal choices in significant daily-living activities—such as shopping, traveling, and preparing food; recreation; and even employment. (Much more support, though, is needed in the moderate than in the mild range.)[46] To this point, learning environments designed for children with mild or moderate intellectual disabilities characteristically are well organized and clearly structured; they also provide extensively for personalized guidance, support, and encouragement.

The most educationally beneficial of such environments also incorporate significant opportunities (within a structured framework) for children to make choices that develop their abilities and judgment in regard to practical deliberation and that express their individuality. Accordingly, although relevant curricula and teaching methods for children with intellectual disabilities in the mild or moderate range differ greatly from those appropriate for nondisabled students, they share one underlying basic objective.

Effort must be directed in both cases toward providing the children a K–12 education reasonably calculated to help them acquire knowledge and develop abilities central to success in seeking the basic human good of self-fulfillment. The second prong of the essential objective of an appropriate education for children in Group A therefore applies clearly with respect to children with mild or moderate intellectual disability condition.

However, the vast majority of educators who are experienced at teaching children with intellectual disabilities in the mild and moderate ranges would say that the attitude intrinsic to democratic deliberation (described under the first prong) presupposes abilities of logical inference and abstract reasoning the children simply cannot develop.[47] The account set forth in this chapter of the moral right of children in Group A to receive an appropriate education thus applies, *but in a limited way*, to children who exemplify intellectual disability in the mild or moderate ranges.

In the case of such children (those with mild or moderate intellectual disability conditions), one key educational objective would be to impart knowledge to them about the public dimensions of their moral world but in a manner limited to utilizing educational materials and methods appropriate for the children's respective individual capabilities of awareness and understanding.

Persons with intellectual disability conditions in the severe and the profound ranges of intellectual disability, according to the DSM-5, "have little understanding of written language or of concepts involving numbers, quantity, and money." Their "spoken language is quite limited in terms of vocabulary and grammar," and "may be single words or phrases." Persons with severe intellectual disability conditions require "support for all activities of daily living," and "cannot make responsible decisions regarding well-being of self or others."[48]

The DSM-5 profile of profound intellectual disability characterizes the condition in terms of even more limited capabilities in the conceptual, social, and practical domains than those enumerated immediately above. For example, according to the DSM-5, "[t]he [profoundly disabled] individual expresses his or her desires and emotions largely through nonverbal nonsymbolic communication," and "is dependent on others for all aspects of daily physical care, health, and safety."[49]

It is apparent that the objective of imparting knowledge and abilities central to (a) American democratic deliberation and (b) having a reasonable chance for success in seeking self-fulfillment, as understood in terms of the two-pronged analysis, are inapplicable to children with severe or profound intellectual disability conditions. These children, nonetheless, have a moral right to receive an appropriate K–12 education. The justification for this belief, however, requires substantially more analysis. This will be developed in the next chapter, which concerns the zero-reject policy in American law of special education.

CONCLUSION

The focus of this chapter has been on ends rather than means. The chapter has analyzed in depth two closely related issues of ends—elucidation of the two-pronged objective of an appropriate K–12 education for American children in Group A and justification of the widespread belief that American children in Group A have a moral right to be provided such an education. This chapter, however, has not broached any of the highly controversial, complex, and difficult-to-resolve issues of K–12 educational practice and policy concerned with the means of providing an appropriate K–12 education for American children in Group A.

When practical, specific issues of means are highly controversial, complex, and difficult to resolve, moral clarity about them requires careful reflection upon abstract, general, deeply interpretive questions of ends. Thus, while the analysis set forth in this chapter alone cannot resolve the contentious disputes over issues of educational practice and policy regarding special education in American K–12 public schools, it nonetheless has special importance for addressing them.

No matter how deep or intense such disputes might be or how bitter, in some instances, they may become, in the vast preponderance of cases the disputants agree that American children in Group A have a moral right to receive an appropriate K–12 education. The analysis in this chapter has been aimed at developing a strongly plausible justification of this belief, and, in doing so, to make explicit and to clarify its underlying values and moral principles.

A successful analysis in these respects can help to (a) identify morally crucial considerations; (b) avoid losing sight of them in the heat of controversy, with the attendant danger of lapsing into, or spiraling downward toward, morally unacceptable conclusions; and (c) reach agreements that all disputants acknowledge as reasonable and fair, even if not optimal from their respective standpoints.

NOTES

1. Andre Agassi, *Open: An Autobiography* (Vintage: New York, 2010), 74–95.
2. Agassi, *Open: An Autobiography*, 78.
3. See Joel Feinberg, "The Nature and Value of Rights," *Journal of Value Inquiry* 4 (1970): 243–59; Robert F. Ladenson, "Two Kinds of Rights," *Journal of Value Inquiry* 13 (131979): 161–72.
4. See Bernard Gert, *Common Morality* (Oxford University Press: Oxford, UK, 2004), 4, 9, 35.
5. Note that the rights have been interpreted extensively by the U.S. Supreme Court.
6. See discussion in chapter 6, pp. 129–54.
7. Robert Cover, "Nomos and Narrative," in *Narrative, Violence, and the Law*, eds. Martha Minow, Michael Ryan, and Austin Sarat (University of Michigan Press:Ann Arbor, MI, 1993), 95.
8. Cover, "Nomos and Narrative," 96.
9. Alan Gewirth, *Self-Fulfillment* (Princeton University Press: Princeton, NJ, 1998), 3.
10. Amy Gutmann and Dennis Thompson, *Democracy and Disagreement* (Harvard University Press: Cambridge, MA, 1996).
11. John Rawls, *A Theory of Justice* (Harvard University Press, Cambridge, MA, 1971), 60.
12. How best to understand the closely related phrases "self-government" and "rule by the people" is a difficult question to answer about which political philosophers and theorists disagree. Under any reasonable answer, however, the following point is apparent: the conditions that these two difficult-to-interpret phrases denote flourish only to the extent that the attitude intrinsic to democratic deliberation ramifies throughout every important area of American life. In the words of the philosopher John Dewey,

> Unless democratic habits of thought and action are part of the fiber of a people, political democracy is insecure. It cannot stand in isolation. It must be buttressed by the presence of democratic methods in all social relationships.
>
> ("Democracy and Educational Administration," *School and Society* 45 (April 3, 1937): 457–67).

The most essential component of the "democratic habits of thought" to which John Dewey referred in the above passage are surely the elements of the attitude intrinsic to democratic deliberation.

13. Gewirth, *Self-Fulfillment*, 35.

14. Joel Feinberg, "The Child's Right to an Open Future," in *Whose Child?* ed. W. Aiken and H. LaFollette (Littlefield & Adams: Totowa, NJ, 1980), 193.

15. John Stuart Mill, "On Liberty" (Indianapolis, 1956), 29.

16. The bitter and deep resentment a person is justified in feeling if deprived of basic educational opportunities for seeking self-fulfillment is reflected strongly in the words that open Shakespeare's play *All's Well that Ends Well*. The speaker, a young man named Orlando, voices the following bitter complaint against his older brother Oliver:

> My brother Jaques he [i.e., Oliver] keeps at school, and report speaks goldenly of his profit. For my part he keeps me rustically at home, or to speak more properly stays me here at home unkept for call you that keeping for a gentleman of my birth that differs not from the stalling of an ox? . . . That is it . . . that grieves me, and the spirit of my father, which I think is within me begins to mutiny against this servitude.

The above passage suggests that Orlando regards being "kept at school" an entitlement due him in virtue of being, in Orlando's words, a "gentleman of my birth." If one replaces this phrase with the phrase "American child" then the above passage expresses the critical relationship for American children between receiving an appropriate K–12 education and being able to avail themselves of the opportunities needed to seek the basic human good of self-fulfillment in a meaningful way.

17. See John Stuart Mill, *Principles of Political Economy*, ed. Jonathan Riley (Oxford University Press: Oxford UK, 1994), chs. X and XI, 295–367.

18. It needs to be emphasized, however, that none of the four major philosophical theories of social justice to be considered in this section ignores or minimizes the moral importance of the three respectively at the cores of the other three major theories. Each theory, however, posits its own core concept as morally fundamental in the following respect. Utilitarianism, Rawlsian Justice as Fairness, Nussbaum's Capabilities Theory of Social Justice, and Moderate Libertarianism each considers its own concept as fundamental for understanding adequately why and how the core concepts of the other three theories are morally significant relative to the subject of social justice.

19. John Stuart Mill, *Principles of Political Economy*, ed. Jonathan Riley Oxford University Press: Oxford, UK, 1994), 160.

20. Rawls, *A Theory of Justice*.

21. John Rawls, "Justice as Fairness—Political not Metaphysical," *Philosophy and Public Affairs* 14 (1985): 227.

22. See note 9.

23. Rawls, *A Theory of Justice*, 62–63.

24. Rawls, *A Theory of Justice*, 63.

25. Rawls, *A Theory of Justice*, 195–201.

26. Martha Nussbaum, *Frontiers of Justice: Disability, Nationality, Species Membership* (Harvard University Press: Cambridge, MA, 2006), 74.

27. Nussbaum, *Frontiers of Justice*, 75.

28. The following list is an abridged version of Nussbaum's presentation of the Central Human Capabilities at *Frontiers of Justice*, 76–78.

29. Nussbaum, *Frontiers of Justice*, 78. (Note that Nussbaum does not discuss trade-off issues.)

30. The bearing of Nussbaum's capabilities account in the case of children with severe or profound intellectual disability conditions is discussed in chapter 3 at 67–69.

31. See Jan Narveson, *The Libertarian Idea* (Broadview Press: Peterborough, Ontario, 2001), Preface.

32. E.g., Jan Narveson says that according to Libertarianism, "The only relevant consideration in political matters is individual liberty: that there is a delimitable sphere of action for each person, the person's 'rightful liberty,' such that one may be forced to do or refrain from doing what one wants to do only if what one would do or not do would violate, or at least infringe, the rightful liberty of some other person(s)" (Narveson, *The Libertarian Idea*, 7).

33. See, e.g., Loren Lomasky, *Persons, Rights, and the Moral Community* (Oxford University Press: New York, 1987), 126–27.

34. This is because, as noted earlier, autonomous, self-determined, choice is essential for both aspiration fulfillment and capacity fulfillment. See discussion at 26–27.

35. E.g., Loren Lomasky acknowledges that impoverished families have a moral right to receive transfer payments to cover the costs of appropriate educational programs for their children but maintains also that K–12 public schools (contrasted with private schools) raise serious problems from a libertarian standpoint. See Lomasky, *Persons, Rights, and the Moral Community*, 174–79.

36. David Friedman, who is one of the most intellectually prominent figures in radical libertarian circles, refers to his position as "anarcho-capitalism." Another intellectually prominent figure among radical libertarians, Murray Rothbard, is credited generally as the first to use this phrase for self-identification purposes. See David Friedman, *The Machinery of Freedom: Guide to Radical Capitalism* (1989) http://digitalcommons.law.scu.edu/monographs/2: Murray N. Rothbard, *Toward a New Liberty* (Ludwig Von Mises Institute: Auburn, AL, 2006).

37. See Narveson, *The Libertarian Idea*, 275–77. Narveson does not explicitly refer to his philosophical position as radical libertarianism, and, indeed, backs away from doing so in the preface to *The Libertarian Idea*. Nonetheless, in an extensive discussion applying his philosophical analysis to issues of practical ethics concerning economic, social, and political questions, he expresses conclusions that coincide, close to exactly, with a radical libertarian outlook. See pp. 187–326.

38. See Narveson, *The Libertarian Idea*, 278–79.

39. See the discussion of Loren Lomasky's conception of "project pursuit" infra at 70–71.

40. See pp. 92–95 infra.

41. It must be emphasized that the five limited kinds of knowledge, awareness, and abilities are necessary but not sufficient for successful development of the attitude intrinsic to democratic deliberation. This attitude, as elucidated in the discussion of rights, responsibilities, and ideals of membership in the American democratic body politic, include: willingness to listen, careful consideration of all viewpoints, restraint, tolerance, and readiness to defend others from violation of their rights as members

of the American democratic body politic. Development of educational approaches to foster such an attitude poses large and diverse challenges of exploration and experimentation. Any such educational approaches, it seems apparent, themselves would have to exemplify the attitude which they seek to develop in K–12 children.

42. Applied ethics also is referred to as practical and professional ethics.

43. 20 U.S.C. 1401 (3) (A).

44. 34 C.F.R. 300.8 (b), (c).

45. American Psychiatric Association, *Desk Reference to the Diagnostic Criteria from DSM-V* (Washington, D.C., 2013), 18.

46. American Psychiatric Association, *Desk Reference to the Diagnostic Criteria from DSM-V*, 19, 20.

47. This conclusion expresses a personal judgment of the author based upon his having heard testimony of educators and read reports of school psychologists and social workers in special education due process hearings over many years.

48. American Psychiatric Association, *Desk Reference to the Diagnostic Criteria from DSM-V*, 21.

49. American Psychiatric Association, *Desk Reference to the Diagnostic Criteria from DSM-V*, 21.

Chapter 3

The Zero-Reject Policy

Timothy W. was born two months premature with severe respiratory problems which resulted in complex developmental disabilities, spastic quadriplegia, cerebral palsy, seizure disorder, and cortical blindness. At the age of five his perceptual, cognitive, and behavioral capabilities were limited to hearing "somewhat," seeing bright lights, smiling, crying, listening to music and television, and responding to talking and touching. Timothy's local public school district concluded that his disabilities were so severe that he was "incapable of benefiting" from an education, and therefore not entitled under federal and state law to receive special education.

In a landmark case, *Timothy W. v. Rochester, New Hampshire, School District 875*, the U.S. Court of Appeals for the First Circuit unequivocally rejected the school district's position. Referring to the federal IDEA, the court declared,

> The language of the Act could not be more unequivocal. The statute is permeated with the words "*all* handicapped children" whenever it refers to the target population. . . . Nor is there any language whatsoever which requires as a prerequisite to being covered by the Act, that a handicapped child must demonstrate he or she will "benefit" from the educational program. . . . The language of the Act in its entirety makes clear that a *zero-reject policy is at the core of the Act* (emphasis added).[1]

This chapter sets forth a moral justification of the zero-reject policy, which the court in the case of *Timothy W. v. Rochester NH School District 875* affirmed lies at the core of the IDEA.

The justification analyzes the policy in terms of the same four theories of social justice drawn upon in chapter 2, where they were used to ground a conception of the moral right to receive an appropriate K–12 education. The analysis in chapter 2 is applicable to all American children, both nondisabled children and children with disabilities, except for children with severe or profound intellectual disability conditions.

The social justice theories employed in the analysis are utilitarianism, Rawlsian Justice as fairness, Nussbaum's capabilities account of social justice, and moderate libertarianism. On first impression it may seem that none of these theories can provide an adequate framework for morally justifying the zero-reject policy. Further analysis, however, indicates that each theory has sufficient conceptual resources for developing a plausible justification.

THE ESSENTIAL OBJECTIVE OF AN APPROPRIATE K–12 EDUCATION FOR CHILDREN WITH SEVERE OR PROFOUND INTELLECTUAL DISABILITY CONDITIONS

According to the analysis developed in chapter 2, the following two-pronged objective is essential to an appropriate K–12 education for children in Group A, defined to consist of (1) all nondisabled children and (2) all children with disabilities except for those with severe or profound intellectual disability conditions as defined in the *Diagnostic and Statistical Manual of the American Psychiatric Association* (DSM-5).

An appropriate K–12 education for children in Group A is one that is reasonably calculated to impart knowledge and develop abilities needed for the following:

(a) exercising the rights, fulfilling the responsibilities, and exemplifying the ideals of membership in the American democratic body politic and
(b) having a reasonable chance for seeking the basic human good of self-fulfillment.

Not only all children in Group A, but also all children with severe or profound intellectual disability conditions (referred to collectively in chapter 2 as "Group B") have a moral right to receive an appropriate K–12 education. It is apparent, however, for the reasons stated in chapter 2, that neither the first nor the second prong of the two-pronged objective applies reasonably to children with severe or profound intellectual disabilities.

Accordingly, the essential objective of an appropriate K–12 education for children in Group B is the following:

> An appropriate K–12 education for an American child with a severe or profound intellectual disability condition is an education reasonably calculated to foster

significant development of dispositions and abilities crucial to central human capabilities relevant in the child's case given the particular aspects of his or her intellectual disability condition.

The above statement raises two immediately apparent interpretive issues. First, to what specific capabilities does the term "central human capabilities" refer? Second, what is (are) the relevant standard(s) for assessing whether significant development of dispositions and abilities critical to such capabilities has taken place in the case of a child with a severe or profound intellectual disability condition?

In answer to the first of the above questions, a central human capability, under Martha Nussbaum's conception (summarized in chapter 2), consists of a combination of diverse factors; primarily, these are opportunities, resource availability, and dispositions and abilities of a person (both physical and mental).[2] Considered together, the factors that make up a given central human capability are necessary for having a reasonable chance to realize one or more particular critical aspects of a good human life. Nussbaum thus distinguishes the capabilities from one another by the various critical aspects of a good human life for which, respectively, they are necessary.

So differentiated, Nussbaum identifies the following ten central human capabilities: (1) life; (2) bodily health; (3) bodily integrity; (4) senses, imagination, and thought; (5) emotions; (6) practical reason; (7) affiliation; (8) other species; (9) play; and (10) control over one's environment.[3]

Most, if not all, of the above ten capabilities could be thought of as applicable to children with severe or profound intellectual disabilities, although the dispositions and abilities crucial to the various capabilities that such children can exemplify are highly limited as compared with nondisabled children. Nonetheless, in many cases children with severe or profound intellectual disabilities reveal in their behavior a diversity of such dispositions and abilities, and often do so in surprising and highly individual ways.

Advancements in educational development of a child with a severe or profound intellectual disability condition, even if very limited when compared with developmental progress of nondisabled students, can be immensely meaningful to parents, caregivers, and others concerned deeply for the child's well-being.[4] This tends to generate firm convictions on their part that a good life for the child must include ongoing opportunities to develop relevant dispositions and abilities they believe she or he has either exemplified or has the potential to exemplify.

The immediately preceding point leads to the second of the key interpretive issues raised by the proposal above concerning the essential objective of an appropriate education for children in Group B (i.e., those with a severe or profound intellectual disability condition). What is (are) the relevant standard(s) for determining whether such a child has made significant progress in developing dispositions and abilities crucial to central human capabilities?

The relevant dispositions and abilities such a child exemplifies are often highly individual. In this regard persons concerned for the child's well-being frequently consider seemingly small developmental advancements deeply significant. One can never specify an appropriate reference group against which to compare the child's progress for purposes of quantitative assessment.

Instead, the appropriate standard involves using a reasonable approach—one that is both qualitative and individualized—for arriving at judgments about developmental progress of a child with severe or profound intellectual abilities. Such an approach presupposes procedures for developing, implementing, and assessing educational progress; these include at a minimum the following procedures:

- annual formulation;
- clear identification both of long-term educational goals and annual benchmark objectives;
- precise specification of key elements in the educational program developed for the child;
- ongoing review throughout the school year to assess developmental progress relative to annual benchmark objectives;
- adequate provision for review and, if needed, revision of the program throughout the school year;
- adequate involvement in development and implementation of the program by individuals experienced in interacting directly with the child both at home and at school and by individuals with relevant specialized knowledge of the child's intellectual disability condition.

The preceding discussion is intended to elucidate the essential objective of an appropriate education for children with severe or profound intellectual disabilities. The remaining discussion in this chapter sets forth a justification of the judgment that such children have a moral right to receive an education reasonably calculated to realize the essential objective of an appropriate K–12 education for them, as so elucidated.

JUSTIFICATION OF THE MORAL RIGHT OF AMERICAN CHILDREN WITH SEVERE OR PROFOUND INTELLECTUAL DISABILITIES TO RECEIVE AN APPROPRIATE K–12 EDUCATION

The justification developed in this section will draw upon the same major philosophical theories of social justice utilized as conceptual resources in chapter

2. In brief, a plausible justification of the moral right of children, whether in Group A or Group B, to receive an appropriate education must clarify the concept of moral requirement as applied to governments. This consideration, as also noted in chapter 2, gives rise to major disputed questions from the standpoint of both substantive moral judgment and philosophical theory.

Four separate arguments were presented (in chapter 2) for the conclusion that every child in Group A has the moral right to receive an appropriate K–12 education. Each argument differed significantly from the others in terms of how it integrates four important moral concepts in the context of analyzing the morally required duties of government. The four theories, each one paired with the concept it treats as morally basic, are as follows:

- utilitarianism—happiness/avoidance of unhappiness;
- Rawlsian Justice as fairness—fairness;
- Nussbaum's capabilities theory—human dignity; and
- moderate libertarianism—liberty (freedom).

All four arguments have strong prima facie plausibility. The overlapping consensus of four arguments, each grounded in a different major theory of justice, accordingly, provided a strong justification for the judgment that every child in Group A has a moral right to receive an appropriate education.

The analysis set forth in chapter 3 applies the same four theories again but directed toward a different objective—justification of the following judgment: every American child in Group B—that is, every child with severe or profound intellectual disabilities—has a moral right to receive an appropriate K–12 education, understood as an education reasonably calculated to foster significant development of central human capabilities relevant given the specific characteristics of the child's disability condition.

Utilitarianism

As noted in chapter 2, according to utilitarianism (developed in its classic form by John Stuart Mill), the idea of assessing human actions in terms of their consequences for promoting happiness and avoiding, or preventing, unhappiness for the greatest number of individuals underpins all the important moral concepts, including social justice.[5] For utilitarianism, a distribution of resources for public K–12 education is just if and only if it maximizes total utility, that is to say, it produces the greatest happiness, and avoids or prevents the greatest unhappiness for everyone affected by it.

Why Should a Utilitarian Consider the Zero-Reject Policy Morally Justified?

On first impression, many individuals might doubt that there is a plausible utilitarian justification for providing K–12 education for *any* children with severe or profound intellectual disabilities, let alone for those—covered under the zero-reject policy—who have the most extreme disability conditions. Someone harboring these doubts might point out the following three considerations:

- First, the cost per student of special education programs for children with severe or profound intellectual disabilities is quite high, requiring efforts of several staff members—for example, a special education teacher, a teacher's aide, and related services providers, such as speech and language, occupational, and physical therapists.
- Second, the number of children with severe or profound intellectual disabilities is small relative to the entire student population.
- Third, students with severe or profound intellectual disabilities make extremely limited educational progress compared with that of other students.

In light of these three considerations, the following two conclusions may seem unavoidable from a utilitarian standpoint to many individuals: first, total utility would not be maximized by providing special education programs for children with severe or profound intellectual disability conditions.

Second, and accordingly, the funds that would be needed for doing so should be devoted to the education of other children; for example, low-achieving nondisabled students living in impoverished conditions, who need additional resources devoted to the education provided for them in order to benefit from it.

The above three considerations are all indisputable. The conclusion, however, that on utilitarian grounds, public resources ought not to be used to fund special education programs for children with severe or profound intellectual disabilities overlooks the following additional consideration.

As noted earlier, the educational progress of a child with severe or profound intellectual disabilities, although minimal compared with that of most nondisabled students, may have enormous significance relative to the child's previously demonstrated abilities and capabilities, thereby resulting in immense benefit (in utilitarian terms) for the child and his or her family.

Thus from a utilitarian standpoint, one may regard special education programs for children with severe or profound intellectual disabilities to exemplify the following three characteristics: (1) high cost per student, (2) relatively small group of beneficiaries (i.e., principally the child with a severe or profound intellectual disability condition and his or her family and close friends, and (3) high level of benefit for those in the relatively small group of beneficiaries.

To analyze the appropriate policy conclusions with respect to use of public funds in the case of programs with the above three characteristics, utilitarians often draw upon the economist's conception of diminishing marginal utility. For the reasons developed immediately below, such an analysis yields a plausible utilitarian argument for public funding of special education programs for children in Group B.

Consider the following example—although unrealistic and oversimplified, it is appropriate for the purpose of illuminating the argument to be developed: Assume a total school district annual budget of $120 million. Assume as well that it would take $75 million to provide minimally adequate programs for all the students who do not have severe or profound intellectual disabilities (i.e., Group A children).

Under this assumption, following the marginal-utility approach, none of the first $75 million in the budget would be spent on educational programs for children with severe or profound intellectual disabilities (i.e., Group B children). The marginal-utility approach, however, dictates analysis at the margin, which in this case means a comparison of spending dollar number 75 million and one on programs for Group B children with spending it for other educational purposes.

The school district may conclude that marginal analysis favors continued expenditures to benefit Group A children (e.g., lunches for children from low-income families, art and music, and so forth). At some later point, however, diminishing returns set in with respect to expenditures for the benefit of Group A students. The critical question in connection with funding special education programs for Group B students, under marginal analysis, is the following: Will the point at which the next dollar spent is likely to result in greater utility for Group B children than for Group A children come before the entire school budget is exhausted?

If one generalizes the preceding example to draw an analogy between the school district's budget and the total resources available in the United States on expenditures of public K–12 education then the following line of argument is plausible: in light of prevailing economic conditions, the United States has sufficient resources to fund public K–12 education at a level that satisfies the minimum-content requirement of the right to receive an appropriate education (as stated in chapter 2) for both Group A and Group B children.[6]

For this reason, when considering the United States as a whole, a marginal-utility analysis would require expenditures on appropriate special education programs for Group B children to be made well before the entire pool of available funds for K–12 public education is exhausted.

Given the realities of public school financing, regrettably, some districts in the United States face the dilemma of choosing between appropriate special education programs for Group B children and minimally adequate programs for high-need Group A students (e.g., those suffering from economic deprivation). The reasons why, however, concern political and legal factors.[7] In terms of a utilitarian analysis, these political and legal factors, admittedly complex and difficult to address, need to be confronted. This is in contrast with acquiescing to a "reality" that forces some school districts to decide which groups will not receive enough resources to provide an appropriate education.

From the standpoint of the well-being of a Group B child and his or her family, very limited educational progress as compared with Group A children can thus have enormous positive consequences. Furthermore, in this regard, one needs to keep in mind that the only alternative to special education and related services under the IDEA for Group B children is a massive reduction in educational programs for them provided by public school districts.

Given the great cost of special education and related services for children with severe or profound intellectual disabilities, few parents could afford them, which, very likely, would result in the return of warehousing as the default alternative. Novelist Robertson Davies has portrayed vividly the complete physical isolation of a child with severe or profound disabilities, as well as the secretiveness and psychological repression, tinged with shame, of the child's family; the term "warehousing" only hints at this.

In his novel *What's Bred in the Bone* Davies describes the experience of Francis Cornish—scion of the most well-to-do family in a tiny Northern Ontario town. At age nine, Francis sees for the first time his older brother—a child with profound intellectual disabilities. Francis's parents have told him that his brother (also named Francis) died at birth. Instead, with the conspiratorial assistance of trusted family, servants, and friends, they staged a fake funeral of the older Francis and then stowed him away in the home of an aunt, Mary Benedetta. There he was looked after by two servants, Zadok and Victoria.

The younger Francis learns of this during a period when his parents, away in England during World War I, have left him in Aunt Mary Benedetta's care. One evening while housebound for several months with whooping cough, the younger Francis hears strange noises coming from a room that Aunt Mary Benedetta has forbidden him to enter. He stealthily climbs a long staircase up to the room in order to eavesdrop; Zadok and Victoria discover his presence. The narrator then relates:

> Francis [was] beckoned into the room, the door of which had been thickened and padded amateurishly but effectively. The room was large and bare, and suggested a sick room. . . . [What] Francis saw first, and what held his eyes for a

long time was the bed. It was a hospital bed with sides that could be slid up and down, so that at need it became a sort of topless cage. In the cage was an odd being, smaller than Francis himself, dressed in crumpled flannelette pajamas.

Because the top of [its] head was so small, the lower part seemed larger than it was, the nose longer, the jaw broader, and the very small eyes peeped out at the world without much comprehension. . . . They were now fixed on Francis.

"Come along Francis, and shake hands with your older brother," said Zadok. Then to the figure in the bed, "This is your brother Franko, come to see you."

Francis . . . walked toward the cage, his hand out, and the figure sank back on its blankets whimpering.

"This is Francis the First," said Zadok. "Be gentle with him; he's not very well."

Francis the Second had been ill for some months, and he was still weak. He fainted. When he came to himself again, he was in his bed and Victoria was sitting by him, dabbing at his brow with a cold towel.

"Now Frankie, you must promise me on your Bible oath that you will never tell where you've been or what you've seen. But I expect you want to know what's going on, and I'll answer a few questions. But not too many."[8]

An educational program for a child with severe or profound intellectual disabilities is costly, the educational goals identified in the program differ vastly from those appropriate for all other students, and efforts at implementing the program usually involve extended periods with no apparent success.

Even taking all these factors into account when considering, in utilitarian terms, the specific interests of children with severe or profound intellectual disabilities and their families, one cannot avoid the following conclusion: provision of special education and related services by public school districts, supported by IDEA funds, is immensely superior to an "educational" approach where the underlying beliefs and values resemble those reflected in the deeply hidden and dark at-home warehousing that Davies portrays in *What's Bred in the Bone*.

The preceding analysis amounts to a plausible utilitarian justification of the judgment that children with severe or profound intellectual disabilities have a moral right to receive an appropriate education. The analysis, however, does not consider specifically the question of why a utilitarian should construe this right on a zero-reject basis which includes even children with disability conditions like those of Timothy W.

In considering this question, one needs to understand clearly what the zero-reject policy requires, and what it does not require, of school districts. This policy requires school districts to deem eligible for special education and related services any child whose profile (as determined by the IDEA-mandated student evaluation process) fits within any of the categories of disability enumerated in the IDEA's definition of a "child with a disability."[9]

After a school district determines a child is eligible to receive special education and related services and develops an IEP for her or him, however, the zero-reject policy does not require the district to persist in trying to implement a specific IEP when it believes doing so would be pointless. If a school district believes that a student's current IEP has failed to provide the student educational benefit, then—according to the IDEA's requirement to provide all special needs students a free, appropriate public education—the school district must convene a new IEP meeting to address the situation and develop another educational approach.

The zero-reject policy says, in effect, that there are no students qualifying for special education and related services under the IDEA upon whom a school district may give up by concluding they cannot be educated at all.

Here one needs to keep the following facts in mind: Most public school districts face enormous pressures from diverse parental constituencies regarding many different kinds of educational and extracurricular programs, all while operating under severely limiting financial constraints. So if the zero-reject policy were eliminated, the number of children in Group B denied public school educational programs would, in all likelihood, quickly expand well beyond the small group presenting disability conditions that approximate those of Timothy W.

Perhaps it overstates the problem to say that the situation would revert quickly to the one that existed before enactment of the IDEA—one with a high prevalence of warehousing in forms that make the custodial keeping of the older Francis in *What's Bred in the Bone* seem benign by comparison.[10] Nonetheless, a utilitarian perspective would have to reflect the deep concern that, in the absence of the zero-reject policy, far more than only a few children in Group B would be denied educational programs that would be highly beneficial in utilitarian terms.

The Bearing of Peter Singer's Views Concerning Infanticide upon a Utilitarian Justification of the Zero-Reject Policy

A proposed justification of the zero-reject policy in terms of utilitarian moral theory would be deficient if it did not consider the controversial views of philosopher Peter Singer, who argues from a utilitarian standpoint on behalf of legalizing infanticide of newly born infants at high risk for serious disabilities.[11] The discussion that follows first summarizes both the argument Singer sets forth and the objections of his critics. It then considers the question of whether—and if so, how—the disagreement between Singer and his critics bears specifically upon a utilitarian justification of the zero-reject policy.

Singer defines the phrase "serious disability" to include not only severe and profound intellectual disabilities under the DSM-5 definition but also a wider range of conditions, both mental and physical; this encompasses, for example, both Down syndrome and hemophilia.[12] Using this definition, Singer writes,

> [T]he important reason why it is a terrible thing to kill an infant is the effect the killing will have on its parents. It is different when the infant is born with a serious disability. Birth abnormalities vary, of course, some are trivial and have little effect on the child or the parents, but others turn the normally joyful event of birth into a threat to the happiness of the parents and of any other children they may have. Parents may, with good reason, regret that a disabled child was ever born. In these circumstances the effect that the death of the child will have on its parents can be a reason for, rather than against killing it.[13]

Many people undoubtedly find Singer's conclusion shocking. On their view high risk of serious disabilities simply is not a relevant consideration that could morally justify taking the life of a newly born infant. Singer presents the following counterargument to this viewpoint:

> A self-conscious being is aware of itself as a distinct entity, with a past and a future. A being aware of itself in this way will be capable of having desires about its own future. For most mature humans these forward-looking desires are absolutely central to our lives, so to kill a normal human being against his or her wishes is to thwart that person's significant desires. Killing a snail does not thwart any desires of this kind because snails are incapable of having such desires. In this respect, however, newborn infants are in the same situation as snails. [Hence] there are fewer reasons against killing both babies and fetuses than exist against killing those who are capable of seeing themselves as distinct entities over time.[14]

Apropos the above line of argument, however, Singer also says the following, by way of clarification to avoid misunderstanding:

> None of this is meant to suggest that someone who goes around randomly killing babies is morally on a par with a woman who has an abortion [which Singer argues elsewhere would be a morally justified choice in a vast majority of cases]. We should put very strict conditions on permissible infanticide, but these restrictions owe more to the effect of infanticide on others than to the intrinsic wrong of killing an infant. . . . Thus infanticide can only be equated with [a morally justified] abortion when those closest to the child do not want it to live. [T]he position taken here does not imply that it would be better if no people born with severe disabilities should survive; it implies only that the parents of such infants should be able to make the decision.[15]

Critics of Singer's views press two principal objections, both of which also happen to cohere with a utilitarian approach to moral reasoning. First, making infanticide legal, the critics object, would convey a devastating message as to both the social and the civic identities of individuals with serious disabilities in Singer's sense (which, as noted above, goes well beyond the DSM-V definition of severe and profound intellectual disabilities).[16] It would express, and thereby validate, say the critics, the attitude that such individuals are at best second-class human beings—an attitude the IDEA and other federal laws concerning disability rights were enacted to eradicate.

Second, the critics contend that sending the above message would open the door wide to the possibility of more legally permissible infanticide, with the consequence that other groups besides newly born infants at high risk for disabilities generally considered serious would be targeted. The critics remind us, in this regard, that extermination of disabled individuals classified as "unproductive" or "unfit" paved the way for the Nazi exterminations of Jews, Roma, and others.[17]

Sorting out the key issues in the controversy between Singer and his critics, to consider their bearing specifically upon the question of whether or not one can develop a plausible utilitarian justification of the zero-reject policy, is not simple. Nonetheless, two principal conclusions can be reached.

First, as noted above, Singer stresses that his position "does not imply that it would be better if no people born with severe disabilities should survive; it implies only that the parents of such infants should be able to make the decision." Allowing the parents to make the decision, however, would not be a morally acceptable approach, *from a utilitarian standpoint*, if the parents could not count upon reasonable assistance in covering the huge costs of health care and education for a severely disabled child. If not, in most cases parents would reasonably conclude they face a decision situation with only one realistic alternative—that is, infanticide.

In terms of the utilitarian moral framework of analysis, addressing the question of what level of assistance is reasonable involves consideration of diverse benefits and harms about which disagreement is possible among individuals who are both impartial and morally conscientious. The utilitarian analysis developed in this section, however, provides a plausible case for the following conclusion: Apropos children with severe or profound intellectual disabilities, reasonable assistance includes the kinds of education and related services, provided at public expense, called for under the zero-reject policy.

Second, both Singer's position and the principal objections to it of his critics focus upon highly significant moral considerations from a utilitarian standpoint. Singer's position places in the foreground the following undeniable fact: while in many cases family members of children with serious disabilities find meaning and gain a deep sense of purpose in their familial roles, in other cases the continual struggle, stress, and strain of caring for a seriously disabled child becomes a crushing burden, devoid of both meaning and joy.[18]

Singer's critics focus upon different, but no less significant, considerations. They believe Singer's espousals of his position have had a significant retarding influence upon efforts to bring about still badly needed change in widespread attitudes that are highly detrimental to children with serious disabilities. More ominously, they also fear that implementing Singer's position could be a very dangerous step backward toward a return to the repugnant attitudes, deplorable practices, and, in a great many instances, horrifying conditions that federal disability law was largely enacted to combat and, hopefully, one day eradicate.[19]

It is extremely difficult to work out a satisfactory accommodation between the above two considerations of immense moral significance raised respectively by Singer and his critics. It is apparent, however, that any serious effort to do so within the framework of utilitarianism would have to include the zero-reject policy, given the preceding moral justification of the policy in terms of a utilitarian analysis.

Rawlsian Justice as Fairness

The core ideas of Kantian moral philosophy reverberate strongly in Rawlsian Justice as Fairness. By way of background, the moral theory first set forth by Immanuel Kant, and developed in diverse ways subsequently by many other philosophers, emphatically rejects the idea that utilitarian assessment of consequences is fundamental in regard to any kind of moral issue, including questions of distributive justice relative to expenditures for public K–12 education.

In his most well-known work on moral philosophy, *Groundwork of the Metaphysics of Morals*, Kant identifies as the ultimate moral standard a principle he calls the Categorical Imperative, which requires that one "should never act except in such a way that [one] can also will that [one's] maxim should become a universal law."[20] According to Kant, the Categorical Imperative is "the universal imperative of duty," from which "all other imperatives can be derived."[21]

Kant views ideas such as moral freedom, human dignity, and the grounds of respect for persons as prerequisites of the capacity for rational choice in regard to questions of morality; such choice is expressed by moral judgment in accordance with the Categorical Imperative.

The affinity of Rawlsian Justice as Fairness with Kantian moral theory becomes evident when considering the philosophical justification Rawls proposes for his two principles of justice. As noted in chapter 2, those principles are as follows:

(1) Each person has an equal right to a fully adequate scheme of equal basic liberties, that is, which scheme is compatible with a similar scheme for all.

(2) Social and economic inequalities are to satisfy two conditions. First, they must be attached to offices and positions open to all under conditions of fair equality of opportunity and second, they must be for the greatest benefit of the least-advantaged members of society.[22]

Apropos the affinity of the above two principles with Kantian moral theory, Rawls contends that when one views human beings as free and equal, his (Rawls's) two principles of justice provide the most appropriate foundation for shaping the basic structure of society. Rawls identifies this structure with the distribution of "fundamental rights and duties and . . . the advantages from social cooperation."[23] By "free" Rawls means that a person is capable of developing a reasonable conception of what he or she wants out of life, and by "equal" he means that a person has as much right as anyone else to try to realize such a conception.[24]

Rawls brings out the relationship between the two principles of justice and the freedom and equality of individuals through a striking thought experiment. Imagine a group of people, all rational and concerned—although not exclusively concerned—with their own well-being, who are called together to deliberate about the fundamental rules determining the basic structure of society.

While deliberating, however, they are placed somehow under a "veil of ignorance" that prevents them from knowing facts that could tempt them to base their respective choices of principles of justice on the desire to promote their own interests to the disadvantage of others. They are then told that they will be bound by the rules they select while under the veil of ignorance; once the veil is removed, they return to their various places in society.[25]

The purpose of the veil of ignorance is to "nullify the effects of special contingencies which put men at odds and tempt them to exploit circumstances to their own advantage."[26] If the people under the veil of ignorance do not know whether they are rich or poor, male or female, old or young, and so forth, then they cannot lobby for particular group interests. By contrast, in the spirit of Kant's Categorical Imperative, they must choose the principles of justice, under which they are to live, purely from a disinterested standpoint.

The capacity for rational choice in moral judgment has immense significance for Kantian moral theory. As previously indicated, Kant directly equates this capacity with human dignity and the grounds of respect for persons. Rawls's views in this regard have a close connection with those of Kant. In another article, widely read by academic philosophers, entitled "The Sense of Justice" (published in 1961), Rawls expressed the following position:

> [T]o whom is the obligation of justice owed, that is, in regard to beings of what kind must we regulate our conduct by the principles of justice? Put another

way, what qualifies a being to hold an initial position of equal liberty, so that in our dealings with him we are required to conduct ourselves in accordance with principles which could be acknowledged in such a position? The answer to this question is that it is necessary and sufficient that the being is capable of a sense of justice.[27]

Rawls's above-stated position has the following clear implication with respect to the zero-reject policy: Children with severe or profound intellectual disabilities are utterly incapable of a sense of justice and, for that reason, do not qualify as the kinds of beings toward which we must regulate our conduct by the principles of justice. From the standpoint of Rawls's position as expressed in the above passage, the zero-reject policy's moral basis, to the extent that it has one, resides in other moral standards than justice. These are standards such as benevolence or charity, which (unlike justice) are not universal in their scope and are discretionary, rather than mandatory, when applicable.

In the above-quoted passage, however, Rawls misstates the appropriate conclusions to draw from his veil-of-ignorance thought experiment in regard to the question of those to whom the obligations of justice are owed. The following four points state the appropriate conclusions correctly:

(i) Given the characteristics, Rawls stipulates the persons under the veil of ignorance possess, the obligation to "regulate conduct by the principles of justice" is required of (contrasted with owed to) all, and only "beings capable of a sense of justice."
(ii) In addition, Rawls's argument implies logically that a being "capable of a sense of justice" is owed the obligation of every other such being to regulate conduct toward her or him by the principles of justice.
(iii) Rawls's argument in terms of the veil of ignorance, however, does *not* logically imply the conclusion that the obligation to regulate conduct by the principles of justice is owed *only* to beings capable of a sense of justice.
(iv) To the contrary, Rawls's analysis in A Theory of Justice of the essential features of political institutions in a just society, as understood from the standpoint of his two principles of justice, provides conceptual resources for a plausible defense of the zero-reject policy; these are developed immediately below.

Legislators in a just society, according to Rawls, have a duty to enact legislation that adheres to his two principles of justice.[28] Furthermore, while the veil of ignorance prevents the individuals placed under it from knowing facts that could tempt them to base their choice of principles of justice on the desire to promote their own interests to the disadvantage of others, the veil does not rule out general information needed to make a rational choice. Such general information could include the following:

Severe or profound intellectual disabilities have a low incidence but require substantial expense to address in educational programs at even a minimally adequate level. Beyond a minimally adequate level, the expense involved in most cases requires making difficult choices between allocation of resources for programs to provide enhanced educational benefit for children with severe or profound intellectual disabilities and other educational programs that serve important needs in a just society.

Complex and controversial matters would come into play in attempting to frame broad basic principles of social justice in a way that also specifically addresses issues of educational need for children with severe or profound intellectual disabilities. These matters would lead the individuals placed under the veil of ignorance in Rawls's thought experiment to adopt the following stance: They would not select principles that address these issues directly but would instead view the issues as an appropriate subject for legislators within a just constitutional order to consider, guided by the principles chosen under the veil of ignorance.

In terms of Rawls's theory, as noted above, legislators are assumed to deliberate subject to requirements of a duty of justice, unlike the parties originally under the veil of ignorance. They are called upon to consider justice paramount when considering proposals for legislative enactment.[29] Implicit in the preceding point, legislators must *deliberate*.

In this connection, the two principles of Justice as Fairness serve to constrain the exercise of legislative authority by articulating its morally legitimate scope and strength. They (i.e., the two principles of justice) neither dictate specific legislation nor, in many instances, even provide significant guidance to legislators relative to fulfilling their principal responsibility. This responsibility was stated succinctly by Thomas Hobbes as the making of laws "needful for the good of the people."[30]

The centrality to Rawlsian Justice as Fairness of the capacity for rational choice in moral judgment does not logically necessitate the idea that duties of justice are owed only to those capable of a sense of justice. Such centrality instead is expressed primarily by the grounding of basic principles of morality in impartial reason—for Kant, the Categorical Imperative and for Rawls, the two principles of justice as fairness.

One may view a just constitutional order, in Rawlsian terms, as one in which legislators deliberate about topics of public concern pursuant to their responsibility to enact needful laws for the good of the people, consistent with the two principles of justice as fairness. Thus the critical issue from a Rawlsian standpoint is the following: What attitude would a legislator within a just democratic constitutional order, motivated by a sense of commitment to Rawls's two principles of justice, adopt toward the zero-reject policy?

For the reasons described above, such a legislator would recognize that a large inferential gap separates any conclusions regarding public expenditures for special education from Rawls's specific formulations of his two principles of justice. (Indeed, this holds true for most other significant public policy issues as well.) Accordingly, the legislator would acknowledge that in order for public deliberation to proceed in a Rawlsian spirit, the two principles of justice must be supplemented by morally plausible mediating principles.

Furthermore, the legislator would find the following two such mediating principles highly persuasive: first, in applying Rawls's principles of justice to matters on the legislative agenda, it would be necessary to distinguish two standards of justification, closely analogous to the distinction between strong and weak scrutiny drawn by the U.S. Supreme Court for the purpose of applying the equal protection clause of the Fourteenth Amendment.

Summarized briefly, in such cases that affect interests of individuals that the Supreme Court has deemed "fundamental," the government must meet a "strict scrutiny" standard of justification, requiring it to demonstrate the necessity of the law at issue to further a "compelling state interest." By contrast, when a challenged law does not implicate fundamental interests then the government need meet only a "weak scrutiny" standard of justification, which involves identifying a rational basis for the law—that is, a reasonable relationship to accomplishing a reasonable objective.[31]

In applying Rawls's two principles of justice to a legislative agenda, a Rawlsian legislator thus would distinguish between morally fundamental interests and interests that, although legitimately within the scope of the legislature's purview, are not morally fundamental. Furthermore, she would consider the standard of moral justification relative to Rawls's principles of justice as far stricter in the former case than in the latter.

The second mediating principle the legislator would deem plausible is that an appropriate K–12 education falls within the category of morally fundamental interests.[32] She would acknowledge the strong consensus of moral judgment throughout the world that an appropriate K–12 public education is a universal human right, reflected, for example, in Article 26 of the United Nations Declaration of Human Rights.[33]

In light of acknowledging the above two mediating principles, a Rawlsian legislator would regard as persuasive the following argument for the conclusion that children in Group B have a moral right to receive an appropriate education: Rawls's second principle of justice, which he terms "the Difference Principle," requires that social and economic inequalities must be to the greatest benefit of the least-advantaged members of society. In other words, their position would be worse off if the inequalities were eliminated.

A Rawlsian legislator would judge that this principle was clearly violated by the policies challenged in the *PARC* and *Mills* cases, summarized in chapter 1.[34] Under these two cases the state of Pennsylvania (*PARC*) and the District of Columbia (*Mills*) each completely excluded from K–12 public education children with diverse disabilities, including severe or profound intellectual disability conditions. All the affected children resided respectively in Pennsylvania and the District of Columbia, where for every other child such residency sufficed as a basis for admission to a public school.

Such unequal treatment would be considered clearly unjust by Rawlsian legislators. Given prevailing economic conditions at the time, no argument purporting to justify it from the standpoint of Rawls's Difference Principle could meet the strict scrutiny standard appropriate for a morally fundamental interest such as public K–12 education.

Having concluded that children with severe to profound intellectual disability conditions have a moral right to receive an appropriate K–12 education, a Rawlsian legislator would then want to determine the measures needed to secure this right. In doing so she would find the following considerations strongly persuasive—considerations which were raised in connection with the preceding utilitarian justification of the zero-reject policy.

Without this policy in place, many public school districts would take the position that some children in Group B cannot benefit from receiving special education and related services; accordingly, the school districts would decline to provide a free, appropriate public education for them.

Furthermore, as also noted in the preceding utilitarian justification of the zero-reject policy, public school districts usually find themselves under immense pressures with respect to decisions concerning resource allocation for diverse educational and extracurricular programs. It is a cause for deep concern that the number of children denied special education and related services on the ground that they cannot benefit from receiving them would thus expand well beyond the small group presenting disability conditions like those of Timothy W.

For the above reasons, a legislator within a just democratic constitutional order, who is motivated by a sense of justice as fairness in Rawls's sense, would conclude that the zero-reject policy is needed to assure that children with severe to profound intellectual disabilities receive the free, appropriate public education to which they have a right under Rawls's principles of justice.

Questions concerning public expenditures for special education and related services in regard to children with severe or profound intellectual disabilities can raise complex and controversial issues, requiring difficult decisions about resource allocation for diverse programs, all of which meet important educational needs in a just society. Nonetheless, based upon the conclusions developed in this section, from the standpoint of John Rawls's theory of Justice as Fairness, the zero-reject policy is morally required under contemporary conditions in the United States.

Nussbaum's Capabilities Account of Social Justice

The capabilities account of social justice (according to its originator, Martha Nussbaum, as summarized in chapter 2) identifies ten central human capabilities which are part of a minimum account of social justice in the respect that "a society that does not guarantee [them] to all its citizens, at some appropriate level, falls short of being a fully just society."[35] The capabilities account, Nussbaum explains, takes its cue from Aristotle's notion of the human being as a political animal by essential nature.

In Nussbaum's opinion, the capabilities approach differs from Rawlsian Justice as Fairness in the respect that

> [I]t sees the rational as simply one determination of the animal and, at that, not the only one that is pertinent to the notion of truly human functioning. Truly human functioning is animal through and through, and what makes for the specifically human dignity of this functioning is the combination of practical reasoning and sociability that infuse it.[36]

Nussbaum contends that "[the] capabilities approach, starting from a conception of the person as a social animal whose dignity does not derive from an idealized rationality, offers a more adequate conception of the full and equal citizenship of the mentally disabled and those who care for them."[37] Under the capabilities approach, says Nussbaum, in a just society every member receives adequate resources to develop capabilities "infused" by a "combination of practical reasoning and sociability," that are constitutive of "truly human functioning."[38]

Capabilities, in Nussbaum's sense, closely resemble the virtues under Aristotle's account in the *Nicomachean Ethics*.[39] Aristotle equates the virtues with dispositions of a human being necessary for her happiness, in virtue of her essential nature as a political, and thus social, animal, which are exemplified when she has to choose among actions or feelings, and in doing so "observes the mean . . . determined by such a rule or principle as would take shape in the mind of a man of sense or practical wisdom."[40]

From the standpoint of the capabilities approach, the basic entitlements of individuals in a just society relate to the conditions needed for the exercise and development of human capabilities understood in a way that tracks closely Aristotle's idea that sociability and practical reasoning lie at the core of essential human nature.

On first impression, it may appear (when viewed in terms of the capabilities approach) that there are morally crucial differences rather than fundamental similarities between the educational initiatives appropriate for children with severe or profound intellectual disabilities and their nondisabled peers.

In this regard, a critic of the claim that the capabilities approach offers an adequate conception of educational rights for such children might direct attention back to the perceptual and cognitive capabilities of Timothy W. As noted at the outset of this chapter, at age five these consisted only of hearing "somewhat," seeing bright lights, smiling, listening to music and television, and responding to talking and touching.

The concept of choice (let alone Aristotle's notion of virtue as the mean between extremes "determined by such a rule or principle as would take shape in the mind of a man of sense or practical wisdom,") has no readily apparent relationship to such simple behaviors. Correspondingly, the critic would conclude, Nussbaum's idea that social justice essentially requires the fostering of capabilities "infused" with "practical reasoning and sociability" appears inapplicable in the case of children with severe or profound intellectual disabilities.

Upon further analysis, the above objection to Nussbaum's capabilities approach has far less weight than it seems on first impression. In this case, one needs to recognize the exceptional profundity of Timothy W.'s disabilities, even compared to those of other children with severe or profound intellectual disabilities. In light of Timothy W.'s educational needs as described by expert witnesses at the trial in his case, an appropriate IEP for Timothy W. would likely not make much provision for other children to interact with him.

The situation is very much otherwise, however, with respect to the vast majority of children with severe or profound intellectual disabilities. Consider the following words of philosopher Eva Feder Kittay concerning the social receptivity and the capability to enjoy both listening to and making music of her (now adult) daughter Sesha and the other residents of the group home in which Sesha resides:

> My daughter was diagnosed as severely to profoundly retarded. She is enormously responsive, forming deep personal relationships with her family and her long-standing care givers and friendly relations with her therapists and teachers, more distant relatives, and our friends. Although she will tend to be shy with strangers, certain strangers are quite able to engage her. (She has a special fondness for good looking men!)
>
> Sesha now lives in a group home with five other severely to profoundly mentally and multiply disabled individuals. . . . I am greeted by smiles and acknowledgments of some sort when I arrive, and my daughter's passionate kisses exhaust both me and my spouse. All her roommates share her real appreciation of music: one, Billie, will "dance" in his wheelchair to rock music. Two others, Matt and Heather, love to sing along, and although they are incapable of

speaking, they vocalize in just the right pitch. . . . Nora is entranced by watching ballet and is a serious participant in the music therapy program. . . . For my own Sesha, "severely-profoundly" retarded though she is, music is her life and Beethoven her best friend. At our home, listening to the *Emperor's Concerto*, she gazes out the window, enthralled, occasionally turning to us with a twinkle in her eye as she anticipates some really good parts.[41]

For children with severe to profound intellectual disabilities, who exemplify capabilities similar to those of Sesha and her fellow group-home residents, the educational benefits of social development, cognitive stimulation, and reinforcement to expend communicational effort call for significant opportunities to interact with nondisabled peers.[42]

Such opportunities may involve full inclusion—that is, placement in a regular educational classroom with an aide—or they may involve a more restrictive placement, but with appropriate provision made for interaction with nondisabled students—for example, at lunch or recess, in strategically selected classes, or through a peer buddies program. Under the IDEA, decisions concerning which of the above kinds of approaches to adopt must be made on a case-by-case basis for each child at an IEP meeting to develop his or her educational program.

The capabilities approach is not only consistent with the procedures specified in the IDEA, it also provides an attractively intuitive account of the moral underpinning of the Act's LRE mandate. According to one way of understanding the mandate, it serves a precautionary purpose—to prevent the warehousing of children with severe to profound intellectual disabilities that prevailed before enactment of the IDEA.

From the standpoint of the capabilities approach, however, the LRE mandate also, and more positively, gives effect to the following three ideas: first, like all other children, those with severe to profound intellectual disabilities realize their human potential through interaction in a human social environment. Second, only such an environment allows for development of capabilities related to practical reason. Third, the more limited the possibilities of development in this connection, the greater the need to foster them through continuing human contact.

As with utilitarianism and Rawlsian Justice as fairness, the zero-reject policy enters into the picture here as well: it assures that public school districts comply with the requirements of the IDEA, including the LRE mandate, in a way that comports with the Act's fundamental purpose.

Moderate Libertarianism

In chapter 2 it was noted that for moderate libertarians the exceptionally heavy burden of justification for governmentally imposed limitation upon freedom, central to libertarian political thought in all its forms, is met in a small number of cases. One of these cases, acknowledged by some moderate libertarians, is taxation to assure that children are provided an appropriate K–12 education. One can articulate a plausible defense of the zero-reject policy within a moderate libertarian framework of moral analysis. Such a defense focuses upon the following three considerations:

(a) the intrinsic relationship between freedom of choice and seeking self-fulfillment;
(b) the central role of family relationships, for a vast number of people, in seeking self-fulfillment; and
(c) the indispensability of the zero-reject policy with respect to seeking self-fulfillment in family relationships for immediate family members of children with severe or profound intellectual disabilities.

The Relationship between Freedom of Choice and Seeking Self-Fulfillment

As noted in chapter 2, the concept of freedom of choice enters into the relationship between self-fulfillment and a good human life in two ways. First, the aspirations and capacities fulfilled when a person has a good life are chosen freely by that person; and second, whether a person fulfills them depends in large part (although not entirely) upon her or his own efforts, which in turn reflect her or his free choices of action.

Loren Lomasky, a prominent philosophical theoretician of moderate libertarianism, justifies a moderate libertarian moral framework in terms of an analysis according to which the notion of human beings as inherent "project pursuers" looms large. Lomasky elucidates the idea of project pursuit in a way that has striking affinities with Alan Gewirth's conceptions of aspiration and capacity fulfillment, which are summarized in chapter 2.

Like both aspirations and capacities for Gewirth, "projects" for Lomasky are (i) indispensable in seeking a good life exemplifying coherence, direction, and purpose; (ii) chosen freely, insofar as they involve a sense of personal commitment impossible to force upon a person; and (iii) pursued primarily through freely chosen—that is, uncoerced—choices of action.[43]

Apropos (iii) above, however, Lomasky recognizes that freedom of choice, while necessary, is not alone sufficient for successful project pursuit. In his judgment, a morally adequate libertarian philosophy must accommodate the idea of welfare rights to assure that no one's share of resources is so deficient for achieving success in project pursuit as to preclude any reasonable chance to have a good life. Lomasky expresses this judgment, on his part, succinctly in the following words:

> The thoroughgoing libertarian who regards all restriction of liberty as impermissible, whatever the grounds on which the restriction is based, will reject the claim there are any welfare rights. Such a libertarianism is indefensible. . . . Individuals have reason to value their own ability to pursue projects. Should that ability be placed in jeopardy by a system of rights such that one can *either* continue to respect other's rights *or* be able to pursue projects, *but not both* then one will no longer have a rational stake in the moral community established by that system of rights.[44]

The Central Role of Family Relationships in Seeking Self-Fulfillment

The immense importance of family relationships, for a vast number of people, in seeking self-fulfillment should be apparent to all. Moderate libertarianism recognizes this importance no less than do other major political philosophies. With respect to this, here again the words of Loren Lomasky are illustrative:

> [H]aving children is often an integral component of persons' projects. . . . For many individuals, the attachments that are most forceful and ripe with meaning are not to abstract ideas or to artifacts of one's creation or to large-scale social and political movements but to particular persons. Love for another makes that person's good one's own. . . . Few people can expect to produce a literary or artistic monument, redirect the life of a nation, or garner honor and glory that lives after them. But it is open to almost everyone to stake a claim to long-term significance through having and raising a child.[45]

In the above passage Lomasky says, "[l]ove for another makes that person's good one's own." This unquestionably true statement surely can apply in the case of parents, siblings, and grandparents of a child with severe or profound intellectual disabilities with respect to the disabled child.

The Need for the Zero-Reject Policy in Seeking Self-Fulfillment for Family Members of Children with Severe or Profound Intellectual Disabilities

Many immediate family members of children with severe or profound intellectual disabilities will acknowledge that they have carried heavy burdens and/or experienced intense emotional/psychological pain in their familial roles as parents, siblings, or grandparents.

Among these immediate family members, however, many also will say that despite, indeed through, the burdens carried and/or pain experienced they have derived a strong and deep sense of self-fulfillment.[46] No matter how personal or family-specific may be their diverse paths to, and definitions of, self-fulfillment, in every case both the paths and the definitions involve far more than only keeping a child with severe or profound intellectual disabilities alive and free from deprivation.

The secretive at-home warehousing depicted in Robertson Davies's novel *What's Bred in the Bone* enabled the older brother of Francis Cornish to survive into his early teen years under conditions that were neither neglectful nor intentionally cruel. No parent of a child with severe or profound intellectual disabilities in the United States at this time, however, who is concerned about his or her child's well-being, would regard as acceptable similar treatment for his or her child.

As noted in the previous section concerning Nussbaum's Capabilities Theory of Social Justice, for most children with severe or profound intellectual disabilities, significant opportunity to interact with nondisabled peers is critical for social development, cognitive stimulation, and motivation to expend receptive and expressive communicational effort.

As for any human being, for a child with a severe or profound intellectual disability condition, once basic needs in relation to survival and comfort are met, the child's quality of life becomes the critical issue for the child's parents and others concerned about his or her well-being.[47] Quality of life, in turn, depends critically upon development of basic human capabilities in the sense Martha Nussbaum sets forth in the capabilities account of social justice.

Identifying the most relevant capabilities in the case of a given child in Group B, then both developing and implementing a successful educational plan to foster them, requires not only deep commitment and strong perseverance, but also enormous amounts of effort by many different highly qualified individuals. No parents could do it by themselves, and very few have sufficient financial resources to cover the complete cost. As underscored by the court in the *Timothy W.* case, the zero-reject policy assures an appropriate K–12 education regardless of the nature and extent of a child's disability condition.

FROM A MORAL STANDPOINT, DOES THE ZERO-REJECT POLICY HAVE A LIMIT?

The preceding analysis and argument, drawing upon four major theories of social justice, provides a strong *prima facie* moral justification of the zero-reject policy at the core of American special education law. The analysis and argument, however, have not yet considered specifically how any of the four theories applies to the circumstances of the *Timothy W.* case. As noted at the beginning of this chapter, that case concerned a child whose disability conditions were especially profound, even when compared to those of other children with profound intellectual disability conditions.

The *Timothy W.* case thus raises the following three questions:

(1) From a moral (contrasted with a legal) standpoint, does the zero-reject policy have a limit?
(2) (a) If the answer to question (1) is "no" then why?
    (b) If the answer is "yes," then what is the limit, and why?
(3) If the answer to question (1) is "yes" then, given the answer to question 2 (b); do Timothy W.'s disability conditions lie within or outside of the moral limit of the zero-reject policy? And, in either case, why?

Here are answers to the above questions:

(1) Yes—morally speaking, the zero-reject policy has a limit.
(2) The limit is passed when a child is in a permanent vegetative state—that is to say, based upon a valid medical determination, the child is permanently unconscious to the extent of not responding to any sensory stimulation whatsoever.
(3) Timothy W. was not in a permanent vegetative state. His case thus fell within the moral limit of the zero-reject policy.

Few people, if any, would disagree with the answers above to questions (1) and (2). Apropos these answers, extensive discussions in this chapter and in chapter 2 were devoted to articulating the essential objectives of an appropriate K–12 education for nondisabled children, and for children with disabilities, including those with severe or profound intellectual disabilities. The entire discussion throughout both chapters (unsurprisingly) presupposed consciousness on the part of children who receive a K–12 education.

From a moral standpoint, the zero-reject policy does not, and (logically) cannot, apply with respect to a child in a permanent vegetative state. Unlike the answers to questions (1) and (2), however, the answer to question (3) is controversial. A person reasonably could doubt whether, from a moral standpoint, being in a permanent vegetative state is the one and only exception to the zero-reject policy. The discussion below sets forth a defense of this position.

The following points were noted in developing a moral justification of the zero-reject policy in terms of utilitarianism—the first major theory of social justice considered in this chapter: K–12 public school districts often face enormous pressures in regard to different kinds of academic and extracurricular programs from diverse parental constituencies, under severely limited financial constraints.

For this reason, if the zero-reject policy were eliminated, in all likelihood, the number of children with severe or profound intellectual disabilities denied educational programs would soon expand well beyond the small group presenting disability conditions that approximate those of Timothy W.

The above problem could not be addressed satisfactorily through the due process hearing procedures mandated by the IDEA. In the absence of the zero-reject policy, whether a child is likely to benefit from receiving special education and related services would be a key threshold issue in regard to initiating or continuing an educational program for him or her. The legal standards adopted to address this issue, it seems clear as a matter of logic, would have to fall into one or another (but only one) of the following three cases:

- Case A: strongly favorable to parents;
- Case B: strongly favorable to neither parents nor school districts; and
- Case C: strongly favorable to school districts.

Case A, would amount to a judicial stance holding school districts to a standard more or less the same as the zero-reject policy but without calling it such.

In regard to Case B, if legal standards, as interpreted and applied by courts, strongly favored neither parents nor school districts, there would be many instances in which parties could not make reliable predictions concerning the outcome of due process hearings. Such hearings, over the question of whether a particular child with severe or profound disabilities would benefit from receiving special education, would not only have uncertain outcomes, but would also put both sides to great expense, expenditure of time, and stress. With respect to Case C, however, in which courts adopted a stance strongly favorable to school districts, parents, but not school districts as well, would have strong incentives not to initiate due process hearing procedures. Public school districts, accordingly, would in all likelihood undertake far less effort than they would under the zero-reject policy to develop and implement programs to address the educational needs of children with severe or profound intellectual disabilities.

For the reasons discussed in this chapter, such an outcome would be morally unjustifiable from the standpoints of utilitarianism, Rawlsian Justice as fairness, Martha Nussbaum's capabilities account of social justice, and moderate libertarianism.

Timothy W. was not a child in a permanent vegetative state. His sensory and intellectual capabilities, nonetheless, were both so limited that a usual response to hearing about them for the first time is inability to think of any measures that could have been educationally beneficial for him. Two different questions, indicated below, however, have primary importance from a moral standpoint:

(1) Could an appropriate educational plan for Timothy W. have been created that
    (a) identified objectives, the attainment of which would constitute significant progress in developing central human capabilities relevant for Timothy W. and
    (b) set forth a program reasonably calculated to help Timothy W. achieve the objectives?
(2) Was it possible to implement such an educational plan without infringing upon the right of other children in the school district to receive an appropriate education?

In the Timothy W. case, the school district presumably collected and analyzed information in the context of an evaluation process. At the completion of the process, but before going any further, the school district concluded Timothy W. could not benefit from receiving special education. Such a conclusion was unwarranted.

As noted earlier in this chapter, there is much variation in the characteristics children with severe or profound intellectual disabilities exemplify. Such different characteristics can affect both how and to what extent different children could benefit from receiving special education. At most the school district could have reasonably concluded, after completing its evaluation of Timothy W. but before undertaking follow-up educational planning and implementation efforts, that such follow-up efforts would pose difficult challenges.

However, interpreted in moral terms, the zero-reject policy requires public school districts *to address such challenges*, albeit in ways that do not infringe upon the educational rights of other children enrolled in the district. Morally, no less than legally, American K–12 public school districts have a responsibility to provide an appropriate education for every child, so long as the child is not in a permanent vegetative state.

CONCLUSION

Strong moral considerations support the zero-reject policy at the core of American special education law. They require, however, a detailed and careful statement, drawing a number of careful distinctions and presenting information, which, while neither complex nor difficult to comprehend, may be unfamiliar to people not involved with special education in some way or other.

The analyses set forth in both this chapter and chapter 2, when considered together, provide a highly plausible justification of the judgment that *all* American children, including children with severe or profound intellectual disabilities, have a moral right to receive an appropriate K–12 education.

Controversial issues remain, however, concerning interpretation and application of this right with respect to children with disabilities. The remaining four chapters of this book will address such issues.

NOTES

1. F.2d 954, 960 (1st Cir, 1989) cert. denied 493 U.S. 983 (1983).
2. See chapter 2 at pp. 19–48.
3. See chapter 2 at pp. 19–48.
4. E.g., see statement by philosopher Eva Feder Kittay about her daughter Sesha who has severe intellectual disabilities at p. 68 infra.
5. See chapter 2 at pp. 19–48.
6. Refer back to statement of minimum content account in chapter 2.
7. The political factors concern the immense difficulties involved in generating the level of public support needed to assure that all children receive a FAPE reasonably calculated to confer educational benefit. The legal problem, put briefly, is the following: Throughout the USA, public school districts rely for their funds primarily from local property taxes. As a result, districts with low bases of taxable property face severe limitations in regard to the amount of money they can raise. Despite the vast differences in per pupil expenditures between school districts with high and low property tax bases, in a major case, *San Antonio Independent School District v. Rodriquez* (411 U.S. 1 [1972]), the Supreme Court upheld the constitutionality, under the Fourteenth Amendment equal protection clause, of using local property taxes as the principal source for funding public K–12 education.
8. (Viking: New York, 1985), 130–31.
9. Here is the statutory definition of "a child with a disability." 20 U.S.C. 1401 3A.

> The term "child with a disability" means a child
> (i) with intellectual disabilities, hearing impairments (including deafness), speech or language impairments, visual impairments (including blindness), serious emotional disturbance . . . , orthopedic impairments, autism, traumatic brain injury, other health impairments, or specific learning disabilities; and
> (ii) who by reason thereof needs special education and related services.

10. Burton Blatt and Fred Kaplan, *Christmas in Purgatory: A Photographic Essay* (originally published, Boston: Allyn and Bacon, 1966).

11. Controversy surrounding Singer's views on infanticide continued for over two decades which included both violent protest demonstrations and cancellations of conferences at which Singer was an invited speaker. To obtain a sense of both the extent and the intensity of feeling involved in the controversy one need only do a Google search on the subject of Peter Singer's views on infanticide.

12. Peter Singer, *Practical Ethics*, 3rd Ed. (Cambridge University Press: Cambridge, UK, 2011), 163–64.

13. Singer, *Practical Ethics*, 161.

14. Singer, *Practical Ethics*, 76–77.

15. Although Singer uses the word "severe" in the last sentence, the context makes it apparent that here he equates "severe" with "serious," in the sense noted above.

16. *Social identity and civic identity*. The term "social identity," as used in this chapter, applies clearly whenever the following conditions jointly apply:

  (a) As a result of processes widely regarded (rightly or wrongly deemed) to be credible, a given individual is regarded widely as classified appropriately under a particular category.
  (b) There is broad (although not necessarily universal) consensus in society concerning characteristics of a person so classified.
  (c) Classification of such a person in terms of a particular category has significant implications for the attitudes other persons in society tend to take toward him or her.

In this discussion, the term "civic identity" refers to the basic rights and responsibilities of a person as a member of the body politic in a particular civil society. The term "civil society" refers to a social order in which morally legitimate governmental authority exists. This means that some person(s) or other has (have) a moral right to govern and, correlatively, every other member of the civil society (considered, collectively, the body politic) has a moral duty to obey. Different civil societies may have different predominant understandings of both the scope and the force of the moral right to govern, and, accordingly, different predominant views of the scope and force of the moral duty to obey.

17. E.g., Wesley J. Smith, "Infanticide Must Be Combated Carefully," *The Human Life Review*, October 4, 2010.

18. Andrew Solomon, *Far from the Tree* (Scribner: New York, 2012), 23–25.

19. Singer opines that implementing the policy he advocates carries with it "only a small but nevertheless finite risk of unwanted consequences." This opinion, some would say, minimizes badly his critics' principal concerns. In this regard, Singer does not, for example, consider the following two issues. First, as noted earlier, in Singer's sense, the term "serious disability" is far broader than the DSM-V definitions of severe or of profound intellectual disability encompassing, for example, both Down syndrome and hemophilia. For this reason, if Singer's proposal went into effect then in many cases children with serious disabilities (in Singer's sense) would be capable of comprehending that others in society regard them as belonging to a group whose members are alive only because their parents chose not to opt for infanticide. What psychological/emotional impact would such comprehension have for a child whose parents had chosen not to authorize infanticide in his or her case? One cannot dismiss

as mere speculation the likelihood it would engender a deep-seated and possibly lifelong devastating inability (either partial or full) to experience either joy or meaning in life.

Second, in regard to concerns that "departing from the traditional sanctity of life ethic" would set a deeply dangerous precedent, Singer avers, "there is little danger it would lead us to slide into the abyss of Nazi style atrocities." Short of this worst-case scenario, however, there are other dangers one needs to consider. Decisions about enactment, implementation, and interpretation of law and public policy apropos a given matter, such as disability rights, on the parts of legislators, administrative agencies, and judges are affected strongly by their perceptions, both of public sentiment and of the directions in which law and public policy are moving. From this standpoint, would making infanticide legal in the case of newly born infants at high risk for serious disabilities worsen badly the situation for seriously disabled children in terms of effective enforcement, protection from retrenchment, and extension when needed, of hard fought for legal rights they now have? Singer does not address this vitally important question in terms of a utilitarian framework of analysis.

20. Immanuel Kant, *Groundwork of the Metaphysics of Morals*, trans. J.W. Ellington (Hackett: Indianapolis, 1981); first published, 1785).

21. Kant, *Groundwork of the Metaphysics of Morals*, 30.

22. Chapter 2, pp. 19–48.

23. Rawls, *A Theory of Justice*, 7.

24. John Rawls, *Political Liberalism* (Columbia University Press: New York, 1993), 278–81.

25. Rawls, *A Theory of Justice*, 142–43.

26. Rawls, *A Theory of Justice*, 136.

27. John Rawls, "The Sense of Justice," *Philosophical Review* 72 (1963): 300.

28. Rawls, *A Theory of Justice*, 195–201.

29. Rawls, *A Theory of Justice*, 198.

30. Thomas Hobbes, *Leviathan*, ed. M. Oakeshott (Collier: New York, 1962), 255 (first published 1651).

31. Gerald Gunther,*Cases and Materials on Constitutional Law*, 12th Ed. (Foundation Press: Mineola, NY, 1985), 819–77.

32. Interestingly, in *San Antonio v. Rodriquez* (cited at n. 10) the opinion of the Supreme Court (reflecting a 5-4 majority) seemed to acknowledge this conclusion even though it ruled that, from a constitutional standpoint, education is not a fundamental interest. In the words of Justice Powell, the author of the opinion, "[N]othing this Court holds today in any way detracts from our historic dedication to public education. We are in complete agreement with the three judge panel below that 'the grave significance of education both to the individual and to our society' cannot be doubted" (411 U.S. 1, 30 [1972]).

33. Article 26 says, "Everyone has the right to an education. Education shall be free, at least in the elementary and fundamental stages. . . . Education shall be directed to the full development of the human personality and the strengthening of respect for human rights and fundamental freedoms." Furthermore, the legislator would be aware of the considerations supporting this judgment, developed in chapter 2, which ground

the moral right to receive an appropriate K–12 education not only in Rawlsian Justice as Fairness, but also in three other major theories of social justice.

34. Chapter 1, p. 4.
35. Martha Nussbaum, "Capabilities and Disabilities: Justice for Mentally Retarded Citizens," *Philosophical Topics* 30, no. 2 (2002): 158.
36. Nussbaum, "Capabilities and Disabilities," 158.
37. Nussbaum, "Capabilities and Disabilities," 135.
38. Nussbaum, "Capabilities and Disabilities," 157.
39. Aristotle, *Nicomachean Ethics*, ed. J. A. K. Thompson (Penguin: London, 2004).
40. Aristotle, *Nicomachean Ethics*, 6 (A1107 1-4).
41. E. F. Kittay, "At the Margins of Personhood," *Ethics* 116 (October, 2005): 126.
42. See A. Gartner and D. K. Lipsky, "Inclusion and School Restructuring: A New Synergy," in *Restructuring for Caring and Effective Education*, eds. R. A. Villa and J. S. Thousand (P.H. Brookes: Baltimore, 2000), 38–55; and M. F. Giangreco et al., "Problem Solving to Facilitate Inclusive Education," in *Restructuring for Caring and Effective Education*, eds. R. A. Villa and J. S. Thousand (P.H. Brookes: Baltimore, 2000), 293–97.
43. Lomasky, *Persons, Rights, and the Moral Community*, 16–36.
44. Lomasky, *Persons, Rights, and the Moral Community*, 127.
45. Lomasky, *Persons, Rights, and the Moral Community*, 167.
46. Solomon, *Far from the Tree*, 24–25.
47. The most well-known articulation in modern psychological theory of this point, rooted in Aristotle's Nicomachean Ethics, is Abraham Maslow's theory of motivation. See "A Theory of Human Motivation," *Psychological Review* 50, no. 4: 370–96, http://psychclassics.yorku.ca/Maslow/motivation.htm.

Chapter 4

Inclusion, Community, and Justice

Beth B. was a child with disabilities who had Rett syndrome—a condition with symptoms that include multiple disabilities in the areas of cognition, communication, and motor functioning. Beth's parents, her private therapists, and the staff of professional educators who worked with her at school estimated her motor abilities to be within the range of five to seven months.

As for Beth's cognitive and communicational abilities, she expressed interest in people, especially in their faces. She smiled, laughed, responded positively to music, and had definite likes and dislikes concerning food, which she expressed through eye gaze, bodily movements, and facial expressions. This was because Beth could not speak but instead communicated primarily through her eye gaze.

For this reason, educational efforts to help her develop her communicational and cognitive abilities relied to a large extent upon computer-based assistive technology equipment, which presented her with arrays of pictures on an adapted keyboard, among which she could focus her eye gaze to indicate a choice.

Beth's parents strongly urged that Beth be placed in a regular education kindergarten classroom, with a one-on-one aide, adapted physical education, and the related service of speech and language therapy. Their school district agreed, and Beth's regular education classroom placement continued through second grade.

However, at the end of second grade the school district decided that, in the opinion of its professional educators who worked with Beth, her educational needs would be better served through placement in a special education classroom with a small number of other students, all having severe or profound intellectual disabilities. Beth's parents strongly disagreed and requested a hearing on the matter, to which they were entitled under federal and state laws regarding special education.

The special education hearing officer in the *Beth B.* case conducted a lengthy hearing that included testimony from numerous individuals over many days.[1] Those testifying included Beth's parents, teachers, and private therapists, as well as expert witnesses called by each side. The hearing officer ultimately issued an opinion upholding the position of the school district.[2] Beth's parents then appealed the decision in the federal courts, where it was upheld by both the Federal District Court and the Federal Court of Appeals.[3] The parents then filed a petition for *certiorari* with the U.S. Supreme Court, which the Court denied.[4]

The *Beth B.* case called for evaluation of extensive testimony and evidence. The legal issues the case presented were far from easy to resolve. This chapter is not intended to re-adjudicate the case many years after its thorough and, at least for the foreseeable future, settled outcome in the U.S. federal court system. Instead the chapter will consider the case as the point of departure for an ethical inquiry which, it is to be hoped, will help to achieve a clearer and deeper moral understanding of a major issue in special education—inclusion in regular education programs of children with disabilities, especially in the case of children with severe or profound intellectual disabilities.

For the purpose of providing background, the chapter will begin by revisiting one of the fundamental aspects of American special education law (already summarized in chapter 1), that define the context in which controversies over inclusion between parents and school districts arise—the LRE mandate of the IDEA.

THE IDEA'S LRE MANDATE

The IDEA requires that "special classes, separate schooling, or other removal from the regular education environment occur only when the nature or severity of the disability of a child is such that . . . education in a regular education classroom with supplementary aids and services cannot be achieved satisfactorily."[5] This requirement raises the question of the proper legal standards to employ for resolving disagreements that may arise about whether education of a child with disabilities "cannot be achieved satisfactorily" in the regular education environment.

Although the U.S. Supreme Court has not addressed this issue, the courts in several circuits of the U.S. Court of Appeals have done so.[6] The legal standards adopted by the various circuit courts, although worded differently, are virtually identical in terms of the crucial considerations they identify. Each standard calls for assessment of the following:

- the academic, as well as the nonacademic but nonetheless educationally relevant, benefits of placement in a regular education program, as compared with a special education program, for the child with a disability;
- the impact of regular education placement of the child with a disability upon the educational progress of the other (nondisabled) students; and
- the financial costs associated with the regular educational placement of the child with a disability.

In cases involving children with severe or profound intellectual disabilities, however, the question of whether a child's education can be "achieved satisfactorily in the regular education environment" tends to merge with the following legal issue: Does the special education program at issue in the case pass the relevant legal test for satisfying the IDEA's requirement to provide a FAPE? That is to say, does the program meet the standard set forth in the U.S. Supreme Court case of *Board of Education of the Hendrik Hudson School District v. Rowley* summarized in chapter 1?[7]

The above issue arises because parents in such cases invariably argue that only a fully inclusive regular educational placement for their child alone meets the *Rowley* standard of being "reasonably calculated to enable the child to receive educational benefit."[8] The school district, however, invariably argues the polar opposite—that is, that regular education placement for the child would not be appropriate in terms of the *Rowley* standard.[9] In such cases, conflicting evidence and arguments about what is educationally appropriate from the standpoint of the *Rowley* standard always loom large.

JUSTICE AND COMMUNITY

States that accept IDEA funding, as noted in chapter 1, are required to provide a FAPE for every child eligible to receive a special education program. As seems evident given the IDEA's essential purpose, the consensus of judicial opinion holds that school districts may not consider the issue of expense in deciding whether or not a particular placement is educationally appropriate for a child.

However, the judicial consensus also holds that in the case of a choice between several placements, each of which is educationally appropriate in legal terms (i.e., which meet the standard set by the U.S. Supreme Court in *Rowley*), a school district may consider their respective costs as a legitimate factor of decision.

Questions of distributive justice thus can, and do, enter into educational placement decisions for children with disabilities. So long as the program options considered for a student satisfy the *Rowley* standard of being "reasonably calculated to enable the child to receive benefit," then questions may arise concerning the allocation of resources to the student's program in relation to other areas of expenditure in the school district's budget.

In some important disputes between parents and school districts over these kinds of matters, however, questions of distributive justice are interrelated with questions that call for interpretation, from a moral standpoint, of the idea of an educational community. These questions can be difficult to disentangle. The nature of such entanglement is brought out by a closer look at some of the sources of contention in the *Beth B.* matter.

At the due process hearing, Beth's parents found much to criticize in the school district's efforts to provide an inclusive educational placement for Beth. The parents opined that the school district provided inadequate training to its staff who worked with Beth, was grossly tardy in the implementation of educationally beneficial assistive technology, and that its teachers and staff members at IEP meetings were preoccupied with Beth's deficits, rather than appreciating her educational progress.

Furthermore, although Beth was placed in a regular education classroom, in the opinion of one of the expert witnesses the parents called to testify, "No concerted effort was made to include [Beth] in the learning activities in the life of [Beth's] classroom."[10] From the parents' perspective, these and other deficiencies stemmed in large part from the school district's refusal to work with them, as well as with specialists retained privately by the parents, in ways the parents considered meaningful.

The school district, in turn, recounted extensive (in its opinion) efforts that it had undertaken to develop and implement a successful regular education classroom inclusionary program for Beth. Both administrators and teachers testified to what they considered frequent interactions with Beth's parents concerning diverse aspects of her program.

The teachers and other school district staff members who worked with Beth testified in great depth concerning the specific reasons they believed that Beth had not benefited educationally despite these efforts; they also explained why, in their judgment, she would benefit from placement in a special education classroom, with opportunities for partial mainstreaming.

Further witnesses called to testify by the school district stated reasons for concluding that even greater difficulties would arise in providing an appropriate (beneficial) education for Beth in higher grades. They also noted the difficulties this would pose for achieving adequate educational progress for the rest of the class.

The decision of Beth B's parents to shoulder the effort, intense emotional strain, and great expense of a special education due process hearing reflected the belief that only placement in a regular education classroom could provide Beth the appropriate K–12 education to which she had a moral right.

Beth's parents believed that any other kind of program, regardless of how well-intentioned on the part of the school district, would consign Beth (and themselves as well) to a subordinate status—that is, to something less than full membership—in the educational community of Beth's school.

Beth's parents recognized that successful implementation of an appropriate educational program for Beth would require a radical transformation of outlook among all members of her educational community. For this reason, the parents believed as well that the school district had significant responsibilities in regard to identifying and undertaking the necessary transformative efforts.

In contrast, the school district dissented vigorously from the parents' perspective that anything other than full regular education classroom inclusion amounted to denying Beth and her parents a status of full membership in their educational community. The school district's view was that, to the contrary—given its efforts to educate Beth—it had treated her and her family as full-fledged educational community members; this fulfilled its responsibility, as a public school district, to accord Beth the same educational respect and concern to which every child has a right.

When people feel marginalized, excluded, or unwelcome in any given particular social context it may or may not be reasonable, from a moral standpoint, to view the situation as requiring rectification. The key morally relevant question in this regard is whether there are, or (morally) ought to be, assignable responsibilities to foster inclusion attached to diverse social roles, statuses, positions, or offices pertaining to the particular social context at issue.

The answer to this question is readily apparent in some cases but in others it can be far from clear-cut. This gives rise to controversies that reflect underlying interpretive disagreement about what community means, from a moral standpoint.

The questions of how best to understand the idea of a classroom, school, or school district as an educational community, and the place of children with disabilities within such a community, thus lie close to the core of controversies presenting the kinds of issues that figured in the *Beth B.* matter. For reasons developed in the next two sections, the idea of an educational K–12 community incorporates two different moral conceptions, which will be referred to respectively as "the ideal of an inclusive educational community" and "the principle of equal educational respect and concern."

In disputes over inclusion, these two conceptions often loom large in the thinking of the disputants about their respective positions' moral justifications. In this regard the moral thinking of parents tends to coincide with central elements of the ideal of an inclusive K–12 educational community and the moral thinking of the school district tends to reflect key ideas underlying the principle of equal respect and educational concern.

THE IDEAL OF AN INCLUSIVE K–12 EDUCATIONAL COMMUNITY

The idea of full inclusion has been a topic of continuing intense controversy among both educators and parents for more than three decades. In the most controversy-laden sense of the phrase, "full inclusion" refers to the idea that children with disabilities should be educated in regular education classrooms regardless of the nature and extent of their diverse disability conditions.[11]

Unsurprisingly, the most highly contested issue in regard to full inclusion, in this sense, concerns whether regular classroom education of children with disabilities is educationally beneficial, with no exceptions whatsoever, for *all* students—both for students with disabilities and for nondisabled students.

The idea of full inclusion, in the above controversy-laden sense, has received much strong criticism.[12] However, considering the idea of full inclusion as worthy of discussion only to decisively identify its flaws forecloses an important opportunity for deepened moral insight and understanding. Such comprehension, if it became widespread, would surely result in educational benefit for children with disabilities and nondisabled children alike.[13]

This section focuses, accordingly, upon developing an outlook referred to henceforth as "strong inclusion." Such an outlook involves strong commitment to a conception referred to here as "the ideal of an inclusive K–12 educational community." Strong inclusionists, in contrast to full inclusionists, hold that the ideal can be exemplified in other ways than by inclusive placements of all children with disabilities in regular education classrooms regardless of the nature and extent of their disability conditions.

However, the difference between the two outlooks does not turn solely upon a difference in preferences concerning the extent of regular inclusion of children with disabilities—a difference analogous to the distinction between "liberal" and "left-leaning middle of the road" used to classify voter behavior. Instead, the distinction consists of a fundamental difference of underlying moral outlook, summarized immediately below.

Full inclusionists conceive of regular classroom educational inclusion as a moral right of children with disabilities—a moral right which asserts an unexceptionable moral responsibility of K–12 public school districts to provide every child with a disability a fully inclusive educational program.[14] According to strong inclusionists, the most important moral considerations that support regular classroom inclusion of children with disabilities lie upon a conceptual axis different from the logically correlative relationship between moral rights and moral responsibilities.

Strong inclusionists regard the crucial moral conception relevant to regular classroom inclusion of children with disabilities as the ideal of an inclusive K–12 educational community. Strong inclusionists believe that this ideal, like all other ideals (contrasted with mere wishes), concerns states of affairs that can be approached but, unlike morally required responsibilities, never realized in full.[15]

Strong inclusionists, however, find such a conception crucial in a morally vital respect. It identifies and clarifies values which the education of *any* child, whether nondisabled or a child with a disability, must embody (in the inclusionist view) in order for K–12 education in the United States—and thus for American society considered as a whole—to flourish.

The following statement by inclusion advocate Tim Villegas provides a good starting point to expand upon and develop the ideal of an inclusive K–12 educational community which underlies the strong inclusionist outlook:

> Part of the big idea of inclusion is to create synthesis where there is dichotomy, restoration where there is brokenness, and healing where there is trauma. . . . [I]nclusion has more to do with complete membership in a community rather than time spent in general education. . . . Membership is about belonging, having full access, being accepted, being supported, and having an environment in which every student can learn.[16]

These words of Villegas point toward the idea of an intrinsic relationship between inclusive education of children with disabilities and the concept of full membership in an educational community.

From the standpoint of the philosopher John Dewey, the highest moral ideal for any kind of community is to exemplify a form of association in which the good of each community member enhances, and, in turn, is enhanced by the good of all the others.[17] Strong inclusionists would say that an inclusive K–12 public school educational community approximates Dewey's ideal if it meets, to a substantial extent, the three conditions specified below:

(i) The actions and attitudes of teachers, school staff members, administrators, school board members, and nondisabled students and their families strongly express an inclusive spirit. Such a spirit, in the words of Villegas, accepts, supports, and provides full access to all children in the school district and their families.

(ii) The children with disabilities and their parents, in turn, on the whole, value and consider themselves as belonging to the educational community of the school district.

(iii) Educational programs for all children, whether nondisabled or with disabilities, are appropriate in a moral sense rather than merely in the legal sense of satisfying the *Rowley* standard.[18] In other words, the programs are reasonably calculated to achieve the basic objectives, articulated in chapters 2 and 3, of the kind of education to which every American child has a moral right.[19]

Strong inclusionists would maintain that in an inclusive educational community, exemplifying the above three conditions to a substantial extent, not only do children with disabilities and nondisabled students both receive significant educational benefit, but also, essential aspects of the benefit for each derive from their interactions with each other as full-fledged members of the educational community.

Apropos this last point, strong inclusionists contend that in the vast majority of cases the best educational placement for a child with a disability, regardless of the disability's nature or seriousness, is a regular education classroom environment, to the maximum extent feasible. From the standpoint of this outlook, a strong presumption favors such placement in a regular education environment that provides meaningful opportunities for interaction with nondisabled peers; such interaction can provide intellectual stimulation, reinforce academic effort, and foster social development.

Numerous manuals, books, articles, and in-service workshops are available that provide suggested teaching approaches and materials to assist educators in their efforts to implement regular education classroom inclusion of children with disabilities.[20] Under the IDEA, however, such efforts cannot be generic; instead, they must address the individual needs of particular students. The ideal of an inclusive K–12 educational community thus calls for deep commitment on the part of teaching staff and school administrators to adapt the above kinds of resources to the specific educational needs of individual children.

Strong inclusionists recognize that problems may arise for education of nondisabled students with regular classroom inclusion of children with disabilities. Nonetheless they maintain that educators should always proceed upon the premise that children with disabilities belong in the regular education classroom. They believe that in most cases such problems will be resolved if approached with an attitude of firm commitment to the ideal of an inclusive educational community.

Strong inclusionists insist that with intelligence, creativity, teamwork, and perseverance, educationally inclusive approaches can be developed in almost every circumstance—approaches that do not interfere with, but actually enhance, the education of nondisabled students.[21]

Well-designed, effectively implemented inclusive classrooms, say the strong inclusionists, facilitate immensely important social learning based on direct experience. Most important in this regard, nondisabled students learn about the educational challenges children with disabilities face, the kinds of educational support that are appropriate for them in diverse cases, and the progress that children with disabilities are capable of achieving with appropriate support.

Strong inclusionists believe that, from a moral standpoint, such experiential learning relates to both prongs of the fundamental objective of an appropriate K–12 education for nondisabled students, as identified and justified in chapter 2.[22] To reiterate the two prongs (according to the aforementioned analysis), an appropriate K–12 education for nondisabled students is reasonably calculated to impart knowledge and develop abilities crucial for

(a) exercising rights, fulfilling responsibilities, and exemplifying ideals of membership in the American democratic body politic, and
(b) having a reasonable chance for success in seeking the basic human good of self-fulfillment.

A strong inclusionist would maintain that the following points about the relationship between disability and objective (a) above are apparent: first, disability affects everyone, either in fact or potentially, in ways that concern the most vital interests of human beings.

Second, the subject of disability enters significantly into public policy issues of great concern for members of the American democratic body politic. Thus strong inclusionists would conclude the following: The experiential learning that takes place in well-designed, effectively implemented K–12 educational programs provides nondisabled students a foundation, seldom obtainable elsewhere, for informed and empathic understanding in later life of issues concerning disability. Such issues are important to vital public matters where the subject of disability looms large.

As for objective (b) above, strong inclusionists would point to considerations such as the following: The formation and realization of aspirations constitutive of self-fulfillment in life depend in large part upon an individual's own choices and efforts.[23] Both choices of aspirations and efforts to realize them require a positive sense of self and strong motivation; and for these, everyone requires both material and emotional support at crucial stages from others, including (but not limited to) family, friends, teachers, mentors, and/or philanthropic or governmental programs.

Strong inclusionists believe that well-designed, effectively implemented inclusive K–12 educational programs, if put in place throughout the entire span of K–12 education, could lay the groundwork for extension of a strongly inclusive outlook to other important areas of American life. This would, in their opinion, have the effect of widening and strengthening the diverse support networks which people need. In short, advocates would say that strong inclusion has the potential to make the United States a more caring society.

The deep significance for American society of the ideal of an inclusive K–12 educational community, the strong inclusionists would maintain, becomes even more apparent when considered in relationship to an outlook termed the "ethics of care," which has been articulated in diverse ways by many contemporary philosophers and educational theorists.[24]

This outlook emphasizes certain important and pervasive elements of a typical human life. Under normal conditions a human life proceeds through stages, from infancy to old age, characterized by varying degrees of dependence and independence. Furthermore, any human being may, at any time, suffer catastrophically irreversible losses of capability to function independently in crucial areas of life.

The ethics of care keeps these facts in the foreground, thereby heightening one's attention to the fact that the moral concerns of most human beings revolve, to a large extent, around relationships in which care is given and received—care as in raising children, providing needed assistance to seriously disabled relatives and friends, and looking after elderly parents.

The ethics of care and the ideal of an inclusive educational community converge upon two conclusions. First, although just legal and political institutions and a productive economy are needed for American society to flourish, they are not enough by themselves. A flourishing American society must not only be just and prosperous but be caring as well.

Second, the lessons in life that nondisabled students can learn in a school environment approximating the ideal of an inclusive educational community benefit not only themselves and their families but these life lessons can also help American society to flourish by fostering attitudes of inclusive care and concern for the well-being of all.

Apart from the above lessons in living related to the ethics of care, strong inclusionists would insist as well that nondisabled children benefit educationally in other immensely important ways, the more closely K–12 school environments approach the full ideal of an inclusive educational community. For example, children with disabilities often have latent strong or even exceptional academic abilities; provision of special education and related services enables them to develop and utilize these in classroom situations to the benefit of fellow classmates.[25]

As a case in point, Amy Rowley (the hearing-impaired child whose IEP figured in the seminal *Rowley* case) has had a successful career in her adulthood as a university professor. The accommodations and services she received—a hearing aid and instruction in cued speech—and which her parents challenged as inappropriate enabled her to hear only half of what her teachers and fellow students said in class.[26] Amy Rowley had potential as a child for development of exceptional academic abilities, which reflected in her career achievement as an adult. Surely not only she alone, but also her fellow classmates, would have benefited educationally had she been provided accommodations and services that increased her access to verbal classroom communication.[27]

A second example is provided by the following passage from an article that describes an inclusive educational program for a child in third grade named Sabrina who, unlike Amy Rowley, had both communication challenges (from a cognitive standpoint) and academic and social delays:

> [R]ecently Sabrina got up in the middle of a lesson, stood very close to Nancy [Sabrina's teacher], and touched her face. Many of the children thought Sabrina would be in trouble. But Nancy paused to explain that although this action could be seen as disruptive, it was simply Sabrina's way of showing that she was interested in the lesson. This turned to a whole class discussion about how everyone's differences make the world a more exciting and interesting place.[28]

The article quoted above goes on to relate that two boys in Sabrina's class, one who had been slow in learning to read and another who had focusing issues, each improved significantly over the school year largely from taking their turns as peer reading tutors with Sabrina.[29]

Attitudes toward children with disabilities have undergone a major transformation since the early 1970s, when one could have described the prevailing outlook as "full exclusion," rather than even partial, let alone full inclusion. This transformation is reflected poignantly in the passage below from an essay by Eva Feder Kittay, whose now-adult daughter Sesha (as described in chapter 3) has severe intellectual disabilities. In this passage Kittay describes how she reacted in 1970 when her mother, upon first becoming fully aware of the severity of Sesha's disabilities, insisted that Kittay place Sesha in an institution:

> Of all the traumatic encounters in that first year and a half of Sesha's life, none, perhaps not even the realization that Sesha was retarded, was as painful as these words from the woman that I loved most in my life. The woman who had taught me what it was to be a mother, to love a child, to anticipate the joys of nursing, of holding, and caring for another, of sacrificing for a child. . . . In time, my mother allowed herself to love Sesha with the fullness of a grandmother's love. And in time I forgave my mother and came to appreciate how her intense, if misdirected, love for me fueled her stubborn insistence that we "put Sesha away."[30]

The deep emotion and firm moral convictions underlying Eva Feder Kittay's choice in 1970 not to "put Sesha away" reflected the incipient major transformation of moral attitudes that has since taken place toward children with disabilities. In his *Republic*, Plato appears to have considered killing children with serious mental or physical disabilities as consistent with his conceptions of both community and justice.[31]

By 1970, society in the United States had come to acknowledge that (as with all other children) those with severe or profound intellectual disabilities ought, at the very least, not to be killed. However, the prevailing view at that time—reflected in the widespread practice of "warehousing" such children—barely went beyond such an acknowledgment.

The IDEA has come to shape the provision of special education programs in the United States in ways that activate the idea that society has significant responsibilities to *all* children, including those with limited or no potential for contributing to aggregate productivity or living independent lives. Strong inclusionists believe that the ideal of an inclusive educational community follows naturally and inevitably, in terms of both moral sentiment and moral logic, from the major transformation in attitudes toward children with disabilities that has taken place over the last half-century.

In the early twentieth century, when special education programs were introduced in American K–12 public schools, educators involved in the programs saw themselves as creating a vastly preferable alternative, both educationally and morally, to the prevalent practices in American society concerning children with disabilities.[32]

Strong inclusionists would say that, similarly, today's educators should take the lead in transforming the attitudes, practices, and policies of American society needed to approach the ideal of an inclusive educational community in most American K–12 public school districts.

THE PRINCIPLE OF EQUAL EDUCATIONAL RESPECT AND CONCERN

The preceding section summarized the reasons why strong inclusionists think the ideal of an inclusive K–12 educational community should guide decisions about the education of children with disabilities. Many would disagree with this conclusion, however, and advance instead another moral outlook—the "principle of equal educational respect and concern."

This principle articulates the moral responsibilities of a K–12 public school district correlative with the "minimum content" (as described in chapter 2) of the moral right of American children to receive an appropriate K–12 education. According to the principle of equal educational respect and concern, every public school district has moral responsibilities to

(i) exert conscientious efforts to develop and implement educational programs reasonably calculated to achieve the basic objectives of the kind of public education which every child has a moral right to receive and
(ii) accord equal educational concern to every enrolled child, whether nondisabled or with a disability.

As noted in chapter 2, the minimum content of children's moral right to receive an appropriate education concerns entitlements that are clearly necessary elements of this right, regardless of other disagreements that may remain about how the moral right should be interpreted.[33]

Similarly, the correlative responsibility of equal educational respect and concern has a number of important implications concerning education for children with disabilities that are reasonably clear, apparent, and widely agreed upon.

First, a teacher, school administrator, or other school staff member involved in the educational process whose attitude accords with the principle of equal educational respect and concern would concur wholeheartedly with the following view: every American child has a moral right to receive an appropriate K–12 education, and, correlatively, K–12 public school districts in the United States have a moral responsibility to provide such an education.[34]

Second, an attitude of equal educational respect and concern toward children with disabilities involves knowledge of, and careful adherence to, rules and regulations of federal and state law intended to provide educational benefit for children with disabilities.

Third, it requires informed understanding of both the moral justification and the historical background behind these laws and regulations. Such informed understanding is essential so that school administrators, teachers, and other school staff members keep in mind—even when they have to meet the law's requirements under tight fiscal constraints—the reasons why children with disabilities need not only special services but also special legal protections.

Fourth, an attitude of equal educational respect and concern involves both complete open-mindedness about educational approaches that might benefit a child with disabilities and unfailing readiness to work with the child's parents to develop and implement a successful educational placement.

Fifth, from the standpoint of an attitude of equal educational respect and concern, however, such placements have to be consistent with a school district's moral responsibility to provide appropriate education for *every* child in the educational community of the district—both children with disabilities and nondisabled children.

In regard to points four and five above, an educator who exemplified the attitude of equal educational respect and concern would always be prepared to seriously consider supporting full regular education classroom inclusion as a placement for a student with disabilities. However, she also would have an open mind toward supporting other educational placement options. One must keep in mind that, from the standpoint of the principle of equal educational respect and concern, the issue would never reduce to a simple choice between full inclusion and full exclusion.

For example, an IEP team might conclude the appropriate placement for a student with a specific learning disability condition, such as dyslexia, is in a classroom with students facing similar challenges for at least a portion of the school day. The team members may reach this conclusion because they agree the student has serious self-esteem issues related to his disability condition which could be addressed best in a learning environment where he experienced a sense of belonging and a level of comfort that increased his receptivity to educational efforts on his behalf.

The team may think this could in turn lead to academic progress that, if combined with appropriate psychological services, could enable him to transition effectively into a complete program of regular education classes.

As for children with severe or profound intellectual disability conditions, any appropriate educational placement for such children would have to provide significant opportunities for meaningful interaction with nondisabled peers. Such opportunities might include mainstreaming for lunch and physical education or a "peer buddies" student-helper program. The goal from the standpoint of the principle of equal educational respect and concern would be to arrive at a just balance between concern for the educational needs of students with disabilities and for those of nondisabled students.

It is worth noting here the significant danger that schools may disregard or marginalize the needs of disabled students. According to the principle of equal educational respect and concern, however, the appropriate means for society to address this danger are twofold: through adoption of social policies and institutional practices (such as those delineated in the IDEA) and through fostering among educators the dispositions, noted above, that constitute the attitude of equal educational respect and concern.

From the perspective of the ideal of an inclusive educational community, achieving justice in American K–12 education will require a major transformation of outlook, as Tim Villegas's statement implies. Strong inclusionists believe that inclusive educational policies and practices are indispensable for creating an educational community whose members—nondisabled students and their families; children with disabilities and their families; and school district teachers, administrators, and other staff members—all share a strong spirit of inclusion.

Such a spirit would be exemplified by a strong conviction on the part of each member of the educational community that his or her well-being, considered as a community member, is closely and inextricably connected with the educational well-being of every other community member.

In contrast, while advocates of the principle of equal educational respect and concern might consider the notion of such an inclusive educational community as an inspiring ideal, they do not consider it fundamental from the standpoint of justice. In this regard, the principle of equal educational respect and concern draws heavily upon another moral conception, which Ronald Dworkin terms "community of principle."[35]

Under Dworkin's conception, the shared attitude at the core of the *morally* significant idea of community relevant to contemporary American society consists of commitment to principles of equality which govern the entitlements of individuals as holders of important rights. These include the fundamental rights guaranteed by the U.S. Constitution but others as well; among these are moral rights, such as the right of every American child to receive an appropriate K–12 education.

The principles at the core of the American democratic body politic, considered as a community of principle, are interpretive in the following sense: commitment to the principles animates the community making it more fully the kind of community it is meant to be, only to the extent that the meaning and application of the principles are subjects of intense, ongoing reflection, debate, and discussion. Thus Dworkin writes,

> Members of a genuine community of principle . . . accept that they are governed by common principles, not just by rules hammered out in a [mere] political compromise. Politics for such people [in large part] is a theater of debate about which principles the community should adopt as a system, which view it should take of justice, fairness, and due process.[36]

In a community of principle, not all, or perhaps relatively few, community members would exemplify a strongly inclusive spirit corresponding closely to the ideal of an inclusive educational community (as developed in the previous section). Nonetheless, justice relative to children with disabilities would be reflected in broadly based support for policies and practices intended to put into effect the principle of equal educational respect and concern, applied specifically with respect to all students, including children with disabilities.

In this regard, K–12 public school educators would always consider proposals for regular education inclusion of particular children with disabilities carefully and with open minds. In doing so, they would be cognizant of, and weigh heavily, the fact that educational placements they authorize for children with disabilities must be consistent with the educators' basic moral responsibility to provide an appropriate education for all children in the educational community. How to do so can raise complex, controversial questions.

THE IDEAL AND THE PRINCIPLE: FURTHER CONTRAST AND COMPARISON

The preceding two sections introduced the ideal of an inclusive K–12 educational community and the principle of equal educational respect and concern.

The suggestion was also made that these conceptions often hover in the background of disputes between parents of children with disabilities and school districts concerning particular children. The specific way they figure in such disputes, however, needs further examination.

The two conceptions do not inherently conflict but rather lie upon different conceptual axes. The ideal of an inclusive K–12 educational community reflects the idea that when each member of an educational community considers his or her well-being (apropos the provision of education) bound up strongly with the well-being, in this regard, of every other member, then the educational community as a whole flourishes.

The principle of equal educational respect and concern pertains to morally fundamental responsibilities of public school educators. These responsibilities lie in their respective spheres of decision-making authority over the education of American children and are correlative with the moral right of every such child to receive an appropriate education.

This suggests, in turn, that disputes concerning inclusion do not involve the unavoidable necessity of making an either/or choice between two diametrically opposed conceptions. On the one hand, realization of the ideal of an inclusive K–12 educational community presupposes that the principle of equal educational respect and concern is upheld. On the other hand, upholding the principle of equal educational respect and concern is not enough for American K–12 education to flourish. It must also significantly approach the ideal of an inclusive educational community.

To the extent that the two conceptions figure in disputes over K–12 regular classroom inclusion of children with disabilities the crux of the matter concerns differing associated views of human nature as spelled out below.

A highly optimistic outlook is required to believe meaningful progress can be made toward approaching the ideal of an inclusive K–12 educational community. As noted earlier, strong inclusionists believe that in a well-designed, effectively implemented K–12 educational environment nondisabled students will acquire informed awareness of learning problems children with disabilities face, appropriate kinds of educational support for them, and the educational progress children with disabilities can achieve if given appropriate support.

Belief that the outlook of strong inclusion could become firmly established throughout America also presupposes the following: If school districts undertake the needed steps to assure that strongly inclusive environments continue in place throughout all the years of students' K–12 education, then a widespread transformational change in attitude will emerge. Strong inclusionists believe that children with disabilities and their families will increasingly be acknowledged by others as fully fledged community members and, correspondingly, will so look upon themselves.

In the above respects, strong inclusionism appears to presuppose highly optimistic beliefs about human nature reminiscent of views held by anarchist philosophers such as Peter Kropotkin.[37] According to Kropotkin, the capacity to empathize with, and the disposition to render assistance to, people in need are both strong natural human tendencies; but they also require the right kind of social environment (which is now badly lacking) for the tendency to be exemplified on a widespread basis throughout society.

A strong inclusionist outlook seems to presuppose that well-planned, effectively implemented K–12 educational programs could provide such an environment. Most K–12 educators, however, even those who support including children with disabilities in regular education classrooms, would consider the scenario described above as ignoring realities such as the following, which most American public school districts face.

Seeking to provide an education that qualifies as appropriate, in the moral sense, for every child is a never-ending struggle. Many other students in addition to children with disabilities have significant or even pressing educational needs. These needs could call for diverse kinds of educational support: for economically deprived students; for curricular development in vital areas such as math, science, social studies, literature, visual art, and music; for programs to address immediate problems, such as a high prevalence of bullying; or for many other areas of concern.

In undertaking to address the above kinds of needs schools face formidable challenges. Thus most K–12 educators would likely consider it exceptionally hard or even impossible for them to play the role of change agent in ways that strong inclusionists would like to see it performed. In their judgment, they could not do so while at the same time fulfilling (or equally important, being perceived by nondisabled students and their parents as fulfilling) their responsibilities in ways that upheld the principle of equal educational respect and concern.

The ideal of an inclusive K–12 educational community and the principle of equal educational respect and concern thus are both open to criticism. It would be a large mistake, however, to reject either out of hand—in the case of the former, as utopian fantasy or in that of the latter, as a rationale for overly easy acquiescence in an unsatisfactory educational status quo.

Rather, each conception embodies important ideas that do not conflict inherently with one another, but which, under favorable circumstances, can be accommodated harmoniously in an educational placement for a child with a disability. There are some important cases, however, when the two conceptions pull in opposed directions.

In this regard, the *Beth B.* case is a prime example. At the due process hearing, the school district called as its witnesses teachers, administrators, and other educational staff members who had been involved in Beth's education.

Each testified to efforts on his or her part to develop and implement a successful inclusive regular education program for Beth.

Nonetheless, all the witnesses expressed the opinion that, despite extensive collective effort, Beth had not benefited educationally. The school district witnesses furthermore all voiced concern that attempting to maintain an inclusive regular education program for Beth in higher grades would have serious adverse effects upon the education of her nondisabled fellow students.

In response, Beth's parents insisted that Beth had benefited educationally during the first three years of her inclusive regular education placement. However, they acknowledged that they had seen far less educational progress during the two years that followed; this period was after the school district had recommended, and the parents had dissented from, a change of placement for Beth.

Apropos the two years following the school district's change of placement recommendation, Beth's parents expressed strong disagreement with the school district witnesses' description of their collective efforts as "extensive." In addition, Beth's parents made it clear they viewed the school district witnesses' conclusion—that provision of a successful inclusive regular education program for Beth would become impossible in future years—as reflecting a deficient level of commitment on the school district's part.

The key *legal* issue the *Beth B.* case presented concerned the relationship between the two core provisions of the IDEA—the (legal) right of American children with disabilities to receive a FAPE and the LRE mandate. From a moral (contrasted with a legal) standpoint, however, the *Beth B.* case comes down to the following crucial question:

How concerted of an effort should the school district have made, and how strong should the school district's commitment have been, to develop and implement a successful inclusive regular education program for Beth B., as well as for other children with severe and profound cognitive disabilities?

A morally thoughtful person's answer to this question will depend, to a large extent, upon where she or he looks primarily for moral guidance—to the principle of equal educational respect and concern or to the ideal of an inclusive educational community.

CONSTITUTIONAL DEMOCRATIC PLURALISM

The analysis and discussion in this chapter has sought to convey, at least partially, the moral force and the intellectual depth of both the ideal of an inclusive K–12 educational community and the principle of equal educational respect and concern. Given the detail and sophistication with which both viewpoints can be articulated, each of them provides its proponents extensive conceptual resources for criticizing, and for responding to criticism from, the other viewpoint.

Academic debate and discussion of these ideas has the potential to continue for a long time. The problem of developing a (morally) just conception of the place of children with disabilities within an educational community, however, not only is a matter for controversy among academics. It arises most importantly in connection with concrete issues concerning educational placements of actual students.

The issue of how best to approach the problem equates in large part with the following question: By what means can American society establish a framework of rules and procedures to help achieve a just balance of competing considerations for particular cases? Such considerations might include the following:

(1) In a large number of cases, children with disabilities benefit educationally from programs that provide significant opportunities for them to interact with nondisabled students in the regular education environment.
(2) The more children with disabilities benefit from educationally successful inclusive programs, the greater the extent to which they and their families identify themselves as fully fledged members of the educational community of the school district. The ultimate result is that all members of the community benefit—children with disabilities and their families, nondisabled children and their families, and school district educators.
(3) Development and implementation of inclusive educational programs for children with some disabilities can require significant expenditures for additions to staff, professional-development education for current staff, and other kinds of resources.
(4) Regular education inclusion programs for children with disabilities must not affect provision of educational services for nondisabled students in ways that deprive them of the kind of K–12 education to which they have a moral right.

Development of a suitable framework of rules and procedures for balancing these considerations presents immense challenges. It requires parties with significantly differing moral perspectives on a matter of great personal importance to participate in a process which calls for extensive debate and discussion. Such discussion seeks areas of convergence in the participants' often-divergent perspectives, in hopes of laying the foundation for a working agreement.

Furthermore, given the importance of the matters at stake to the participants in the debate and discussion, as well as the extent of divergence in their moral perspectives, no framework arrived at could ever come close to satisfying everyone completely. For this reason, one needs to understand the processes through which harmony is sought among parties with deeply divergent perspectives as necessarily operating over the long run and tending to achieve only partial success at any given time.

Thus all parties must understand that even if the processes of debate and discussion of the terms of a framework result in a statutory enactment, any proposal considered and rejected—no matter how much at odds with the one ultimately enacted—may always be brought up again at a later time for reconsideration.

To develop rules and procedures suited to the task of finding a morally just balance among the aforementioned factors, a society's governmental practices must include two elements that are not easy to combine.

The society must be able to make and to implement decisions on various controversial matters. At the same time, it must positively encourage and promote both discussion and debate on such matters, even when the society has collectively arrived at closure on these matters by enacting legislation. That is to say, the processes of discussion and debate must be ongoing (literally) and always regarded by those participating in them as capable of generating meaningful results.

Far more than in any other kind of government, constitutional democracy combines the above-described two elements. A constitutional democratic government, like any other, has its procedures of decision making, and it requires strong deference to their outcomes on the part of everyone subject to the government's authority.[38] At the same time, however, a constitutional democracy contains elements which encourage and promote, to a much greater extent than in the case of any other kind of government, the processes of ongoing and meaningful discussion and debate needed in difficult cases. This is relevant to the need to harmonize the perspective of parents concerned about their own children with special needs and the perspective of K–12 public school educators who are answerable for providing an appropriate education for every child in their educational community.

The essential elements in this regard concern three synergistically related areas:

(a) practices involving exercise of communicational rights, such as freedom of speech, press, and assembly, which make possible discussion and debate whereby individuals and groups may express their viewpoints in regard to the necessity, desirability, or appropriateness of contemplated legislative enactments;

(b) procedures of democratic decision making, through which a constitutional democratic government can demonstrate meaningful responsiveness to the activities of the individuals and groups exercising their communicational rights; and

(c) judicial practices and procedures that make possible the challenging of interpretations adopted by government officials of enacted rules and regulations in specific cases, and which, in virtue of the principle of stare decisis, provide for discussion and debate to take place even after enactment of a law, with tangible effects upon how the law will be applied in the future.[39]

Constitutional democratic government is not an absolute prerequisite for developing a framework of rules and procedures to determine educational programs for children with disabilities. Frameworks for this purpose could be devised under other governmental systems; these might even have certain important advantages, such as clarity, consistency, and efficiency of administration, over the kind of framework likely to emerge under constitutional democracy (e.g., the IDEA).

It seems highly unlikely, however, that such frameworks could address satisfactorily the problem of (moral) justice with regard to regular education inclusion of children with disabilities posed in this chapter. The problem in this connection relates to harmonizing significantly divergent reasonable interpretations of the idea of an educational community, and of the place within such a community of children with disabilities.

For the philosopher Plato, such harmonizing would require that someone invested with authority to govern transcend the realm of mere opinion and gain knowledge which can ground a correct understanding of what makes a classroom, school, or school district an educational community. This sense was articulated by John Dewey as an association in which the educational good of any student enhances and is enhanced by the educational good of all the others.

A diametrically opposed philosophical viewpoint (maybe postmodernism in some of its forms) would reject the idea of knowledge in the realms of morality and educational theory as, in the worst cases, pure myth, embodied within an ideology propagated by the powerful in society to maintain their dominant position.

A third viewpoint says that unless we assume the reality of knowledge in connection with morality and educational theory, the entire enterprise of K–12 education lacks a coherent point. What exactly it means to speak of knowledge in these areas, however, is very hard to explain fully and adequately. Nonetheless, some points in this regard seem apparent.

Knowledge about morality and educational theory is immensely difficult to obtain. For this reason, at any given time, understanding of what it means for a classroom, school, or school district to constitute an educational community can only be partial and highly subject to change. One has to assume that in the long run and with great effort, and despite—or more accurately, in virtue of—countless disputes, such understanding tends to advance both morally and intellectually.

The reasons developed above provide a strong argument that the institutions and practices of constitutional democracy are indeed indispensable.

CONCLUSION

Hope was expressed at the beginning of this chapter that the discussion to follow might contribute to a clearer and deeper sense of what justice means relative to a major issue in special education—inclusion of children with disabilities in regular education classes and school activities. The discussion and analysis that followed, however, did not advance a specific recommendation about the meaning of justice in this context.

Given the complexity and depth of the issue, such a recommendation would have been a bold, or more accurately, a wrongheaded objective. If this chapter has helped to clarify and deepen understanding of what justice means relative to regular education inclusion of children with disabilities, it has done so in a more modest way, by developing the following point.

Regular education inclusion of a child with a disability—especially a child with profound intellectual disabilities, such as Beth B.—can raise difficult problems regarding allocation of the classroom teacher's time between the needs of the disabled student and those of her nondisabled classmates. Such issues raise problems of distributive justice of a kind deeply interconnected with questions about what it means from a moral standpoint for a classroom, school, or school district to constitute an educational community.

The resolution of these issues is complicated by the fact that there is no universal and objective combination of regular education academic objectives, teaching methods, and learning environment that can serve as a standard for assessing the effects upon nondisabled students when a child with disabilities is included in a regular education classroom or school activity. Schools can choose from a wide array of options concerning the educational programs for nondisabled students; their choices will be influenced by many different factors.

As stressed throughout this chapter, one especially important factor in such choices is the school's understanding of what it means for a classroom, school, or school district to be an educational community.

Two interpretations of this idea were identified, each having a different crucial concept at its core—respectively, the ideal of an inclusive educational community and the principle of equal educational respect and concern. The discussion and analysis of these two different core conceptions sought to bring out the moral force and intellectual depth in each one. It did not, however, proceed to the point of considering the question of whether one or the other, or a particular synthesis, of these conceptions most closely approximates justice relative to the inclusion of children with disabilities in regular education classroom and school activities.

The ideal of an inclusive educational community and the principle of equal educational respect and concern do not inherently conflict with each other. In some difficult cases, however, such as the *Beth B.* matter, they pull in opposed directions. When this happens reconciliation can only come in either of two ways.

First, if a conflict involves educational placement of a particular child with a disability, reconciliation may emerge through structured opportunities, provided within the framework established by the IDEA, for discussion between the child's parents and educators in the child's school.

Second, conflicts over inclusion that involve broader issues of educational policy can be reconciled only through legislative decision-making and/or judicial adjudication. In either case, reconciliation of the ideal of an inclusive K–12 educational community and the principle of equal educational respect and concern, to the extent possible, must come through the processes available for discussion, debate, and search for compromise distinctive to constitutional democratic government.

NOTES

1. The author was the special education due process hearing officer in the case of *Beth B.*
2. Decision and Rulings in the Matter of Elizabeth B. and Lake Bluff (IL) School District 65, May 26, 2000.
3. Beth B. v. Van Clay, 126 F. Supp. 2d 53 (2001); 282 F. 3d 493 (2002).
4. Cert. denied 537 U.S. 948 (October 15, 2002).
5. 20 U.S.C.A. sec. 1412 (a) (5).
6. Roncker v. Walter, 700 F. 2 1058 (6th Cir. 1983); Daniel R.R. v. State Board of Educ., 847 F. 2d 1036 (5th Cir. 1989); Oberti v. Board of Educ., 995 F. 2d 1204 (3rd Cir. 1993); Sacramento City Unified School District v. Rachel H. by Holland, 14 F. 3rd 1398 (9th Cir. 1994).
7. 458 U.S. 176 (1982).
8. *Rowley*, 207.
9. E.g., see the summary, in the immediately following section of this chapter of key points presented by each side at the due process hearing in the *Beth B.* matter.
10. Decision and Rulings in the Matter of Elizabeth B. and Lake Bluff (IL) School District 65, May 26, 2000.

11. E.g., Gartner and Lipsky, "Inclusion and School Restructuring" in *Restructuring for Caring and Effective Education*, eds. R. A. Villa and J. S. Thousand (P.H. Brookes: Baltimore), 38–55; T. M. Skrtic, W. Sailor, and K. Gee, "Voice, Collaboration, and Inclusion," *Remedial and Special Education* 17 (1996): 142–57; W. Stainback and S. Stainback, "Schools as Inclusive Communities," in *Controversial Issues in Special Education: Divergent Perspectives*, eds. W. Stainback and S. Stainback (Allyn and Bacon: Boston 1992), 29–43.

12. E.g., J. M. Kauffman and D. P. Hallahan (eds.), *The Illusion of Full Inclusion* (Pro-Ed. Inc.: Austin, TX, 1995).

13. As John Stuart Mill states in chapter 2 of his classic essay "On Liberty," however, viewpoints one has strong reasons to reject, from either a theoretical or a practical standpoint, nonetheless may contain a "portion of the truth," providing significant insight and understanding, which otherwise would be insufficiently appreciated or even completely ignored. See "On Liberty" (London, UK, 1969, 57–65).

14. See, e.g., W. Stainback and S. Stainback (eds.), *Controversial Issues Confronting Special Education: Divergent Perspectives* (Allyn and Bacon: Boston, 1992).

15. See chapter 6.

16. "What Does Full Inclusion Really Mean?" (August 7, 2014), www.thinkinclusive.us/what-does-full-inclusion-really-mean Note that Villegas appears to reconceptualize full inclusion to coincide with strong inclusion, as characterized in this chapter.

17. John Dewey, *The Public and Its Problems* (Chicago: Gateway Press, 1944), 49.

18. See chapter 1.

19. For summary statements of basic objectives of an appropriate K–12 education see chapter 2 at 22–23 and chapter 3 at 50–52.

20. E.g., M. A. Mastropieri and T. Scruggs, *The Inclusive Classroom 6th ed.* (Pearson: London, UK, 201); D. J. Sands, B. Kozleski, and N. K. French, *Inclusive Education for the Twenty-First Century* (Wadsworth: Belmont, CA, 2000); R. Stokes and G. Hornby, *Meeting Special Needs in Mainstream Schools: A Practical Guide for Teachers* (Routledge: London, UK, 2000).

21. See Gartner and Lipsky (cited at n. 11); Giangreco et al., "Problem Solving to Facilitate Inclusive Education," 321–460; J. S. Thousand and R. A. Villa, "Collaborative Teaching: A Powerful Tool in School Restructuring," 254–91 (in *Restructuring for Caring and Effective Education*, eds. Villa and Thousand (Paul H. Brookes: Baltimore, 2000).

22. See chapter 2.

23. See chapter 2.

24. E.g., C. Gilligan, *In a Different Voice* (Harvard University Press: Cambridge, MA, 1982); V. Held, *Feminist Morality: Transforming Culture, Society, and Politics* (University of Chicago Press: Chicago, 1993); V. Held (ed.), *Justice and Care* (Westview Press: Boulder, CO, 1995); N. Noddings, *Caring: A Feminine Approach to Ethics and Moral Education* (University of California Press: Berkeley, 1984); S. Ruddick, *Maternal Thinking* (Beacon Press: Boston: 1989).

25. See Rich Weinfeld, Linda Barnes-Robinson, Sue Jeweler, and Betty Roffman Shevitz, *Smart Kids with Learning Difficulties*, 2nd ed. (Prufrock Press: Waco, TX,

2013). See also, Jonathan Mooney and David Cole, *Learning Outside the Box* (Simon and Schuster: New York, 2000).

26. *Rowley*, 185.

27. For a thorough analysis of the importance for a conception of justice concerning disability to give development of talent due consideration, see Anita Silvers, "No Talent? Beyond the Worst Off! A Diverse Theory of Justice for Disability," in *Disability and Disadvantage*, eds. Kimberley Brownlee and Adam Cureton (Oxford University Press: Oxford, UK, 2009), 163–199.

28. Kate MacLeod, Julie Caulston, and Nelia Nunes, "Sabrina's Story," *Rethinking Schools* 31 (2017): 24–27.

29. MacLeod et al., "Sabrina's Story," 27.

30. *Love's Labor* (Routledge: New York, 1999), 152–53.

31. *Republic* 460c.

32. See Ch. 1.

33. See discussion in chapter 2 at 19–48.

34. The relationship between (a) the moral responsibility of K–12 public school educators to provide all children the kind of education to which they have a moral right and (b) the educators' legal responsibility to provide the FAPE mandated by the IDEA poses issues identified and addressed in chapter 7.

35. Ronald Dworkin, *Law's Empire* (Harvard University Press: Cambridge, MA, 1986), 211–15.

36. Dworkin, *Law's Empire*, 211.

37. Peter Kropotkin, *Mutual Aid: A Factor in Evolution* (New York, 1909).

38. See P. Soper, "Legal Theory and the Claims of Authority," *Philosophy and Public Affairs* 18 (1989): 209–37.

39. See R. Ladenson and M. Malin, "On the Scope of Legitimate Authority," *Journal of Social Philosophy* 29 (1998): 59–73.

Chapter 5

K–12 Public School Suspensions and Expulsions

In chapter 1 it was noted that the IDEA places stringent legal requirements upon K–12 public school suspensions and expulsions of children with disabilities that do not apply in the case of nondisabled students.[1] This chapter will present reasons for concluding that the basic *moral*, contrasted with legal, issues concerning K–12 public school suspensions and expulsions are the same for all students, whether or not they have disability conditions entitling them to receive special education and related services under the IDEA.

There is widespread agreement that disciplinary authority in K–12 public schools must be extensive and strong in order to assure a school environment where learning can take place.[2] Morally legitimate disciplinary authority in K–12 public schools, however, has limitations. By their nature suspensions and expulsions withhold the provision of educational services from students.

For the reasons developed in chapters 2 and 3, the idea that every American child has a right to receive an appropriate K–12 education, however, is central to the moral justification of public K–12 education in the United States. The key moral issues regarding suspensions and expulsions of K–12 public school students thus are the following:

- What considerations are relevant for deciding in specific cases whether or not a suspension or expulsion violates an American student's moral right to receive an appropriate K–12 education?
- In the case of each relevant consideration, why?
- Are there rules or guidelines for attaching weights to the relevant considerations?
- If so, what are they, and what are their bases?
- If not, what procedures should one follow to arrive at a decision, and why?

This chapter has three sections. Section 1 contains two case vignettes concerning K–12 public school expulsions. The first vignette involves the expulsion of a child with a disability, while the second concerns expulsion of six nondisabled students. Although the vignettes have different factual circumstances, each raises the same morally basic issue—how to resolve the prima facie conflict between K–12 public school suspensions and expulsions, on the one hand, and the idea that every American child has a moral right to receive an appropriate K–12 education, on the other hand.

Section 2 develops an analysis of the limits of morally justified disciplinary authority of K–12 public school districts in regard to suspensions and expulsions that addresses the five crucial issues enumerated above. Section 3 returns to the two case vignettes and discusses the particular moral issues each poses from the standpoint of the analysis developed in section 2.

TWO CASE VIGNETTES

The Matter of *James M.*

James M. caused an explosion at his school toward the end of his freshman year by placing a quarter stick of dynamite in a toilet. The school district expelled him for two years, with no provision for receiving alternative educational services.[3] In late December of the following school year, James M's mother requested a special education due process hearing on the ground that the expulsion violated James's rights under the IDEA.

As relief she requested annulment of the expulsion and James's reinstatement as a student in good standing. She also requested an order directing the school district to develop an appropriate Individualized Educational Plan (IEP) for him. In addition, James's mother asked for the issuance of orders directing the school district (a) to provide additional education and related services as compensation for the period of time James was not educated under an appropriate IEP and (b) to pay the full costs of placement for him in an appropriate out-of-district residential placement.

The author was assigned to serve as due process hearing officer in the *James M.* case. The following two items of background information are essential to understand the key legal issues the case presented. First, five months before the expulsion school district staff had considered whether to conduct a case study evaluation of James to determine whether he was eligible to receive special education and decided that doing so was unnecessary.[4] For this reason he was designated as a regular education student by the school district.

Second, as noted in chapter 1, the requirements of the IDEA are stringent relative to disciplinary sanctions imposed upon special education students.[5]

These requirements apply also under the IDEA with respect to a student who has not been designated as eligible for special education if the school district "had knowledge," as defined in terms of conditions set forth in the IDEA, that he or she was "a child with a disability," at the time of his/her disciplinary infraction.[6]

The evidence and testimony presented in the case pointed clearly to the following two conclusions. First, James M. qualified for special education at the time of his expulsion under the IDEA eligibility category of emotional disturbance.[7] Second, the statutory conditions, in the IDEA, for determining whether a school district had knowledge of a child's disability, applied clearly to the circumstances of the case. Accordingly the author, in his position as due process hearing officer, ruled in favor of James M. and granted all the above mentioned relief James's mother had requested.

Although clear cut legally, the *James M.* case poses troubling *moral* issues. In many, if not most, instances a two-year expulsion, without alternative education provided, would result in a child dropping out of school. Such, in all likelihood, would place a child upon a trajectory toward a bleak future at the margins of society that includes unemployment, necessity to rely on public assistance, substance abuse, and/or incarceration for criminal activity.

What if the facts of the *James M.* case had been different in such a way that the explicit statutory conditions under the IDEA were not satisfied for concluding that the school district "had knowledge" that James M. was a "child with a disability" at the time of his expulsion? There would not then have been any legal basis to issue an order annulling James's expulsion.

Did expelling James M. for two years, without providing any alternative education, violate not only his legal rights under federal special education law but also a *moral* right he possessed, along with every other American child, to receive an appropriate K–12 education? If so, why? If not, why not?

The Decatur Six

On September 17, 1999 a fight broke out in the stands during a football game at Eisenhower High School in Decatur, Illinois. The fight disrupted the game. About half of the nearby spectators scattered to avoid getting hurt. The fight, however, involved no weapons and resulted in no serious injuries to anyone. Six students, all African American, who had taken part in the fight, which had been recorded on videotape by a spectator, received immediate suspensions.

Upon further investigation, school authorities learned the fight was gang related. The students belonged to rival notorious gangs—the Vice Lords and the Gangster Disciples—based in Chicago, which had spread throughout the state to smaller cities, such as Decatur—located 175 miles south of Chicago.

In late October of 1999 the school board voted, with only one dissent, from the sole African American board member, to expel the six students for two years, with no provision for alternative education. The school board's decision generated immense controversy. Reverend Jesse Jackson and other members of the Push/Rainbow Coalition, which he led, came to Decatur to take up the students' cause. In early November the Governor of Illinois and the State Superintendent of Education met with the school board and Jesse Jackson in an effort to defuse the situation.

The Education Superintendent proposed that the students be given an opportunity to receive alternative schooling at a regional educational center while expelled. He suggested also that the school board allow the students to apply for readmission at the end of the fall semester contingent upon satisfactory academic work and conduct in the alternative school setting. On behalf of the students and their families, Jesse Jackson indicated that he considered the Education Superintendent's suggestions fair and reasonable.

The school board, however, rejected the proposals, but owing to intense persuasive efforts by the Governor of Illinois, reduced the expulsion order to the remainder of the 1999–2000 school year, with provision of alternative schooling. Push/Rainbow Coalition attorneys filed a lawsuit in federal court protesting the expulsion of the six students. The U.S. District Court for the Central District of Illinois issued a decision that upheld the school board's action.[8]

A video recording taken by one of the spectators, presented as evidence at the trial, established to the court's satisfaction that the fight at the football game was a serious altercation, and that all six expelled students took part in it. The district court concluded that the Decatur School District clearly acted within the limits of its disciplinary authority under the Illinois School Code. Also, the district court rejected as legally insufficient arguments the Push/Rainbow Coalition attorneys presented for considering the expulsions unconstitutional and racially discriminatory.

As with the *James M.* matter, the *Decatur* case, although legally straightforward, raises a troubling moral issue. Even if the Decatur School Board's decision was found to be in accord with Illinois law, and withstood challenges based upon the U.S. Constitution and federal civil rights laws, did the decision, nevertheless, violate the students' moral right to receive an appropriate K–12 education?

RELEVANT FACTORS FOR DECIDING IF A SCHOOL SUSPENSION OR EXPULSION VIOLATES A STUDENT'S MORAL RIGHT TO RECEIVE AN APPROPRIATE K–12 EDUCATION

If a disciplinary decision involving a student falls within the scope of a school district's morally legitimate authority then although reasonable people may disagree with the decision, nonetheless, those in disagreement (morally) must defer to it.[9] Deference in the relevant sense has two key aspects dealing respectively with action and belief. The first is simply accepting a decision. The second involves a belief that the decision maker holds a position such that the fact of her holding it constitutes (within limits) a morally decisive reason to accept the decision, apart completely from consideration of its merits.

In the case of a K–12 public school disciplinary decision relative to a student, acceptance by the student's parents amounts roughly to the following: even if the parents consider the decision morally unjustified, nonetheless they try to help their child get it behind her, and move forward educationally, which requires that the parents maintain efforts to cooperate with school district personnel.

By contrast, the concept of deference, understood as above, cannot apply when parents believe a disciplinary decision imposed upon their child exceeded the limits of the school district's morally legitimate authority. In such a situation parents may choose not to protest. If so, however, their choice indicates "acceptance" only in a minimal sense of concluding that efforts to have the decision rescinded would be futile.[10] Rather than expressing deference, the choice reflects an alienating and embittering awareness that they have no realistic alternative to acquiescing in treatment of their child they consider deeply unjust.

Insofar as suspensions and expulsions necessitate withholding educational services, one cannot justify them on the basis of their educational benefit for suspended or expelled students, other than for "teaching students a lesson"—that adverse consequences they want to avoid result from unacceptable conduct at school. Considered solely as an educational approach, such "teaching," it is apparent, often fails to achieve its intended purpose.

Nonetheless, most educators, even those who decry widespread excessive reliance upon suspensions and expulsions, would say that no public school can accomplish its fundamental purposes without authority to suspend or expel. Educators would point, in this regard, to considerations such as maintenance of an environment in which learning can proceed, providing basic safety and security for students, and affirmation of respect for indispensable rules of school conduct by communicating an unmistakable message that certain kinds of violations are forbidden completely.

Under what circumstances, however, do the preceding kinds of considerations provide a sufficient moral justification for withholding educational services? The discussion that follows identifies four relevant factors for deciding in specific cases whether or not a suspension or expulsion violates a student's right to receive an appropriate K–12 education.

Relevant Factor 1: Adherence to Mandated Procedures under the IDEA Concerning Discipline of Children with Disabilities

As stated earlier, the IDEA places stringent requirements upon school districts that do not apply to nondisabled students when imposing disciplinary sanctions on children with disabilities. In such cases, the most prominent disability category is "serious emotional disturbance," defined by the IDEA's associated federal regulations as a condition exhibiting one or more of the following five characteristics over a long period of time to a marked degree that adversely affects a student's educational performance:

(a) an inability to learn that cannot be explained by intellectual, sensory, or health factors;
(b) an inability to build or maintain interpersonal relationships with peers and teachers;
(c) inappropriate types of behaviors or feelings under normal circumstances;
(d) a general pervasive mood of unhappiness or depression; and
(e) a tendency to develop physical symptoms or fears associated with personal or school problems.

Each of the above five characteristics has numerous differences of degree. Differentiations in this regard often require nuanced, subtle, and, to a great extent, unavoidably subjective judgments. The responsibility for deciding whether the IDEA definition of "serious emotional disturbance" applies in a particular case rests with a "team of qualified professionals and parents of the child."[11] Predictably there are frequent close calls.

Though often difficult to apply, nonetheless, the IDEA definition of "serious emotional disturbance" has a plausible rationale. The first of the above five characteristics involves, by explicit wording, an "inability to learn." As for the other four, without question each can have a significantly adverse effect upon a child's capability of benefiting from educational efforts on his or her behalf.

If any one of the five characteristics persists to a marked degree, for a long period of time, a child has serious problems that a school district must identify and address to fulfill its responsibilities correlative with a child's rights to a reasonable educational program and to equal educational concern as developed in chapter 2.

Furthermore, as noted earlier also, the IDEA specifies conditions under which a school district is deemed to have had knowledge that a disciplined student was a child with a disability even if at the time of his infraction he had not been evaluated and found eligible to receive special education. If a hearing officer finds that such conditions obtain, he/she has authority to annul the disciplinary action and issue an order directing the school district to adhere in the case of the student to the relevant procedures mandated by the IDEA.

A child's rights to a reasonable educational program and to equal educational concern thus dictate the following two requirements. First, school districts must undertake reasonable efforts to identify and address disability conditions, defined by the IDEA, which could result in behavior warranting suspensions or expulsions under school district rules. Second, if a student engages in such behavior, the school district's disciplinary decisions must adhere to mandated procedures concerning discipline of children with disabilities.[12]

Relevant Factor 2: Heightened Attention to At-Risk Students

Insofar as most suspended or expelled students do not fall within the disability categories enumerated in the IDEA, the Act's procedural protections relative to discipline of children with disabilities do not apply to them. A child's right to receive an appropriate K–12 education, set forth in chapters 2 and 3, however, entails that a school district's responsibilities include also heightened attention in the case of any student whose disciplinary infractions appear at risk of escalating in frequency and/or seriousness.

Heightened attention to every at-risk student, regardless of whether he or she qualifies for special procedural protections under the IDEA, responds to the complex, multidimensional realities of human development throughout the K–12 school years. At every stage—primary grades (including kindergarten), middle school, and high school—school staff must hold a child accountable for his or her behavior while simultaneously providing significant support to help the child develop in diverse ways (e.g., emotionally, socially, and academically) that foster educational progress.

Doing so often calls for firmness, combined with sound judgment, reflecting fairness, understanding of developmental stages in childhood, and empathy with the circumstances of the disciplined child.

Heightened attention to at-risk students may take a number of different forms. To respond effectively when there appears to be a close causal relationship between academic difficulties (cause) and unacceptable behavior (effect), some schools have a resource person on the staff to help a student's teacher develop a plan for additional academic support.[13]

In cases where a student's problems relate to fighting with other students, either physically or verbally, an in-school suspension that includes components such as anger management counseling or a restorative justice program can help resolve conflicts and provide the student valuable learning experiences about ways to settle disagreements without fighting, or to prevent them from escalating out of control.[14]

If a student's behavior problems stem from low self-esteem, interventions can be directed to helping the student develop a more favorable perception of himself or herself. An imaginative effort at positive behavior intervention toward this end, for example, in one school involved providing a student an opportunity to spend time during the day tutoring children in the classroom of a former teacher of his, with whom he had had a highly positive relationship.[15]

Under a minimum content interpretation, the right to an appropriate K–12 education encompasses a child's right to receive a reasonable educational program and to equal educational concern.[16] Both of these rights imply a responsibility of school districts to make reasonable efforts with regard to developing and implementing approaches aimed not only at placing, but also maintaining students on a trajectory of educational success. The limitations upon morally legitimate disciplinary authority in K–12 public education thus include a requirement of heightened attention to at-risk students.

Relevant Factor 3: Keeping Open the Door to Educational Opportunity

Suspensions and expulsions, by their nature, involve withholding provision of educational services to children. Despite this, as noted earlier, most, if not all, K–12 public school educators would say circumstances can arise in which suspension or expulsion of a student is unavoidable. Even in such circumstances, however, the action taken must keep the door to educational opportunity open for the student.

Such a requirement looms most large relative to long-term expulsions of a year or more. Given their immensely adverse effects upon academic progress and motivation to stay in school, long-term expulsions may be imposed justifiably only if a school district has compelling reasons to do so. An expelled student's infractions must be exceptionally severe, taking all relevant considerations into account.

In addition, long-term expulsion must be a final resort measure. Before imposing it, school authorities must consider with utmost thoroughness, whether they can identify a significantly less severe sanction such that every important reason supporting long-term expulsion in the given case equally support the lesser sanction.

If school authorities conclude they have no reasonable alternative to imposing a long-term expulsion, the expelled student must be provided an opportunity to receive alternative education. A meaningful alternative education must place substantial emphasis upon utilizing educational approaches to maintain, or help strengthen, a student's motivation to succeed and to increase his level of self-understanding, especially concerning the aspects of his behavior and attitudes which led to the long-term expulsion.

The program must have sufficient academic content, taught competently, so that the students who make reasonable effort avoid falling hopelessly behind. In the case of some students, however, a meaningful alternative educational program may focus upon other objectives than facilitating return to a regular public school placement. Such a program, for example, may provide academic preparation needed for obtaining a general education diploma (GED).

Such alternative preparation, however, must be combined with vocational training and transition services reasonably planned and implemented to help a student make intelligent choices concerning an initial career direction, and to get off to a good start along his chosen path upon leaving the program.[17]

As developed in chapter 2, an appropriate K–12 education for all American children (except for children with severe or profound intellectual disability conditions) must be designed and implemented to help children acquire knowledge and develop abilities central to the following:

1. exercise of rights, fulfillment of responsibilities, and exemplification of the ideals of membership in the American democratic body politic and
2. having a reasonable chance for success in seeking the basic human good of self-fulfillment.

From the standpoint of the above two basic objectives, one is hard pressed to think of a worse approach to discipline than long-term expulsion without meaningful alternative education. Such an approach makes it all but certain that expelled students will drop out of school, which is a consequence correlated strongly with a bleak future that includes unemployment, necessity to rely upon public assistance, substance abuse, and/or incarceration for criminal activity.

An American child's moral right to receive an appropriate K–12 education encompasses a responsibility of public school districts to provide meaningful alternative education for students upon whom long-term expulsions are imposed.

Relevant Factor 4: The *Internal Morality* of Discipline and Punishment

Morally legitimate disciplinary authority in K–12 public education must satisfy reasonable requirements concerning (i) notice, (ii) due process, (iii) impartiality, and (iv) proportionality. Such moral requirements apply, although in different ways, to any system of authority to impose discipline or to punish, as found in K–12 public schools, but also, for example, in the criminal law, the military, the family, and the workplace.

Moral requirements relating to notice, due process, impartiality, and proportionality are intrinsic to any system of discipline and punishment with morally justified purposes, insofar as they differentiate discipline and punishment under the system from, in the words of the philosopher Thomas Hobbes, mere expressions of "hostility."[18] Adapting Lon L. Fuller's terminology, one may refer to the above requirement as the *internal morality* of discipline and punishment.[19]

State school codes typically specify legal requirements for school districts concerning notice and due process apropos suspension or expulsion of a student. In regard to due process, the U.S. Supreme Court's decision in *Goss v. Lopez* sets out requirements for short-term suspensions (ten days or less), which the opinion of the Court grounded in the Fourteenth Amendment due process clause of the U.S. Constitution.[20]

Questions about the adequacy of due process protections in the case of particular suspensions or expulsions can generate strong dispute. Widespread agreement exists, however, on two important points. First, due process rights of K–12 public school students with respect to suspensions and expulsions must achieve a reasonable accommodation between assuring fair treatment to students and avoiding encroachment upon morally legitimate decision-making authority of school personnel.

Second, a system of due process rights much narrower than the full range of protection to which a defendant in a criminal trial is entitled can achieve such reasonable accommodation.

Anyone duly authorized to impose discipline or punishment has a duty of impartiality. The duty requires that the actions of an authorized person concerning discipline and punishment with respect to a group subject to her authority must not be influenced by which individuals in the group will be harmed or benefited.[21]

Breaches of the authorized person's duty of impartiality stemming from negative attitudes on her part toward a specific individual—for example, imposing more severe discipline upon the individual than upon others in similar circumstances—constitutes animus, while breaches reflecting positive attitudes toward a specific individual—for instance, leniency toward the individual not accorded others—display favoritism.

Animus and favoritism are discriminatory when an authorized person bases her actions upon an attribute belonging to all members of a subgroup within the group over which her authority to discipline or punish extends. Discrimination, in the above sense, upon any basis, violates the duty of impartiality that is part of the internal morality of discipline and punishment.

As for proportionality, the critical question is, To *what* must suspensions and expulsions be proportional? The minimum content account of an American child's moral right to receive an appropriate K–12 education, set forth in chapter 2, suggests the following plausible answer.[22] Suspensions and expulsions exemplify the attribute of proportionality to the extent they satisfy the following two conditions:

(a) A given suspension or expulsion takes into account adequately the moral right of other students to receive a reasonable K–12 educational program and to be accorded equal educational concern.
(b) The suspension or expulsion is implemented in a manner that takes into account adequately the suspended or expelled student's moral right to receive a reasonable educational program, and to be accorded equal educational concern.

Major differences of opinion can arise about how to apply conditions (a) and (b) above to circumstances surrounding particular suspension or expulsion decisions. Nonetheless, the vast majority of disputants in such cases would acknowledge both conditions as essential to a common moral framework within which to discuss and debate their disagreements on reasonable terms. Apropos the second condition specifically, all agree, insofar as they reasonably consider the issue, that a suspended or expelled student, like any other, has rights to a reasonable educational program and to equal educational concern.

What these rights mean, however, in light of the circumstances giving rise to a decision to suspend or expel is not readily apparent. Their principal elements, however, relative to suspended or expelled students concern relevant factors (1), (2), and (3) discussed above—that is, adherence to mandated procedures concerning discipline of children with disabilities under the IDEA, heightened attention to at-risk students, and keeping the door open to educational opportunity.

Can one enunciate plausible rules or guidelines for attaching weights to the four relevant factors for deciding if a suspension or expulsion violates an American child's right to receive an appropriate K–12 education?

The four relevant factors referred to in the above question are given as follows:

(1) adherence to mandated procedures under the IDEA concerning discipline of children with disabilities;
(2) heightened attention to at-risk students;
(3) keeping open the door to educational opportunity; and
(4) the internal morality of discipline and punishment.

The first three of the above relevant factors all are direct corollaries of the minimum content of an American child's moral right to receive an appropriate K–12 education developed in chapter 2—that is, the rights to a reasonable educational program and to equal educational concern. The fourth relevant factor concerns moral requirements intrinsic to any authority system for imposing discipline or punishment.

Accordingly, if a suspension or expulsion is gravely deficient from the standpoint of one or more of relevant factors 1 through 4 then it violates the moral right of every American child to receive an appropriate K–12 education, and thereby exceeds a public school district's legitimate disciplinary authority.

Development of guidelines for deciding when a suspension or expulsion is gravely deficient with respect to each factor calls for an effort to arrive at general conclusions based upon thoughtful consideration of many diverse specific cases. Toward this end, the section that follows immediately revisits the *James M.* and the *Decatur, Illinois* cases, discussing them in terms of the analyses set forth in this section.

THE *JAMES M.* CASE AND THE *DECATUR SIX* CASE REVISITED

The *James M.* Case

Six months before the school district expelled James M, it had considered if it should conduct an evaluation of James to determine his eligibility to receive special education, and, as a result, declined to do so. Based upon evidence and testimony presented at the due process hearing in the *James M.* case, however, it was apparent that at the time of the expulsion the IDEA's conditions for deeming a school district to have had knowledge that a student was a child with a disability applied clearly with respect to James.[23]

The expulsion thus was gravely deficient from the standpoint of the first of the four relevant factors identified and discussed in the immediately previous section—adherence to mandated procedures for discipline of children with disabilities under the IDEA. The expulsion, however, had grave deficiencies as well in terms of the other three relevant factors, each of which is discussed immediately below.

Heightened Attention to At-Risk Students[24]

James's grades fluctuated between mediocre and failing throughout the 1999–2000 school year. After the midterm grading period in the first term (of four) during the school year James was placed in a class designed to provide academic support, including help with homework and developing study skills. At the time of his expulsion, however, when his grades reached their lowest point (two Fs and a D+), James was no longer enrolled in the program. The school district provided no explanation at the hearing as to why this was the case.

At the time James was expelled he had amassed nineteen disciplinary infractions throughout the school year. Early in the fall, prior to the time of expulsion, James's mother communicated her concerns that James was using drugs to the assistant principal with responsibility for dealing with disciplinary issues.

She expressed interest in a program she had heard about under which, with parental consent, a student is subjected to random drug testing in school. The assistant principal said he would make inquiries about it and report back to her but did not do so. Later in the fall (December 1999), a truant officer found James and a friend smoking marijuana in the friend's home during school hours and returned them to school.

James was sent home from school in April of 2000 for shouting profanities in a school corridor. That evening he attempted suicide by ingesting twenty-six tablets of Ritalin—his prescribed medication for Attention Deficit Hyperactivity Disorder (ADHD). James's mother brought him to a hospital emergency room immediately. He was released the next day fortunately alive and unharmed. James's mother promptly informed the assistant principal of the attempted suicide, discussing it with him at school for approximately a half hour.

The following conclusions are readily apparent: (1) James M. was a seriously at-risk student and (2) the school district failed to meet its responsibility of heightened attention with respect to James.

Keeping Open the Door to Educational Opportunity

In the case of a student who receives a long-term suspension or expulsion, keeping open the door to educational opportunity requires provision of meaningful alternative education. The expulsion imposed upon James M. provided for none at all.

The Internal Morality of Discipline and Punishment: Proportionality

James explained his behavior as an intended prank, instigated by another student, to get them both sent home for the day. None of James's prior disciplinary infractions indicated either specific intention or desire to inflict harm upon other students.

One cannot reasonably minimize the seriousness of the disciplinary infraction resulting in James's expulsion, which could have caused a grave injury to other students or himself. Under the 1994 Gun-Free Schools Act, in order to receive federal funding support for K–12 education, states must assure that every school district has promulgated disciplinary rules mandating expulsion of no less than one year for students found possessing weapons or explosives at school.[25]

The two-year expulsion, with no provision made for alternative education, imposed upon James, however, was completely unjustified from a moral standpoint. The disciplinary sanction called for, at most, would have consisted of a one-year expulsion, with availability of a meaningful alternative educational program, designed to help James address his serious behavioral concerns, avoid falling far off track academically, and understand the dangerously irresponsible character of his behavior that resulted in expulsion.

The *Decatur Six* Case

The *Decatur Six* case continued to generate intense differences of opinion even long after the events in controversy took place. Despite the widespread media attention the case received, however, only limited information is available concerning a number of important matters apropos the analysis of relevant factors, developed in the second section of this chapter, for determining whether a suspension or expulsion violates an American child's right to receive an appropriate K–12 education.

The analysis, nonetheless, provides useful guidance for identifying the kinds of additional information one would need to make such a determination in the *Decatur Six* case. One point is indisputable at the outset. The Decatur School Board's initial decision to impose two-year expulsions, with no alternative education, violated the moral right of the six expelled students to receive an appropriate K–12 education.

The key moral issue requiring further analysis, however, is whether the same conclusion applies to the board's subsequently imposed one-year expulsions, with alternative education provided. No one can deny reasonably that fighting in school is a very serious matter. One also needs to acknowledge, however, that it occurs often, in many different kinds of K–12 public school environments. Expulsion of one year (even with alternative education) for fighting in school, when neither weapons were involved nor serious injury resulted, far exceeds the disciplinary norm under such circumstances.

One must recognize, however, conditions relative to a given situation could justify school authorities in concluding they needed to convey an especially strong message about the impermissibility of fighting—for example, if they had specific well-founded concerns about dangerously violent gang conflict spilling over into a school. The media coverage of the *Decatur, Illinois* case, however, provides no information concerning whether school officials had good reason to believe such conditions existed when the fighting at the football game took place.

The one-year expulsion the Decatur School Board imposed upon the six students, reduced from two years to one year after intense persuasive efforts by the Governor of Illinois, provided for the students to receive alternative education during the expulsion period. Press reports indicate in this regard that an alternative education center agreed to admit the six expelled students at the request of the State Superintendent of Education.

As stated in this chapter, the kind of alternative education required for a long-term expulsion to avoid violating an American child's moral right to receive an appropriate K–12 education must be meaningful. It must, for example, place substantial emphasis upon utilizing educational approaches to maintain, or help strengthen, a student's motivation to succeed and to increase his level of understanding, especially concerning the aspects of his behavior and attitudes which led to the long-term expulsion.

The program must have sufficient academic content, taught competently, so that students, who make the necessary effort, can avoid falling hopelessly behind. The press reports about the *Decatur Six* controversy contain no specifics at all about the content of the alternative educational program made available to the six expelled students.

The press reports on the *Decatur Six* case provided insufficient information as well on the following morally crucial questions: Were any of the six students at risk of getting into serious trouble in school, warranting a long-term expulsion, prior to the fight at the football game? If so, did they receive reasonable heightened attention from school staff?

One can never say with certainty that heightened attention to an at-risk student would have prevented behavior resulting in his expulsion. Given that the student was at risk, however, his moral right to receive an appropriate K–12 education entailed a correlative school district responsibility of reasonable heightened attention that might have made the difference. When school district staff members fail to meet the above responsibility, and an at-risk student then gets into serious trouble, the question of what to do next becomes very difficult to resolve.

To bring the point of the preceding discussion into focus, the following three matters, about which it appears the available information is insufficient, have great significance for analyzing the *Decatur Six* case in terms of a school district's morally legitimate authority to suspend or expel students:

(i) Were there reasons why specific conditions at Eisenhower High School made it imperative to convey an especially strong message through the disciplinary sanction imposed on the six expelled students, about the unacceptability of fighting in school, including school-sponsored events?
(ii) Did the alternative education provided for the six expelled students include the essential features of a meaningful educational program?

(iii) Were any of the six expelled students at risk prior to the expulsion, and, if so, did they receive reasonable heightened attention from school staff?

After the Decatur School Board reduced the expulsion to one year, with alternative education, the controversy might have ended had the school district been able to provide reasonable answers to the above questions at the meeting with the Illinois Governor, the State Superintendent of Education, and Jesse Jackson.

The preceding discussion has emphasized the moral importance for the *Decatur Six* case of the following two among the four relevant factors identified in this chapter—heightened attention to at-risk students and keeping open the door to educational opportunity. Many of the commentators who voiced opinions on the *Decatur Six* case at the time it drew widespread media attention took hard lines against the six expelled students, expressed in severe words, but without articulating explicitly the key moral premises underlying their diverse tough stances.

Most of the commentators, however, it is apparent, would have expressed the following two views emphatically.

First, they would have warned of the grave harm that, in their view, would result if school district personnel allowed themselves to become preoccupied with heightened attention to at-risk students and keeping the door open to educational opportunity in their decisions concerning suspensions and expulsions. Such, in their view, inevitably would place school districts on a slippery slope downward toward a norm of morally unjustifiable leniency, which would make it impossible to provide students who avoid getting into serious trouble an appropriate K–12 education.

Second, the commentators would have rejected the premise that *at the time they were expelled* the six students had a moral right to receive an appropriate K–12 education. To the contrary, the commentators would have maintained instead that the six students indeed had this right *before* taking part in the fight but forfeited it by doing so.

Apropos the first of the above views, one cannot reasonably deny that were a norm of morally unjustified leniency to become entrenched, it would erode the sense of personal responsibility upon which successful functioning of any social order depends. The conclusions that the commentators would draw from this unarguable point, however, are unacceptably one-sided.

The sense of personal responsibility needed badly in American society at this time, would be developed most effectively in schools by adopting disciplinary practices and policies that hold children accountable if they misbehave, while, at the same time, providing emotional, social, and academic support that fosters educational progress.

Such policies and methods must be firm but also reflect sound judgment, fairness, understanding of developmental stages in childhood (including adolescence), and empathy with the circumstances of the disciplined child.

Concern to avoid contributing to the establishment of a morally unjustifiable norm of leniency cannot justify an expulsion likely to place a child on the road to a life no rational person in America would consider worth living.

As for the second view, to consider thoughtfully the claim that, by their behavior, the six students forfeited their right to receive an appropriate K–12 education, one needs first to consider the following general issue. What conditions must be obtained in any case where one has reasonable grounds for concluding that a person has forfeited a moral right through morally unacceptable conduct? The following two conditions are essential:

(1) The person is aware fully, or should be aware fully, that his/her morally unacceptable behavior (e.g., intentional killing of a human being) could result in forfeiture of a moral right (e.g., the right to freedom).
(2) It is morally justifiable for an authority system (e.g., the legal order of a given civil society) to mandate forfeiture of the moral right as a consequence of the person's morally unjustifiable conduct (e.g., laws specifying the punishment for homicide).

The next question in order of logical priority is how the above two conditions apply to the question of whether a student has forfeited through his conduct the right to receive an appropriate K–12 education. In cases where disciplinary authority lies with public school districts (rather than elsewhere) the following two conclusions are apparent.

First, it is unreasonable to regard condition 1 as applicable under any circumstances to students below the age of sixteen, given their lack of experience and maturity.[26] Second, while condition 1 could apply in diverse cases involving some older students, for reasons developed immediately below, condition 2 never applies to K–12 students of any age.

In regard to the second of the above two conclusions one needs to keep in mind that, from the standpoint of the moral right of American children to receive an appropriate K–12 education, the relationship between a student and a school district is not bilateral, as in a contractual relationship between two purely private parties. In contrast, school districts are public bodies established to serve a public purpose of the utmost importance.

The fact that a student engaged in unacceptable conduct with full awareness that doing so could result in a disciplinary sanction tantamount to losing his right to receive a K–12 education—for instance, a two-year suspension with no alternative education—therefore does not suffice to justify imposing the sanction upon him. To the contrary, the sanction is morally unjustifiable insofar as it cannot be justified in terms of the four relevant factors identified and described in this chapter for assuring that an expulsion does not violate the child's moral right to receive an appropriate K–12 education.

CONCLUSION

Imposing discipline upon any K–12 public school student, whether a child with a disability or a nondisabled child, is never enjoyable, and, often painfully difficult. The difficulty for thoughtful individuals can include among its aspects an uncomfortable gnawing sense of moral uncertainty that stems from the following realization.

Hovering in the background of specific matters for decision in a school discipline case often are broad, deep, and fundamental, issues about the limits of morally legitimate authority to discipline students in K–12 public schools that are insufficiently analyzed. Hopefully, the analysis set forth in this chapter helps to identify, clarify understanding, and gain insight into factors which underlie a morally justifiable approach concerning K–12 public school suspensions and expulsions of any student, whether nondisabled or a child with a disability.

NOTES

1. See chapter 1, pp. 1–18.
2. The following words of Justice Harry Blackmun express a highly prevalent view in this regard:

> Maintaining order in the classroom can be a difficult task. A single teacher often must watch over a large number of students, and, as any parent knows, children at certain ages are inclined to test the outer boundaries of acceptable conduct and to initiate the misbehavior of a peer if the misbehavior is not dealt with quickly. . . . Thus the Court has recognized in [*Goss v. Lopez* 419 U.S. 565, 580 (1975)] that "events calling for discipline are frequent occurrences and sometimes require immediate effective action." (*New Jersey v. T.L.O.* 469 U.S. 325, 352 [1984])

One of the few strong expressions of disagreement with the above view is found in the following words of Tolstoy, which, to understate the matter, most people would consider implausible: for example, ". . . [L]eave [children] alone and see how simply and naturally [conflict] will settle itself. . . . I am convinced that . . . the school has no right and ought not to reward and punish; that the best police and administration of a school consist in giving full liberty to the pupils to study and settle disputes as they know best."

Leo Tolstoy, "The School at Yasnaya Polyana," in *Patterns of Anarchy*, eds. Leonard I. Krimmerman and Lewis Perry (Doubleday Anchor, 1966), 476–77.

3. *Reed Custer CU School District 255* (2001) 35 IDELR 246 (The author was the due process hearing officer in this case.)

4. At the time the meeting took place to determine whether a case study evaluation should be initiated, James was passing all of his courses with no grade lower than C, and the frequency of his disciplinary citations had diminished.

5. See chapter 1, pp. 1–18.

6. The relevant provisions of the IDEA in 2001, at the time of the *Matter of James M.*, stated that a school district shall be deemed to have "had knowledge" that a student was "a child with a disability" when

> (i) the parent of the child has expressed concern in writing . . . to personnel of the appropriate educational agency that the child is in need of special education and related services;
>
> (ii) the behavior or performance of the child demonstrates the need for such services;
>
> (iii) the parent of the child has requested an evaluation of the child . . . ; or
>
> (iv) the teacher of the child or other personnel of the local educational agency has expressed concern about the behavior or performance of the child to the director of special education of such agency or to other personnel of the agency (20 U.S.C. 1415 (k) (8) (B)).

Under the federal regulations associated with the above statutory provision, however, a school district would not be deemed to have had knowledge that a student was a child with a disability if, as a result of obtaining the kind of information specified in any of the conditions specified in 20 U.S.C. 1415 (k) (8) (B):

> (1) the school district conducted an evaluation and determined that the student was not a child with a disability; or
>
> (2) determined that an evaluation was not necessary (34 C.F.R. 300.327 (c)).

Under the IDEA, as reauthorized in 2004, the relevant statutory provisions for deeming a school district to have had knowledge that a student was a "child with disability" differ slightly from the 1997 provisions. Under IDEA 2004 the provisions state the following: A school district is considered to have had such knowledge if before the behavior that precipitated the disciplinary action occurred (a) the parent of the child expressed concern in writing to supervisory or administrative personnel of the appropriate educational agency, or a teacher of the child, that the child is in need of special education and related services; (b) the parent of the child has requested an evaluation of the child pursuant to 20 U.S.C. sec. 1414 (a) (1) (B); or (c) the teacher of the child, or other personnel of the local educational agency, has expressed specific concerns about a pattern of behavior demonstrated by the child directly to the director of special education of such agency or to other supervisory personnel of the agency.

An exception to the above rule applies, however, if the parent of the child has not allowed the school district to evaluate the child, has refused services, or if the child has been evaluated and it was determined that the child is not a child with a disability (20 U.S.C. sec. 1415 (k) (5) (C) (Supp. 2004)).

7. For a brief discussion of issues that applying the category of emotional disturbance presents for a special education due process hearing officer see the discussion at p. 6.

126 Chapter 5

8. *Fuller v. Decatur Public School Board of Education School District 61* 78 F. Supp 812 (2000).

9. In more formal/theoretical terms, legitimate authority may be considered as a relation between an authority holder and a subject such that the authority holder has a moral right to deference of the subject, and, correlatively, the subject has a moral duty of deference to the authority holder. On the relation between the concepts of authority and deference see Joseph Raz, *The Morality of Freedom* (Oxford University Press: Oxford, 1986), 38–69.

10. Public School officials possess broad, powerful, and, for the most part, legally unfettered authority under state school codes, which courts, including the U.S. Supreme Court, have upheld consistently with only a few exceptions. For example, as noted in the preceding summary of the *James M.* case, the Illinois School Code authorizes school districts to expel students for up to two years, with no provision made for alternative education (105 ILCS 5/10-22.6(d)).

As for constitutional limitations upon the disciplinary authority of public schools, in *Ingraham v. Wright* 430 U.S. 651 (1977) the Supreme Court held that the protection of the Eighth Amendment, with respect to the imposition of cruel and unusual punishment only applies to punishment under the criminal law, and not to school discipline. (The petitioner in *Ingraham v. Wright* complained that he was struck with a paddle twenty times while being held over a table in the principal's office. The paddling was so severe, he reported, that he suffered a hematoma requiring medical attention and keeping him out of school for eleven days.)

The Supreme Court has held that students have Fourth Amendment rights to freedom from unreasonable searches and seizures (*New Jersey v. T.L.O.* 469 U.S. 325 [1985]), but the Court interprets these rights narrowly. The Court ruled in *New Jersey v. T.L.O.*, for example, that a search only needs to be based upon reasonable grounds to believe that the student has violated rules of the school. School district officials need not obtain search warrants and are not subject to the Fourth Amendment requirement of probable cause to believe that the subject of the search has violated the law.

The Supreme Court also has held that K–12 public school students have a right, under the Fourteenth Amendment, to a disciplinary hearing upon suspension. Such a hearing, however, in the case of suspensions of ten days or less, need only afford "rudimentary precautions against unfair or mistaken findings of misconduct and arbitrary exclusion from school" (*Goss v. Lopez* 419 U.S. 565, 582 [1975]). The Court has not considered the issue of whether the Fourteenth Amendment requires more stringent procedural safeguards relative to longer term suspensions or expulsions.

11. 20 U.S.C. 1414(b) (4) (A).

12. By far the most problematic aspect of the IDEA's rules and regulations relative to discipline of children with disabilities concerns the manifestation determination process, which comes into play after a child has been suspended for ten school days (34 C.F.R. 300.530 (e)). The process requires school district staff to decide in the case of the next disciplinary infraction warranting suspension under school rules whether the student's conduct was a manifestation of his disability, in which case extensive further requirements apply in regard to providing the student an appropriate educational placement (34 C.F.R. 300.530(f) (g)).

The manifestation determination process has been criticized strongly for the following reason: Educators can (although often with difficulty) make determinations as to whether or not a student qualifies for services under the IDEA category of serious emotional disturbance. There is no objective test, however, to determine whether a student's identified serious emotional disturbance condition was among the causes of unacceptable conduct at school in a particular circumstance.

The question at the heart of the manifestation determination process thus raises a problem that parallels closely the fundamental difficulty besetting the insanity defense in criminal law—that the task of applying the relevant legal standard poses questions that require judgments for which there is no objective standard.

It is extremely difficult to avoid the above difficulty with the manifestation determination process. As with the insanity defense, abolishing the process would pose equally, if not more, troubling issues. Similar to the insanity defense, there are essentially two alternatives to requiring that school districts determine whether the conduct precipitating a disabled student's eleventh day of suspension was a manifestation in part of his disability:

First, every student with a disability could be treated no differently from nondisabled students relative to discipline. Such an approach, however, has the unreasonable consequence of eliminating "serious emotional disturbance" as a category of disability altogether, given that, under the IDEA, the indicators of "serious emotional disturbance" all are exemplified through behavior often of a kind involving disciplinary infractions—for example, truancy, disruption, insubordination, fighting, and so on.

Second, at the other extreme, students with disabilities could receive differential treatment from nondisabled students in every circumstance—that is, without undertaking a manifestation determination review. Apart from the justified resentment this approach would arouse from nondisabled students, it conflicts as well with a disabled student's right to receive a reasonable educational program for the following reason.

The manifestation determination process, albeit unsuccessfully, attempts to address an *educationally relevant issue*—does a student possess the knowledge, understanding, and capability for self-control needed in order for imposing of school discipline, at least under highly favorable circumstances, to be a learning experience for him or her? If so, then disciplinary sanctions predicated on the opposite premise deprive the student of an important educational experience, and therefore conflict with his right to receive a reasonable educational program.

13. Interview with Carol Steiner, Principal (Ret.), Parkwood-Upjohn Elementary School, Kalamazoo, MI (January 10, 2009).

14. See Alan J. Borsuk, "A Circular Path to Peace," *Milwaukee Journal Sentinel* (March 17, 2009): 1B.

15. Interview with Edis Snyder, principal (Ret.), Chicago Public Schools (January 12, 2009).

16. Cite to chapter 2.

17. For reasons why preparation for passing a GED examination alone would not suffice see, James J. Heckman, *Giving Kids a Fair Chance* (MIT Press, Boston: 2013), 8–9.

18. See Hobbes, *Leviathan*, 230.

19. Lon L. Fuller, *The Morality of Law* (Yale University Press: New Haven, 1963).

20. 419 U.S. 565 (1975).

21. For full development of the account of impartiality this analysis draws upon, see Bernard Gert, *Morality* (Oxford University Press: Oxford UK, 2005), 131–55.

22. See chapter 2, pp. 19–48.

23. Decision and Orders in the *Matter of James M. v. Reed Custer Community Unit School District 255u* (March 29, 2001) (The Author was the Due Process Hearing Officer in this case.)

24. The additional information that follows in this subsection consists of factual findings, based upon a review of the evidence and testimony presented in the *James M.* case.

25. 20 U.S.C. 8921 et seq. The Gun-Free Schools Act also contains the following two mandates. First, schools must refer students found in possession of weapons or explosives in school to the criminal justice system or juvenile justice system. Second, the statute requires that state law "allow the chief administrating officer of [the] local educational agency to modify [the] expulsion requirement for a student on a case by case basis." 20 U.S.C. 8921 (b) (1).

26. U.S. Supreme Court Justice Clarence Thomas recommended in his concurring opinion in *Morse v. Frederick 551* U.S. 393 (2007) that the Supreme Court adopt an exceptionally strong version of the in loco parentis doctrine. Justice Thomas's recommendation appears to authorize every kind of disciplinary action currently deemed unconstitutional in virtue of Supreme Court precedents relating to constitutional guarantees of free speech, protection from unreasonable searches and seizures, and procedural due process insofar as they apply to K–12 public schools.

Such a sweeping interpretation of the in loco parentis doctrine could not legally justify a two-year K–12 public school expulsion for the following reason. Under in loco parentis the disciplinary authority of K–12 public schools is no greater than that of parents. Parents, however, have responsibility to assure their children receive an appropriate education. Accordingly, school districts lack in loco parentis authority to impose a disciplinary sanction, such as a two-year expulsion, with no alternative education provided, which is likely to result in the end of a child's K–12 public education.

As a counterargument, a supporter of Justice Thomas's strong interpretation of in loco parentis might respond that every parent has a choice in the first place of whether or not to send his/her child to a public school, rather than enrolling the child in a private school or homeschooling the child. Therefore, according to the counterargument, by choosing to send his/her child to a public school a parent thereby authorizes all the school district's disciplinary decisions. Justice Thomas's Supreme Court colleague Justice Samuel Alito, however, in his concurring opinion, rightly characterized the above counterargument as based upon a "dangerous fiction."

Chapter 6

Special Education Due Process Review
A Hearing Officer's Moral Responsibility

Chapter 5 began with a summary of the matter of *James M.*, a special education due process case, involving a student who was expelled from high school for two years—the maximum length allowed by the School Code of Illinois—with no provision for alternative education. Five months before the expulsion occurred, school district staff had considered whether they should conduct a case study evaluation to determine James's eligibility status for receiving special education and decided that doing so was unwarranted. In this regard, the school district staff noted, James was passing all his courses with grades of C or better, and the disciplinary infractions he had committed up to that time were relatively minor. Accordingly, when James was expelled five months later, he was not designated as a "child with a disability" under the IDEA's statutory definition.[1]

The critical issue in the due process case was whether conditions specified in the IDEA for judging a school district to have "had knowledge" that a student was a "child with a disability" even though the student (as in James M.'s case) had not been evaluated and found eligible to receive special education, nonetheless, applied with respect to James M. If so, then the IDEA's procedural safeguards regarding discipline of children with disabilities would dictate annulment of the expulsion.[2] If not, then the expulsion order would stand.

As noted in chapter 5, it turned out that the above statutory conditions applied apropos James M. There was thus a solid legal basis for issuing orders that annulled James's expulsion, and for granting all the relief James's mother had requested.[3]

The following issue in regard to the matter of *James M*, however, raises troubling moral questions. It is one thing for a hearing officer to uphold a suspension or expulsion about which he disagrees personally, and yet believe not only that it comports with pertinent legal standards, but also that it falls within the limits of the school district's morally legitimate authority to discipline students.

It is another thing entirely, however, for a hearing officer to conclude that in rendering a decision he has no other alternative than to uphold the legality of a suspension or expulsion that, in his judgment, exceeds vastly the limitations upon a K–12 public school district's *morally* legitimate disciplinary authority over any student.

Suppose a hearing officer had to decide a case with facts similar exactly to those in the matter of *James M.*, except for the following: circumstances were *not* present in the case such that under the IDEA a school district must be deemed to have "had knowledge" that an expelled student was a "child with a disability" at the time of the expulsion. What moral issues would such a case pose for a hearing officer, and how could he/she deal with them?

Framing adequate answers to these questions requires both widening and deepening the scope of inquiry beyond the particular morally difficult and emotionally wrenching situation a hearing officer would have to face under the above circumstances. One needs, in this regard, to consider the issues listed below, which are essential for seeking to understand the relationship between the special education due process review system and the moral right of American children with disabilities to receive an appropriate K–12 education:

(1) From a moral standpoint, what is the primary function of the special education due process review procedure?
(2) In light of this function, what are the primary moral responsibilities of a special education due process hearing officer?
(3) What are the moral limits of a hearing officer's primary moral responsibilities relative to his/her role in the due process review procedure?

This chapter has four sections. Section 1 addresses issue (1) above, setting forth reasons which justify the conclusion that a legal right of due process review for children with disabilities, and their parents, is indispensable to effectuate in a meaningful way the children's moral right to receive an appropriate K–12 education.

Section 2 considers both issues (2) and (3). It contains an analysis of the special education hearing officer's duty of fidelity to the rule of law that draws heavily upon philosopher Bernard Gert's conception of common morality.[4] The analysis focuses upon the duty's presumptive moral force—that is, (a) the extent to which the requirements of the duty, for someone in a judicial position, take precedence over other morally relevant considerations and (b) the limits beyond which the duty loses its moral force.

Section 3 introduces an analytical framework for identifying morally permissible choices a hearing officer would have in a case with a factual pattern exactly similar to the pattern in the matter of *James M.* but for one crucial exception. The evidence and testimony presented are *insufficient* for concluding that, under the IDEA, the school district must be regarded as having had knowledge at the time of an expulsion that the expelled student was a child with a disability.

Finally, section 4, drawing upon the analyses in sections 2 and 3, considers an approach a hearing officer could take in a case similar to the matter of *James M.* except for the facts in the *James M.* case that provided a valid legal justification for annulling the expulsion.

WHY A LEGAL RIGHT OF K–12 SPECIAL EDUCATION DUE PROCESS REVIEW IS MORALLY NECESSARY

A legal right of due process review is indispensable for giving meaningful effect to the moral right of children with disabilities to receive an appropriate K–12 education. In explaining why, it helps to start with some general points about the relationship between the concepts of due process and moral rights. Authority systems are a pervasive feature of human life, as contemporary Americans know it. In such systems some persons occupy roles or positions conferring the right to exercise authority over other persons.

Hierarchies of authority make it possible for institutions or organizations such as schools, businesses, and governmental agencies to accomplish their diverse essential purposes. Given both the nature of institutional/organizational hierarchies and human psychology, however, abuses or misuses of authority by superiors within an authority system over subordinates, in the sense of those subject to their authority, are inevitable.

Due process is a means of addressing this problem. Described broadly it is a procedural method with the following four essential elements:

(i) rules of the authority system which forbid diverse kinds of behavior (or omissions) which violate moral rights of subordinates;
(ii) provision for subordinates to initiate an adjudicatory proceeding conducted by an impartial person (or group of persons);
(iii) fair opportunity at the proceeding for the subordinate to present reasons why in his/her opinion acts or omissions of a superior violate his/her moral rights in ways proscribed expressly by the rules of the authority system; and
(iv) authority of the adjudicator(s) to order appropriate remedial action.

Due process is not the only conceivable way to avoid, limit, or remedy abuses and/or misuses of authority within an authority system. Investigation and direct enforcement by a regulatory agency within the system may be effective in this regard. To cite another example, a scheme for decentralized decision making in a given institutional/organizational context may enable stakeholders to participate significantly, under fair conditions, in decision-making processes with respect to important issues affecting them.

Philosopher Thomas Scanlon lists the following four questions as central in deciding whether due process, rather than some other scheme, would be the best means of protection against abuses and/or misuses of institutional/organizational authority:[5]

(1) How likely is it that a given form of power—if unchecked—will be used outside the limits of its [moral] justification?
(2) How serious are the harms inflicted by its [abuses] or misuses?
(3) Would due process be an effective check on the use of this power?
(4) Would the costs of a requirement of due process in cases of this kind be excessive? Is the additional effectiveness of due process over other forms of control worth the additional cost?

When one answers the above four questions, specifically in relation to K–12 education of children with disabilities, the moral indispensability of a legal right of due process review becomes apparent. Regarding question (1), as noted earlier, given human nature, as well as the nature of institutions/organizations, abuses and/or misuses of authority in K–12 public schools are inevitable. Apropos question (2), an abuse or a misuse of authority that results in failure to provide a child with a disability an appropriate K–12 education, to which he or she has a moral right, surely qualifies as a matter of utmost seriousness.

As for question (3), the orders issued in the matter of *James M.* summarized in chapter 5 illustrate the effectiveness of due process review for addressing such a serious abuse or misuse of authority. For example, the orders directed the school district to (i) reinstate James M. as a student in good standing, (ii) provide compensatory education for the time period he was expelled, and (iii) pay the full costs for an out-of-district residential school placement appropriate in light of James M's ADHD and serious emotional disturbance conditions.[6] All the above orders were well within the scope of a special education due process hearing officer's remedial authority under the IDEA.[7]

In regard to question (4), there are two principal kinds of measures for giving meaningful effect to the educational rights of children with disabilities besides due process review as provided for in the IDEA. These are (i) regulatory investigation and enforcement by a government agency such as the Office of Civil Rights of the U.S. Department of Justice and (ii) procedures for dispute mediation, both voluntary and mandatory.[8] Both kinds of measures can reduce the volume of cases in which parents of children with disabilities, or school districts as well, consider it necessary to initiate due process hearing procedures.

Extending and refining these kinds of measures undoubtedly is very important and should be encouraged strongly but, in all likelihood, doing so never could eliminate completely the need for due process review procedures. When one looks beneath the contested legal issues which the parties in a due process hearing identify as the reason for the hearing one finds in many, if not most, instances highly contentious *moral* questions concerning interpretation of the moral right of American children to receive an appropriate K–12 education in cases involving children with diverse disability conditions.

As chapters 2 through 5 make apparent, such matters of interpretive controversy implicate disagreement over how to understand and to apply philosophically deep concepts such as happiness, justice, human dignity, and freedom relative to education programs for specifically identified children with disabilities. The most difficult of such cases can only be resolved for practical purposes, at least temporarily, through a decision with the force of law behind it. The cases of *Timothy W.*, *Beth B.*, and *James M.*, with which chapters 3, 4, and 5 respectively began, each provide a persuasive example in this regard.

The right to special education due process review under the IDEA thus serves the following indispensable function, from a moral standpoint. It upholds the moral right of American children with disabilities to receive an appropriate K–12 education by providing a method, with the force of law behind it, to effectuate the right meaningfully in diverse difficult-to-resolve individual cases.[9]

THE HEARING OFFICER'S JUDICIAL DUTY OF FIDELITY TO LAW: MORAL BASES AND MORAL LIMITS

The function of a special education due process hearing officer within the procedures of due process review is thoroughly judicial. A hearing officer carries out her/his function by conducting hearings at the conclusion of which she/he must issue a written decision.

Hearings are characteristically judicial in nature, including opening and closing statements by the parties, direct and cross-examination of witnesses, introduction of documentary evidence, and (frequently) post-hearing briefs submitted by the parties. The written decision of a hearing officer must explain its justifying bases, which calls for identifying, applying, and interpreting pertinent sources of legal authority such as provisions of federal and state statutes concerning special education, and case law (i.e., court decisions) that apply and interpret such provisions.

The basic moral responsibility of a special education hearing officer, intrinsic to her/his judicial function, is adherence to the judicial duty of fidelity to the rule of law. This duty has two key parts: first, a hearing officer must make conscientiously researched and carefully thought out efforts to identify the pertinent law in a case before her. Second, she must apply that law even if it conflicts with the decision she would have rendered if she could have based it solely upon her conclusions about the moral rights and duties of the parties in light of the presented evidence. The judicial duty of fidelity to law thus can, and often does, function as a morally relevant consideration to justify subordination of moral to legal judgment on the part of a hearing officer in virtue of her judicial role.

Like other duties attaching to roles or positions, however (e.g., of parents, teachers, military personnel, and members of professions, such as law, medicine, and journalism), from a moral standpoint, the judicial duty of fidelity to the rule of law is not absolute. What kinds of considerations could take precedence over the judicial duty of fidelity to the rule of law, and upon what grounds?

In order to address such questions, one must develop an account of the duty's moral foundations, which in turn leads directly to issues at the core of legal philosophy about the requirements of morality that concern obedience to law. The philosophy of law has two predominant approaches in regard to the essential relationship between law and morality—natural law theory and legal positivism—each of which emphasizes a different central idea.

Natural law theory, expressed in its classic form by Saint Thomas Aquinas, regards the central idea as justice, in a broad sense that encompasses basic moral requirements concerning actions of human beings that affect the well-being of other human beings.[10] Aquinas and other natural law theorists identify justice with precepts of conduct that, according to their theory, are as follows:

- morally paramount—they take precedence over any other kinds of consideration when making a moral decision or moral judgment;
- universal—every human being (beyond a relatively young age) with normally functioning cognitive abilities, is aware of, and understands them; and
- morally foundational—the relationship law bears to morality (in the natural law sense) is the moral foundation of legal authority.

In contrast, for legal positivists, exemplified paradigmatically by John Austin, the central idea is order.[11] Specifically, the kind of order legal positivists consider central to the concept of law is realized in a system of norms that

- has the purpose of determining the rights and duties of persons within a given society;
- contains formal procedures for settling disputed issues; and
- possesses de facto authority—that is, the system is recognized widely throughout the given society as authoritative.

Setting forth an adequate account of how the ideas of justice and order relate to one another for purposes of clarifying the relationship between morality and law is extremely difficult. Nonetheless, one can say safely that everyone, upon reflection, would recognize *both* justice (in the broad natural law sense) and order as central considerations. In this regard, the purpose a legal system serves of providing formal and authoritative procedures for settling moral disputes within a society is morally fundamental. This purpose alone justifies the rule "Obey the law" as a basic moral rule.

"Obey the Law," as a Basic Moral Rule

The following discussion sets forth an analysis in support of considering "Obey the law" a basic rule of morality, which draws heavily upon ideas of philosopher Bernard Gert.[12] The analysis will then be extended, making it applicable as well to the idea of a special education due process hearing officer's duty of fidelity to the rule of law. The extended analysis in the second subsection will both identify the moral foundation of the duty and clarify implicit judgments of thoughtful morally conscientious individuals concerning the force of the duty's requirements in diverse circumstances.

Gert defines common morality as "the moral system that thoughtful people implicitly use when making moral decisions and judgments."[13] So conceived, according to Gert, the system of common morality serves the purpose of lessening harms to human beings caused by actions of other human beings.[14] The harms that the system seeks to lessen, according to Gert, specifically, are death, disability, pain, loss of freedom, and loss of pleasure.[15] Common morality contains, at its core, the four elements identified and described briefly below:

(i) *Basic moral rules*: rules of morally required conduct under the system of common morality. The rules are general, in the sense of being phrased without specified exceptions, but not absolute. That is to say, the rules may be violated justifiably depending upon circumstances. Gert identifies the following ten rules as basic moral rules:

> 1. Do not kill; 2. Do not disable; 3. Do not cause pain; 4. Do not deprive of freedom; 5. Do not deprive of pleasure; 6. Keep your promises; 7. Do not deceive; 8. Do not cheat; 9. Obey the law; 10. Do your duty.[16]

(ii) *Moral ideals*: objectives of human action which, from the standpoint of common morality, are *not* morally required but, nonetheless, morally praiseworthy for a person to seek to achieve or realize. Actions that exemplify moral ideals are morally praiseworthy because they aim to prevent the harms, identified above, which the purpose of the system of common morality is to lessen. Examples of such ideals thus are prevention of death, disability, pain, loss of freedom, and/or loss of pleasure.[17]

(iii) *Morally relevant features*: considerations to which primary importance must be attached regarding decisions or judgments as to whether a given violation of a basic moral rule is (or was) justified in a given set of circumstances. In this regard, morally relevant features are facts regarding a situation in which a basic moral rule is violated (or in which violation is contemplated) which, if different, could affect whether some rational impartial persons would consider such violation morally justified.

(iv) *Decision procedure*: sequence of morally crucial issues to consider when making a moral decision or judgment. The sequential steps of this procedure are (a) determining whether a basic moral rule has been violated (or if such a violation is contemplated); (b) if so, then identifying the morally relevant features of the situation; and (c) asking oneself this question: What consequences would result if "this kind of violation"— that is, violation of the basic moral rule at issue in this situation, given the morally relevant features in this situation—was publicly allowed?

As Gert understands it, common morality is grounded in three universal aspects of human nature: vulnerability, fallibility, and rationality. *Vulnerability*: the harms that common morality serves to lessen, according to Gert—that is, death, disability, pain, loss of freedom, and loss of pleasure—all are ones to which every human being is vulnerable.

Fallibility: An invulnerable and infallible being would have no need for the kind of guidance common morality provides which, in the words of the philosopher Thomas Hobbes, "redound to the damage or benefit of his neighbors."[18] In contrast, the content and structure of common morality—that is, the basic moral rules, moral ideals, morally relevant features, and decision procedure—all, in diverse ways, facilitate decision making of vulnerable, fallible human beings not immune from error when considering the consequences of their actions for others.

Rationality: Considered as an aspect of human nature, common morality reflects rationality in the following two key respects. First, all rational human beings want to avoid the five harms common morality seeks to lessen—death, pain, disability, loss of freedom, and loss of pleasure—except in specific circumstances when they have an adequate reason for not wanting to do so.[19]

Second, every rational human being is capable of (a) full understanding of the content of common morality and making decisions or judgments in terms of it, (b) acting in accordance with its requirements, and (c) comprehending the reasons why common morality serves the purpose of lessening harms to human beings caused by the actions of other human beings.[20]

Gert's argument for considering "Obey the law" a basic rule of common morality is best understood along the following lines:[21] disputes over moral issues occur often and concern always, although with varying degrees of urgency in diverse circumstances, the most fundamental kinds of human interests—specifically, avoidance, or prevention of harms, which Gert defines as death, pain, disability, loss of freedom, and loss of pleasure.

Furthermore, common morality, as Gert points out, has two significant limitations. First, it is incomplete—that is, it cannot provide a unique correct answer to every moral question. Second, common morality is informal in the sense that the decision procedure it contains is a framework for seeking to reach a decision, rather than an explicit procedure to settle disputed questions.

The quality of life in any human society would be intolerable for any rational person if the society lacked a formal method, regarded widely throughout society as authoritative for settling moral disputes, at least temporarily.[22] Common morality thus needs to be supplemented by a formal system—namely law. Law cannot serve its morally indispensable function of settling moral disputes, however, unless members of society act in accordance with its requirements.

For this reason, according to Gert, all rational impartial individuals would agree that the rule "Obey the law" should be included in common morality, considered as an informal public system applying to all rational persons.[23]

The phrase "presumptive moral force" refers to the extent to which, in diverse kinds of situations, a basic moral rule takes precedence over other morally relevant factors supporting justified violation. Gert's account of why common morality includes the rule "Obey the law" makes apparent a crucial aspect of the way in which morally conscientious thoughtful individuals conceive of the rule's presumptive moral force.

To identify and clarify this aspect, however, requires first introducing into the analysis a distinction between two different viewpoints, which could be taken toward the violation of a basic moral rule. The two viewpoints, identified immediately below, draw heavily upon a distinction Gert draws between "strong" and "weak" justification of a basic moral rule violation.

- A person considers a violation of a basic moral rule as *strongly justified* if and only if she believes that all qualified impartial rational persons would consider the violation justified.[24]
- A person considers a violation of a basic moral rule as *weakly justified* if and only if she believes some, but not all, qualified impartial rational persons would consider the violation justified.

Suppose a particular thoughtful, morally conscientious person concludes that a given law, whether enacted statutorily or announced in the context of judicial adjudication, is not even weakly justifiable in the above sense. To avoid inconsistency, he ought then to regard the basic moral rule "Obey the law" as having *no* presumptive moral force relative to the given law, that is to say, as not applying with respect to it.

According to Gert's theory, the indispensable role legal systems play in settling disputed moral issues alone justifies including "Obey the law" among the basic rules of common morality, conceived of as a public system applying to all rational persons. This morally fundamental role can be played only by laws that are, at least, weakly justifiable in Gert's sense.

Consider, for example, the famous passages in *Huckleberry Finn* where Huck describes the pangs of conscience he experienced while rafting down the Mississippi with the runaway slave Jim as it dawned upon him that he was helping Jim attempt an escape to freedom.[25] A person would badly miss the intended irony of these passages if he thought they were meant to raise a genuine moral issue about the moral justifiability of violating the State of Missouri's antebellum criminal laws, which forbade aiding and abetting a runaway slave.

Tragic situations arise at times in which a qualified impartial rational person could conclude, all things considered, that common morality requires compliance with a morally unjustifiable law. In such situations, however, the reasons concern morally compelling factors other than those with an intrinsic connection to the fundamental purposes of a legal system from a moral standpoint. For this reason, questions about the presumptive moral force of the rule "Obey the law" do not come into play.[26]

Gert's account, as described above, of why "Obey the law" is a basic moral rule of common morality thus helps one understand, with enhanced clarity, the principal reasons why the natural law theory conception of justice and the legal positivist understanding of order *both* are central to the concept of law. Apropos the former, for reasons set forth in Gert's account, all rational impartial persons would agree the rule "Obey the law" should be included in common morality and considered as a public system applying to all rational persons.

At the same time, however, thoughtful morally conscientious persons believe that the rule has no presumptive moral force in a particular circumstance unless the pertinent law is morally justifiable, at least in the weak sense that some, but not all, qualified impartial rational persons regard it as morally justified.

As for the legal positivist understanding of order, to serve the morally (and also socially) indispensable function of settling disputes over moral issues, a legal system not only must contain formal procedures for doing so but, in addition, the settlements must be considered authoritative as a matter of social consensus. Most members of society must believe that the moral requirement to comply with the law, although not absolute, nonetheless, has presumptive moral force in a vast majority of circumstances.

The Judicial Duty of Fidelity to the Rule of Law

Up to this point the discussion has focused solely upon "Obey the law," as a basic moral rule, rather than upon the judicial duty of fidelity to the rule of law. Such focus has not been a digression. It provides important conceptual resources that aid in identifying and clarifying the views of thoughtful morally conscientious individuals about both the moral foundations and the presumptive moral force of the judicial duty of fidelity to the rule of law.

In regard to moral foundations, the judicial duty of fidelity to the rule of law and the basic moral rule "Obey the law" are related closely. The morally fundamental purpose of law is to supplement common morality with formal and de facto authoritative procedures to settle moral questions. Law cannot serve this purpose, however, unless most members of society share the attitude that the rule "Obey the law" has strong presumptive moral force whenever laws are morally justifiable, at least in in Gert's weak sense. That is, they regard violations of such morally justifiable laws as always requiring moral justification.

The above attitude would have no point, and thus not be shared widely, if even held by anyone at all, in a society, however, without consistent enforcement of law. Application of constantly changing legal standards would result in the same conditions of pervasive chilling uncertainty that would make human life intolerable in a society lacking any kind of formal and de facto authoritative procedures for settlement of disputed moral questions.

Consistent law enforcement requires, however, that anyone performing a judicial function, such as a special education due process hearing officer, regard her judicial duty of fidelity to the rule of law as highly stringent to the extent of resolving all reasonable doubts she might have concerning whether a given law is morally justified in favor of upholding the law. This means regarding herself as bound by the duty of fidelity to the rule of law even if she considers the law morally unjustified, so long as she acknowledges that some qualified impartial rational persons could consider it morally justified.[27]

As for circumstances where a law is not even weakly justified, in Gert's sense, thoughtful morally conscientious individuals share an attitude concerning the presumptive moral force of the judicial duty of fidelity to law that parallels their views in this regard apropos the basic moral rule "Obey the law." Such a law cannot serve as a standard to apply for settlement of moral issues.

Imagine, for example, there was once a kingdom which adopted as a rule of law the method King Solomon proposed for settling a dispute over custody of an infant between two harlots in his harem (i.e., splitting the baby in two).[28] The judicial duty of fidelity to law never (logically speaking) could take *moral* precedence over the basic moral rule "Don't kill," for purposes of settling such a dispute, and thus it would not do so even in the above imaginary kingdom.

It makes no sense, accordingly, to suppose that the judicial duty of fidelity to the rule of law, considered, as a *moral* responsibility, requires a person in a judicial role to enforce a rule that all qualified impartial rational persons consider morally unjustifiable.

A critic might raise the following objection to the above line of argument: no legal system can be perfect. A particular system may contain several laws that are morally unjustified, in the sense of not being even weakly justified. Nonetheless, considered as a whole, the system may do close to the best job one could reasonably expect of supplementing common morality with formal and de facto authoritative procedures for settling moral disputes.

Common morality, however, provides no objective test to determine whether a given law is not even weakly justified in Gert's sense. Accordingly, no imperfect (but arguably close-to-best attainable) system whatsoever could be realized if judges considered their own independent moral judgment the appropriate standard to apply in this regard.

The above objection calls for a considered response to the following question: When is a person in a judicial role, such as a special education due process hearing officer, justified in concluding that a given law is not even weakly justified from the standpoint of common morality?

One must acknowledge that the preceding objection makes a valid and important point. The system of common morality does not provide a clear and decisive test to apply for differentiating weakly justified laws from laws that no qualified impartial rational person would consider morally justified. Recognizing this point, however, it is crucial to avoid jumping to the extreme opposite conclusion—that considering a law morally unjustifiable, in Gert's sense, consists of nothing more than harboring strongly negative sentiments toward it.

To the contrary, for thoughtful morally conscientious persons the judgment reflects the outcome of careful, detailed, and comprehensive analysis, which utilizes in an implicit way, the decision procedure the system of common morality provides for making moral decisions and judgments, according to Gert.

The first step of this procedure, as noted earlier, involves determining whether in a given situation a violation of one or more basic moral rules has occurred or is contemplated. If so then the second step comes into play—identifying the morally relevant features of the violation(s). The third step calls for one to address the following morally decisive question: What consequences would result if this kind of violation—that is, violation of the basic moral rule at issue, in light of its identified morally relevant features—was publicly allowed?

Under Gert's analysis the following questions are crucial to consider when utilizing the above decision procedure to analyze the moral justifiability of a given law: *What violations of basic moral rules are intrinsic to the law in question, in the sense of being present or highly probable, whenever the law is enforced or action is taken pursuant to the law?*

Enforcing a law, by its nature, deprives people of freedom, at least to some extent, thereby violating the basic moral rule "Do not deprive of freedom." Also, in some circumstances, other violations of basic moral rules may be intrinsic to a given law, in the sense indicated above. For these reasons, to assess the law's moral justifiability one must begin by determining clearly and fully any and all violations of basic moral rules present or highly probable whenever the law is enforced or action is taken pursuant to the law:

What features intrinsic to the given law are relevant to the question of whether the law is morally justified?

A morally relevant feature of a basic moral rule violation, according to Gert is a fact such that if it were different it could affect whether some qualified impartial rational person would consider the violation morally justified.[29] Gert enumerates ten questions in this regard, the answers to which, in diverse circumstances, help identify morally relevant features.[30] All ten questions relate to the basic point of the system of common morality—to lessen harms suffered by human beings:[31]

(1) What basic moral rule is being violated?
(2) (a) What harms are caused by the violation? (b) What harms are avoided by the violation? (c) What harms are prevented by the violation?
(3) What are the morally relevant desires and/or beliefs of the person toward whom the rule is being violated? (E.g., did the person toward whom the rule is violated provide his informed consent?)
(4) Is the relationship between the person violating the rule and the persons toward whom the rule is being violated such that the former has a duty to violate moral rules with regards to the latter independent of their consent (e.g., the right of parents to discipline their children or of law enforcement authorities to use legally authorized force)?
(5) What goods (i.e., benefits) are promoted by the violation?[32]
(6) Is the rule being violated toward a person in order to prevent her from violating a moral rule when the violation would be unjustified?[33]
(7) Is the rule being violated toward a person because he has violated a moral rule unjustifiably?[34]
(8) Are there any alternative actions or policies that would be preferable from a moral standpoint?
(9) Is the violation being done intentionally or only knowingly?[35]
(10) Is the violation an emergency such that no person is likely to plan for being in that kind of situation?

Could a qualified impartial person consider a given law morally justifiable taking into account (a) the violations of basic moral rules intrinsic to the law and (b) all other features intrinsic to the law relevant to questions of whether the law is morally justified?

Addressing the above question would require anyone in a judicial role to identify and to consider issues concerning whether, and, if so, for what reasons qualified, impartial rational persons could have different and conflicting views about the moral justifiability of a law in question. In this regard a judicial role carries special responsibilities requiring stringent adherence to the judicial duty of fidelity to the rule of law so long as pertinent law in a case is at least weakly justified from a moral standpoint, in Gert's sense.

Such special responsibilities concern willingness to listen and to ponder carefully moral reasons advanced to support diverse positions contrary to one's own from the inside—that is, to grasp the fundamental concerns, both normative and factual, motivating the positions, and to appreciate their force to the (limited) extent of recognizing why some morally responsible persons could find them persuasive. Anyone addressing the above three questions carefully, fully, and impartially would conclude in the vast majority of cases that applying pertinent law is at least weakly justifiable from a moral standpoint.

Contrary to the preceding objection, one thus may draw the following conclusions. First, independent moral assessment by thoughtful morally conscientious adjudicators in a judicial role would lead them to consider their judicial duty of fidelity to the rule of law as having strong presumptive moral force in by far, most cases. Second, given the moral foundations that underlie the judicial duty of fidelity to law, all thoughtful morally conscientious adjudicators in a judicial role would consider the duty as highly stringent, overridden, at most, only in exceptional circumstances.

WHAT IF THE LEGALLY RELEVANT FACTS IN THE MATTER OF *JAMES M.* HAD NOT JUSTIFIED ANNULMENT OF JAMES'S TWO-YEAR EXPULSION WITHOUT ALTERNATIVE EDUCATION?

For the reasons developed in section 2, the judicial duty of fidelity to law has very strong, *but not absolute*, presumptive moral force. In this regard, the morally fundamental purpose of legal systems is to provide formal and de facto authoritative procedures for settlement of disputed moral questions. It is logically impossible, however, for a hearing officer to resolve a morally problematic situation he/she faces in a case by issuing a decision that upholds an expulsion that *no* qualified impartial rational person would consider morally justified.

Had the legally relevant facts in the matter of *James M.* been such that the IDEA's procedural safeguards failed to support annulment of James's two-year expulsion, then the following two questions would have arisen:

(1) Was the expulsion of James M. morally unjustifiable in Gert's sense? That is to say, is it the case that no qualified, impartial, rational person could consider the expulsion morally justified?
(2) If the answer to question (1) is "Yes," then what *morally* justified courses of action are available in the case?

The account of the judicial duty of fidelity to the rule of law developed in section 2 of this chapter suggests that in addressing question (1) a hearing officer would have to undertake an analysis that included the following two critical elements. First, she would have to try to identify fully reasons that could be advanced to morally justify the two-year expulsion of James M. Second, she would have to make a best effort at considering carefully whether, even though she may disagree with such reasons, nonetheless, she understands why some qualified, impartial, rational persons could find them persuasive.

The above-described kind of careful consideration supports a firm conclusion that the answer to question (1) is "Yes," for the reasons set forth in chapter 5. To summarize, a two-year expulsion, with no alternative education provided, in many cases, has irreparably devastating developmental consequences. It puts the expelled student on a trajectory toward a bleak future likely to include unemployment, necessity to rely on public assistance, substance abuse, and/or incarceration for criminal activity.

The discussion in chapter 5 acknowledges the seriousness of James M's disciplinary infractions, which could have resulted in badly disabling permanent injuries for other students as well as for James himself. It recognizes also the importance of concern to avoid initiating a descent leading ultimately to a disciplinary norm of morally unjustified leniency, with its eroding effect upon the sense of personal responsibility indispensable for any human society.

As noted in chapter 5, however, surely there are morally preferable alternatives for addressing these important concerns to long-term K–12 public school expulsions, which push already at-risk children further down the road toward a life no rational person would want to live.

The above points lead directly to question (2). What morally justified courses of action, if any, would have been available if the legally relevant facts in the *James M.* case had not supported annulling the expulsion of James? A useful starting point to address this second question is suggested by the following words of the Chinese philosopher Mencius (372–289 B.C.E), which concern a different but closely related kind of issue—proper conduct of an adviser to a ruler when the adviser concludes the ruler has acted unjustly:

> Even when in a low position, . . . "a man was not willing as a good man, to serve a bad ruler." Such was Po Yi. Another went five times to T'ang, and five times to Chieh. Such was Li Yin. Yet another was not ashamed of a prince with a tarnished reputation, nor was disdainful of a modest post. Such was Liu Hsia. These three followed different paths, but their goal was one. What is meant by "one"? The answer is "benevolence." All that is expected of a gentleman is benevolence. Why must he be exactly the same as other gentlemen?[36]

Mencius identifies three courses of action in the preceding passage. Each exemplifies a different category of response available to organizational/institutional dissenters. Adopting Albert O. Hirschman's well-known terminology, one may refer to them respectively as "exit," "voice," and "loyalty."[37] The three categories encompass diverse difficult choice situations including those faced by the officials Mencius refers to in the above passage, and also by special education due process hearing officers who consider apparently applicable law in a pending case strongly unjustifiable in terms of the system of common morality.

Each category can be exemplified in a wide variety of ways depending upon the opportunities for relevant action either available in, or precluded by, different organizational/institutional contexts. In this regard a chosen course of action may be a hybrid of two, or even all three, categories.

Furthermore, Mencius's statement that "All that is expected of a gentleman is benevolence" and the question Mencius poses of "Why must he be exactly the same as other gentlemen?" both point to the highly situation-specific character of the choices organizational/institutional dissenters, including those in a judicial role, must make.

The discussion that follows concerns respectively three courses of action that exemplify respectively exit, voice, and loyalty as responses of a special education due process hearing officer to question two concerning the matter of *James M.* The discussion does not exhaust all available possibilities but, instead, is intended simply to foreground difficult issues the hearing officer would need to address in answering the question.

The choice to exit is exemplified when an organizational/institutional dissenter resigns to avoid personal complicity in organizational/institutional decisions, actions, policies, or practices she considers morally unjustified in the sense of being not even weakly justified in Gert's sense. Doing so, however, raises troubling moral issues in the kind of situation described below by C. A. J. Coady:

> An extrication problem exists when an agent has embarked on a course of immoral actions or has instituted an abiding immoral state of affairs and now repents it and seeks to extricate herself from the mess. . . . [A]n agent may not have initiated the immorality herself but may be part of a group which did, or . . . the agent may have inherited responsibility for the situation. Believing the situation to be seriously immoral, she must surely try to change it, but just stopping may sometimes cause greater harm than temporary persistence in an evil with a view to extrication. Whether she stops or persists, the agent will cause harms for which she must take responsibility.[38]

The moral problem of a hearing officer who had to confront question (2) above concerns extrication, as Coady elucidates the problem in the above quotation. By resigning from her position as a special education due process hearing officer, with the case well underway, she would not address the problem, and instead, would aggravate it, in all likelihood. Granted, it was not her who created the problem but rather the school district, which expelled James M. for two entire years, and the state legislature, which enacted the School Code authorizing such an expulsion.

Nonetheless, in virtue of becoming a special education due process hearing officer, the principal responsibility of addressing the problem rests with the hearing officer. In Coady's words, she has "inherited responsibility for the situation." Unless she could find some other way to exemplify the exit option, which, unlike withdrawing from the case, would have been morally permissible in the circumstances, she would need to consider closely the next two options—voice and loyalty.

The voice option involves expressing dissent through organizationally or institutionally established channels—that is to say, through working within the system. Anyone in a judicial position or role who confronts an apparently applicable law in a pending case which she considers strongly unjustified from the standpoint of common morality thus may seek to work within the system by searching for a way, in Robert Cover's aptly chosen words, "to translate moral imperatives into legal ones."[39]

The following two interrelated aspects of legal systems in complex societies enable persons in judicial positions or roles within such societies to address the above problem satisfactorily in many, although not in all, of the situations when it arises. First, a complex society necessitates a multitude of complex laws, which, in turn, raise issues continuously about how the laws relate to one another. These issues must be resolved in order to achieve and maintain a level of interpretive coherence that allows the society to function.

Second, many of the formal procedures of legal systems in complex societies for settling disputed moral questions possess features that either, explicitly or implicitly, accord persons in judicial positions or roles in wide areas of judicial discretion. Given the above two aspects of complex legal systems, laws that appear unjustified in terms of common morality often can be interpreted in morally justified ways, as applied to the specific circumstances of diverse cases.

The matter of *James M.*, however, does not appear to present any opportunity for utilizing the voice option effectively in the above-described way. A special education due process hearing officer's subject matter jurisdiction authorizes her only to decide whether the IDEA's explicitly specified conditions for deeming a school district to have "had knowledge" that a student was a "child with a disability" apply with respect to the child in the case before her.[40]

A negative conclusion in this regard would place the case outside the scope of the hearing officer's jurisdictional authority over persons, which, does not extend to any actions of a K–12 public school district taken with respect to regular education students.[41] It thus is highly doubtful that she could find bases in the law to draw upon for translating moral imperatives into legal ones apropos the expulsion of *any* K–12 public school student for two full years, with no provision of alternative educational services.

An organizational/institutional dissenter exemplifies loyalty, the third option, when

(1) he regards a given organizational/institutional decision, action, policy, or practice as morally unjustified and
(2) he believes, nonetheless, that expressing his opposition to it would result in such grave harms that, all things considered, it is morally justified for him not to speak out in protest.

In *Justice Accused* Robert Cover describes a momentous example of loyalty in the above sense.[42] Joseph Swan, who had been selected chief justice of the Ohio supreme court as an antislavery advocate, authored the opinion of the court in *Ex Parte Bushnell*—an 1859 case rejecting a constitutional challenge directed at the federal Fugitive Slave Act of 1850.[43]

By way of background, several months before the proceedings in *Ex Parte Bushnell* commenced, the U.S. Supreme Court had upheld the constitutionality of the 1850 federal Act in the case of *Ableman v. Booth*, the majority opinion of which had been written by Chief Justice Roger Taney, author of the infamous *Dred Scott* decision.[44] The Ohio supreme court adjudicated *Ex Parte Bushnell* against a background of impending national crisis. Two dissenting judges advocated that the court no longer recognize the appellate authority of the U.S. Supreme Court.

At the crux of Judge Swan's majority opinion, Cover believes, was an "attempt to draw the balance between order and rebellion."[45] "I must refuse the experiment," Swan wrote, "of initiating disorder and governmental collision to establish order and evenhanded justice."[46]

The evidence in the matter of *James M.* indicates clearly that, under the IDEA's explicit statutory conditions, the school district did not have knowledge that James M. was a child with a disability. Accordingly, withdrawal from the case would not be morally justified. It would put each party in the position of having to respond to entirely unanticipated circumstances, of crisis proportions, after already investing vast amounts of time and effort, and having undergone intense emotional strain.

Neither the exit option nor the voice option would have been available to the hearing officer. As summarized above, there would have been no legally plausible interpretation of the relevant provisions of the IDEA and the relevant state laws that supported annulment of James M.'s two-year K–12 public school expulsion.

Opting for loyalty, the third option, as did Judge Joseph Swan, in the case of *Ex Parte Bushnell*, however, would express a profoundly sad conclusion—that a tragic choice situation morally requires rendering a decision in conflict with, but, nonetheless, overriding, the morally fundamental purpose of law.[47]

Following Bernard Gert, this purpose is provision of formal and *de facto* authoritative procedures to settle disputed moral questions. Such, in turn, requires that laws relied upon as the bases for a judicial decision themselves must be morally justified, at least in Gert's weak sense. For the reasons developed in this section the provisions of the Illinois School Code which allow for a two-year school expulsion, with no alternative education provided, are not even weakly justified from a moral standpoint.

CONCLUSIONS

As noted at the beginning of this chapter, a deeply troubling moral issue hovers in the background of the due process case in the matter of *James M.* Suppose the facts of the case had turned out to indicate clearly that, under the IDEA's statutory conditions, the school district did not have knowledge that James M. was a child with a disability at the time his two-year expulsion, with no provision for alternative education, was imposed. What could a hearing officer do in such a case given the analysis set forth in this chapter?

The possibilities would be very small, or, perhaps, nonexistent, for either a morally justified exercise of the exit option, or an exercise of the voice option that involved framing a plausible argument, grounded in statutory and case law, to justify annulling the expulsion. A hearing officer thus would have no other choice than opting for loyalty. Doing so, however, in a way limited simply to a statement of the legal basis for allowing the expulsion order to stand (and saying no more) would leave any morally thoughtful person with an enduring residue of deeply uncomfortable uncertainty about whether this was all he/she could have done.[48]

A morally preferable course would be a hybrid approach combining elements of both loyalty and voice. Such an approach could involve strenuous effort in the hearing officer's written opinion both to convey the following points clearly and to state them as best he or she could in a way that might strike a resonant chord with both of the parties in the case, especially with the school district.

Under the IDEA's explicit conditions for deeming a school district to have "had knowledge" that a student was a "child with a disability," James M. was considered properly a regular education student at the time he was expelled. Furthermore, the subject matter jurisdiction of a special education hearing officer, under the IDEA, does not extend to any issues concerning disciplinary actions taken by a K–12 public school district in regard to regular education students.

The hearing officer would make it clear that he/she lacked authority to render a legally binding judgment that annulled the disciplinary action the school district had taken toward James M. He/she would make it equally clear, however, that in his/her judgment, the school district's expulsion decision was morally unjustified (for the reasons set forth in chapter 5).

Furthermore, the hearing officer would emphasize in the opinion that the IDEA's provisions regarding discipline of children with disabilities are not meant to grant children with disabilities special privileges and/or immunities. They are meant instead to assure that school districts avoid violating the moral right of all American children, including children with disabilities, to receive an appropriate K–12 education. Expulsion from a K–12 public school for two years, with no provision whatsoever for alternative education, violates this basic moral right.[49]

At the beginning of this chapter a morally troubling issue raised by the matter of *James M.* was posed that was not considered in chapter 5. The focus of chapter 6 then widened and deepened to cover not only the moral justification of the due process review system, but also the content and limits of the judicial duty of fidelity to the rule of law. The latter topic, in turn led to consideration of questions about the relationship between law and morality central to the justification of "Obey the law" as a basic moral rule. A summary statement thus is in order about how these wide-ranging subjects relate to each other.

Section 1 of this chapter contains a moral justification of the due process review procedures mandated by the IDEA. In this regard reasons are set forth for the indispensability of these procedures to effectuate in a meaningful way the moral right of all American children with disabilities to receive an appropriate K–12 education.

Section 2 contains an analysis of the content and limits of a special education due process hearing officer's judicial duty of fidelity to law. Sections 3 and 4 seek to bring the discussion in the two sections preceding them to bear upon the troubling issue just beneath the surface in the matter of *James M.* Hopefully, the analyses in these sections have succeeded in making apparent how and why the issue calls for a philosophically informed analysis of a special education due process hearing officer's basic moral responsibility.

The analysis developed in this chapter does not result in a conclusion that is strongly justified, in Bernard Gert's sense, about the troubling moral issue raised by the matter of *James M.* The analysis nonetheless enables one to apprehend clearly the moral crux of the issue, identify crucial questions one needs to ask in addressing it, and analyze morally relevant considerations in regard to such crucial questions.[50] Most importantly, the analysis directs one's attention to basic questions about the moral responsibility of due process hearing officers within the special education due process review procedures indispensable for giving meaningful effect to the moral right of American children with disabilities to receive an appropriate K–12 public education.

As a separate point, Bernard Gert's conception of the system of common morality and especially Gert's distinction between strong and weak moral justification, both of which were drawn upon extensively in this chapter, have immense value also in other contexts, for analyzing issues of basic moral responsibility. They will be utilized again as conceptual resources in chapter 7, the final chapter, that follows to analyze basic moral responsibilities, in regard to K–12 education of children with disabilities, of lawmakers, K–12 public school educators, and parents of children with disabilities.

NOTES

1. See chapter 5, pp. 3–4.
2. Chapter 5, n. 4.
3. Chapter 5, pp. 18–21.
4. *Common Morality* (Oxford, UK: Oxford University Press, 2004; *Morality Its Nature and Justification, Revised Edition* (Oxford, UK: Oxford University Press, 2005).
5. Thomas Scanlon, "Due Process," in *Nomos XVIII*, eds. J. Roland Pennock and John W. Chapman (New York University Press:New York, 1977), 97.
6. Ch. 5, pp. 3–4.
7. Under the IDEA the subject of a complaint needed to initiate a due process hearing must concern "identification, evaluation, or educational placement of the child, or provision of a free appropriate public education to the child" (20 U.S.C. 1415 (b) (6) (A)). The IDEA states that the decision of a hearing officer "shall be made upon substantive grounds based upon a determination of whether the child received a free appropriate public education" (20 U.S.C. 1415 (f) (3) (E) (i)).
8. In this regard, the IDEA requires states that accept funds under the statute to "ensure . . . procedures are established and implemented to allow parties to disputes involving any matter prior to the filing of a [due process] complaint, to resolve such disputes through a mediation process (20 U.S.C. 1415 (e) (1)). Such procedures must be voluntary on the part of the parties, and "not used to deny or delay a parent's right to a due process hearing" (20 U.S.C. 1415 (e) (2) (A) (i) (ii)).

In addition, the IDEA mandates that when a due process complaint is filed, prior to the hearing the school district must convene a Resolution Session. At the Resolution Session the school district and the parent have an opportunity to discuss the complaint, and the school district then is given thirty days to attempt resolving the matter. If at the end of the thirty-day period, the complaint has not been resolved then the due process hearing commences (20 U.S.C. 1415 (f) (1) (B)).

9. For a discussion responding in thorough detail to highly critical assessments of special education due process review that have been advanced recently, see Mark Weber, "In Defense of Due Process," *Ohio State Journal of Dispute Resolution* 29, no. 3 (2014): 501–30.
10. Thomas Aquinas, *Treatise on Law* (Summa Theologica, Questions 90–98), ed. R. J. Regan (Hackett: Indianapolis, IN, 2000).

11. John Austin, *The Province of Jurisprudence Determined*, ed. J. Rumble (Cambridge University Press: Cambridge, UK, 1995).
12. Gert, *Morality,* 201–209; Gert, *Common Morality*, 47–4.
13. Gert, *Common Morality*, 4.
14. Gert, *Morality*, 12; Gert, *Common Morality*, 109.
15. Gert, *Morality*, 90–92.
16. Gert, *Morality*, 218; Gert, *Common Morality*, 20.
17. Gert, *Morality*, 246–71; Gert, *Common Morality*, 22–26. The ideal of an inclusive educational community, discussed in chapter 4, is a social ideal. At the same time, however, it is also a moral ideal in Gert's sense. This is because seeking to promote a society in which attitudes and actions are widespread that exemplify enthusiastic welcome of, and meaningful support for, inclusion of children with disabilities in K–12 regular education programs necessarily involves working to prevent pain, loss of freedom, and loss of pleasure.
18. Hobbes, *Leviathan*, 123.
19. Gert, *Morality*, 56–60; Gert, *Common Morality*, 112–14.
20. Gert, *Morality*, 11–14; 159–62.
21. Gert, *Morality*, 201–6; Gert, *Common Morality*, 47–49. The argument presented here differs in some respects from the one Gert sets forth expressly in his writings in order to bring to the foreground a number of important points implicit in Gert's argument.
22. Granted, not every moral disputes need be resolved in order for a society to function adequately. Nonetheless, given the combined effects of human vulnerability and fallibility, the lives of most people in a society with no formal authoritative procedures whatsoever to settle disputes over moral issues would be, in Thomas Hobbes's famous words, "solitary, poor, nasty, brutish, and short" (Hobbes, *Leviathan*, 100).
23. Gert defines a public system as a guide to conduct with the following two features: (1) All those whose behavior is to be guided and judged by that system, understand it, and know what kind of behavior the system prohibits, requires, discourages, encourages, and allows. (2) It is not irrational for any of these persons to accept being guided and judged by that system (Gert, *Morality*, 11).
24. Gert, *Morality*, 221–22. Here is how Gert understands the terms "qualified person," "impartial person," and "rational person." A qualified person is aware of all the morally relevant features of a situation in which a person violates a basic moral rule (Gert, *Morality*, 57). An impartial person is one whose conclusion about whether or not a violation of the law is unjustified does not depend upon her beliefs concerning what moral agents are harmed or are benefited by the violation (Gert, *Morality*, 132). As for "rational person," a person is rational if he/she is not irrational. Irrational persons are those who act irrationally in the sense of harming themselves with no adequate reason, doing so frequently, and/or in seriously harmful ways (Gert, *Common Morality*, 33, 138–39).
25. Mark Twain (New York, 2003), 82–85.
26. See the discussion that follows at pp. 19–20 of this chapter.
27. Although they have closely related moral foundations the judicial duty of fidelity to law and the basic moral rule "Obey the law" thus differ from one another in

a crucial respect. The system of common morality does not require moral agents to resolve all reasonable doubts in favor of obedience to law whenever qualified impartial rational persons disagree concerning the presumptive moral force of the basic moral rule "Obey the law"—that is to say, in every circumstance when disobedience is weakly justified. As Gert stresses, however, according to common morality, in such circumstances to regard the violator as *liable* to punishment is strongly justified (Gert, *Morality*, 224; Gert, *Common Morality*, 152).

28. 1. Kings: 3, 25.
29. Gert, *Morality*, 226; Gert, *Common Morality*, 58.
30. Gert, *Morality*, 226–36; Gert, *Common Morality*, 59–73.
31. Gert, *Morality*, 270–71; Gert, *Common Morality*, 20–26.
32. This morally relevant feature, Gert notes, comes into play, for the most part, only under circumstances in which the immediately preceding morally relevant feature is present. For example, the good promoted by a violation of the basic moral rule "Don't deprive of freedom" is morally relevant in cases such as the following: A has a duty to promote the well-being of B. In some circumstances carrying out this duty may necessitate A violating the basic moral rule "Don't deprive of freedom" with respect to B (e.g., a parent making his child do her homework).
33. Self-defense and defense of others are prime examples in this regard.
34. As with the fifth morally relevant feature, this feature as well comes into play, for the most part, only under circumstances in which the fourth morally relevant feature applies. Punishment of wrongdoers, for example, is an inherently public function, carried out by public officials charged with the duty to do so.
35. Here is a prime example of a situation where this morally relevant feature looms large: physicians conclude they can only save the life of a pregnant woman by performing a procedure, which they know will result in the death of the fetus.
36. *Mencius*, Tr. D. C. Lau (Penguin: London, UK, 1970), 175.
37. Albert O. Hirschman, *Exit, Voice, and Loyalty* (Harvard University Press:Cambridge, MA, 1970).
38. C. A. J. Coady, "Politics and the Problem of Dirty Hands," in *A Companion to Ethics*, ed. Peter Singer (Oxford University Press: Oxford, UK, 1995), 380.
39. Robert Cover, *Justice Accused* (Yale University Press: New Haven, 1975), 198.
40. 20 U.S.C. 1415 (k) (5) (A).
41. 20 U.S.C. 1415 (b) (1).
42. Cover, *Justice Accused*, 255.
43. Ohio St. 77 (1859).
44. 21 How. 506 (1859). 19 How. 393 (1857).
45. Cover, *Justice Accused*, 255.
46. Cover, *Justice Accused*, 255.
47. In this regard, Cover relates that Joseph Swan was not recommended in 1859 as chief justice of the Ohio supreme court owing to the opinion he wrote in *Ex Parte Bushnell*. After the civil war ended, however, according to Cover, Swan was again offered the position several times but always refused. Cover speculates that Swan did not wish to relive the agony of decision he experienced in the case of *Ex Parte Bushnell* (Cover, *Justice Accused*, 256).

48. Captain Edmund Fairfax Vere, in Hermann Melville's novella *Billy Budd* was tormented by such uncertainty to his dying breath *Billy Budd and Other Stories* (Penguin Books: New York, 1986), 381–82.

49. For a hearing officer to express the above kinds of opinions, which are unrelated to his specific legal conclusions in a case, is frowned upon because to do so can invite serious misunderstanding. Many would agree, however, that this important concern is not decisive when

    (a) a hearing officer concludes that a given law is unjustified from the standpoint of common morality after making significant effort to resolve all reasonable doubts in favor of considering the law morally justified, at least in Gert's weak sense;

    (b) the hearing officer states her legal conclusions with heightened care and precision; and

    (c) there is a chance (however slight) that a clear, thorough, and well-reasoned statement of the reasons why a legally allowed action, pursuant to the given law, is morally unjustified could persuade the party taking the action to reconsider.

50. As a separate point, recognizing and appreciating Gert's distinction between weakly and strongly justified violations of basic moral rules points one toward a view of the relationship between law and morality implicit in any morally justifiable conception of the judicial role. In this regard, Richard Posner writes,

> [Judges] do not think, "This is an awful rule but it is the law, so I have a dilemma—can I get around it?" The business of judges is enforcing law. (*How Judges Think* (Harvard University Press: Cambridge, MA, 2008], 213)

A judge who tried to get around pertinent legal rules in a case whenever he considers them "awful" would fail to act in accordance with his judicial duty of fidelity to law. The reason why, however, from Gert's standpoint, is the following: the informal system of common morality requires supplementation by the formal system of law, which, in turn, cannot function effectively unless judges regard the duty of fidelity to law as highly stringent in cases where the relevant law is at least weakly justifiable in Gert's sense.

Posner's statement, "The business of judges is enforcing laws," although applicable in the great majority of cases, nonetheless is too sweeping. It overlooks, for example the anguishing kinds of problems that faced Judge Joseph Swan in *Ex Parte Bushnell*.

Chapter 7

Appropriate K–12 Education for Children with Disabilites: Whose Moral Responsibility?

Chapter 1 identified six philosophically basic issues raised by the idea that every American child with a disability has a moral right to receive an appropriate K–12 education.[1] Chapters 2 through 6 each has analyzed and/or set forth a justification for a position concerning a different one of the first five such issues. The following discussion in chapter 7 addresses the sixth philosophically basic issue—the principal moral responsibilities correlative with the moral right of every American child with a disability to receive an appropriate K–12 education.

How to fulfill such correlative responsibilities poses complex multidimensional issues that give rise to challenges no one organization or (unorganized) aggregate of individuals, let alone single individual person, could address adequately.

The responsibility therefore must be thought of as shared. Chapter 7 thus analyzes the duties of the three principal co-bearers of the moral responsibility to assure that every American child with a disability receives an appropriate K–12 education. Those co-bearers are as follows:

(i) lawmakers (elected legislators and judges);
(ii) K–12 educators (school administrators, teachers, and other educational staff members); and
(iii) parents of children with disabilities.

Because this shared responsibility is *moral*, in the sense of correlative with the moral right of American children with disabilities to receive an appropriate K–12 education, the analysis in chapter 7 draws extensively upon ideas developed in the preceding six chapters.

The term "moral responsibility," as used in this chapter, refers to duties, in the sense of, morally required actions of a person in virtue of her/his diverse roles. The word "role," in turn, refers not only to prime examples, such as nuclear family relationship categories, but also, more broadly, to various jobs, positions, offices, statuses, and the like. Sometimes requirements of role-related duties are set forth explicitly—for example, in a contract (written or oral) or a covenantal agreement such as an oath or vow. In other cases, role-related duties are grounded in prevailing practices of a social group.[2]

In still other cases, however, questions of whether or not a particular requirement attaches at all to a given role, or of whether acknowledged general requirements of a role do not apply in a specific circumstance, give rise to significant differences of interpretation.[3] Such is the case, as the discussion that follows will make apparent, regarding the duties of the three principal co-bearers of the moral responsibility to assure that every American child with a disability receives the kind of K–12 education to which she/he has a moral right.

LAWMAKERS (ELECTED LEGISLATORS AND JUDGES)

Lawmakers (Elected Legislators)

As used in this chapter, the term "elected legislators" refers to all persons elected, under the system of government in the United States, to offices in which they vote on policies which will have the force of law behind them. Relative to K–12 special education, accordingly, the following kinds of elected legislators are most important: (a) members of K–12 public school district boards, (b) members of state legislatures, and (c) members of the U.S. Congress.

The basic moral responsibility of elected legislators in regard to education of children with disabilities is to support enactment of legislation aimed at giving meaningful effect to the children's moral right to receive an appropriate K–12 education. Such legislation includes the following:

- explicit legal declaration that children with disabilities have a right to receive an appropriate K–12 education;
- authorizations for adequate funding of special education;
- promulgation of reasonable regulations for provision of special education; and
- establishment of means for effective monitoring and compliance enforcement.

Legislative initiatives to accomplish the above objectives have generated intense and deep moral disagreements, exemplified by the issues analyzed and discussed in chapters 2 through 6. A question arises thus of how to decide whether or not in a given case a legislator has fulfilled her/his moral responsibility apropos assuring that every American child with a disability receives an appropriate K–12 education.

The answer to this question is that she does so to the extent her words and actions relative to pertinent legislation exemplify the attitude intrinsic to democratic deliberation from the ideal standpoint characterized in chapter 2. According to that characterization the ideal encompasses four principal elements listed below:[4]

(1) commitment to values and principles that define and shape one's conception of the moral bases of democratic government, including, but not limited to, the following rights, which John Rawls terms the system of basic liberty: "freedom of speech and assembly, liberty of the person, along with the right to hold personal property, and freedom from arbitrary arrest and seizure, as defined by the rule of law";[5]
(2) awareness that reasonable persons differ in their commitments to a number of different values and principles;
(3) realization that, for practical purposes, no value is ultimate and no principle is absolute; and
(4) willingness, therefore, to listen to, and to consider carefully, the viewpoints of other deliberators, with whom one disagrees.

In regard to the fourth item on the above list, willingness to listen involves a good faith effort to become fully aware of the key arguments advanced on behalf of positions with which one disagrees. It also includes the effort to view such positions from the inside—that is, to understand the fundamental concerns motivating arguments advanced, or sentiments expressed, in their favor and even to appreciate their force to the (limited) extent of recognizing why some reasonable people find them persuasive.

Careful consideration of a viewpoint on a public issue with which one disagrees consists of applying high reasoning standards both as to logical and to factual inferences. Apropos logical inference, careful consideration about controversial matters often calls for hard thought about how one's commitment to a given value or principle is logically relevant to the matter at hand given the specific circumstances of the issue in controversy, or of whether it bears upon it at all.

As for factual inferences, careful consideration requires both the ability to recognize when factual evidence clearly supports a particular conclusion and respect for fact, in the sense of readiness to exercise the ability regardless of the resulting conclusion. Such reasoning ability and respect for fact are immensely valuable for democratic deliberation. When opposing parties on a public issue come to agree on what each party considers all relevant facts, they often discover that they no longer have reasonable grounds for disagreement.

Two points are critical to recognize about debate and discussion among the members of any democratic body politic:[6] First, opposing sides do not always reach convergence of judgment. Furthermore, the likelihood of arriving at anything close to it in regard to controversial, complex, difficult-to-resolve, and highly viewpoint-dependent issues is remote.[7] Second, however, debate and discussion exemplifying the attitude intrinsic to democratic deliberation and grounded in mutually reasonable, responsible, and principled accommodation can increase the possibility of compromise on difficult public issues.

Through such debate and discussion, opposing sides apprehend each other's positions more fully and clearly (e.g., key arguments the other side presents and fundamental concerns motivating the arguments). As a corollary, each side tends to develop a fuller, clearer, and deeper understanding of its own position—of both its strongest and its less than strongest arguments, and of the core moral commitments implicit in its strongest arguments.

Debate and discussion of public matters within a legislative body whose members exemplify the attitude intrinsic to democratic deliberation thus does not, and is not intended to, result inexorably in convergence of judgment. It increases, however, the likelihood of compromise on difficult public issues, of which there are many related to support for K–12 public school special education provided by the IDEA, that both sides can justify in terms of their respective views of the facts and important moral commitments.

Actions and words exemplifying the attitude intrinsic to democratic deliberation not only are a moral ideal for lawmakers (as for all members of the American democratic body politic) but also are a moral responsibility in virtue of their official public lawmaking role.

The preceding account of an elected legislator's basic moral responsibility leaves room for much disagreement in specific cases concerning decisions of legislators about support for K–12 special education. In one legislative district, for example, advocates for children with disabilities and their families may consider a legislator's voting record apropos support of K–12 special education funding inadequate, while other constituents, with strong concerns focused upon other kinds of significant public issues, may disagree. In another district, the array of constituent viewpoints on the issue may differ.

In either case, however, it is one thing for voters to decide not to vote for reelection of a legislator because they disagree with her stance on an issue, and another thing entirely to conclude that, in virtue of her stance, she failed to fulfill her moral responsibilities as a legislator concerning support for K–12 special education. The relevant standard to apply in regard to the latter judgment is whether her actions and words relative to her official public lawmaking role reflect with consistency the attitude intrinsic to democratic deliberation.

Judges

In cases that call for application of statutory enactments, judges are lawmakers from the standpoint of the morally fundamental purpose of law, as identified in chapter 6.[8] That is to say, judicial decisions in such cases set forth interpretations of statutory enactments that resolve (at least temporarily) disputed moral issues that, as a practical matter, must be settled in order for a society to function.[9]

The most important example in this regard relative to K–12 special education in the United States, by far, is the decision of the U.S. Supreme Court in the case of *Board of Education of the Hendrik Hudson School District v. Rowley*.[10] As summarized in chapter 1, the Supreme Court set forth in its *Rowley* decision a legally binding interpretation of the statutory phrase FAPE, which denotes the basic right of American children with disabilities under the IDEA but nonetheless is not defined explicitly in the statute.[11]

The judge's role is complex from both intellectual and moral standpoints. The intellectual complexities are brought out well in the following quotation from *The Nature of the Judicial Process*, written by Benjamin Cardozo:

> What is it that I do when I decide a case? To what sources of information do I appeal for guidance? In what proportions do I permit them to contribute to the result? In what proportions ought they to contribute? If a precedent is applicable when do I refuse to follow it? If no precedent is applicable, how do I reach the rule that will make a precedent for the future? If I am seeking symmetry of the legal structure, how far shall I seek it? At what point shall the quest be halted by some discrepant custom, by some consideration of social welfare, or by my own or the common standards of justice and morals?[12]

The judicial role not only is complex intellectually but morally also in virtue of including at its core a duty of fidelity to the rule of law, which seems to presuppose the idea that law (however it may be defined and understood) is something judges must follow rather than create, as if writing on a blank slate. In this regard, the discussion in chapter 6 noted that the judicial duty of fidelity to the rule of law has two key aspects.[13]

First, a judge must undertake conscientious research and carefully pondered efforts to identify pertinent law for deciding a case. Second, she must apply the law she concludes is pertinent even if doing so conflicts with the decision she would have rendered if she could have based it upon her personal views of the moral rights and duties of the parties in light of the evidence presented.[14]

The analytical framework judges should adopt in trying to reconcile the lawmaking function of judicial decisions in cases requiring statutory interpretation with the underlying premises of the judicial duty of fidelity to the rule of law is a matter of intense and enduring controversy among jurists and legal scholars. The three most well-known and eminent jurisprudential scholar/public intellectuals in the United States over the past quarter century—Antonin Scalia, Richard Posner, and Ronald Dworkin—engaged, over many years, in intense and at times sharply worded three-cornered disputes.[15]

Each of the three views regards a different value as resting at the core of the judicial duty of fidelity to the rule of law applicable to American democracy. For Scalia the core value was order, for Judge Posner it is instrumental means–end rationality, and for Dworkin it was a concept he referred to as "law as integrity."

All the above mentioned values are intrinsic to the judicial duty of fidelity to the rule of law in the context of American democratic government. Setting forth an adequate analysis of how the values interrelate, however, is extremely difficult.

The core idea of Scalia's view, which he called "textualism," is that, even in difficult cases, to the greatest extent reasonably possible, judicial interpretation of a statute should construe the statutory language at issue in the case either as it is ordinarily understood or as it was ordinarily understood at the time the statute was enacted. More broadly, Scalia conceived of the textualist approach he advocated as crucial to American society for providing an ordered formal dispute resolution procedure intrinsic to the concept of law itself.[16] In this regard, he wrote,

> Of all the criticisms leveled against textualism the most mindless is that it is "formalistic." The rule of law is about form . . . Long live formalism. It is what makes a government a government of laws and not men.[17]

Judge Posner advocates strongly a view he terms "Pragmatism," according to which the most valuable resources, by far, a judge can draw upon when a case calls for him or her to perform a lawmaking function is social science.[18] Judge Posner includes the following subjects under the category of especially pertinent social science for judicial decisions: empirically oriented political science and sociology, psychology (both normal and abnormal), evolutionary biology, statistics, and historiography.[19]

The critical issue for judges in the vast majority of cases that require judicial lawmaking, Judge Posner believes, concern identifying the best means to accomplish essentially agreed-upon objectives. In this regard, he characterizes the issues to involve weighing of costs and benefits for the purpose of arriving at a socially beneficial legal rule, and he maintains that social science, in his broad sense, can provide judges immensely valuable information and analytical frameworks to address such cost-benefit issues.[20]

For Ronald Dworkin resolving the tension between the judicial duty of fidelity to the rule of law and the lawmaking function of judges in difficult cases that involve statutory interpretation requires that judges consider themselves to perform this function within, what Dworkin termed, a "community of principle." As noted in chapter 4, according to Dworkin,

> Members of a genuine community of principle accept that they are governed by common principles, not just by rules hammered out in a [mere] political compromise. Politics for such people is a theater of debate about which principles the community should adopt as a system, which view it should take of justice, fairness, and due process.[21]

In difficult cases when neither statutory language nor previous legal decisions provide adequate guidance, from Dworkin's perspective, judges within a community of principle would adopt an outlook he calls "law as integrity," which consists in "trying to find in some coherent set of principles the best constructive interpretation of the political structure and legal doctrines of the community."[22]

Antonin Scalia's, Judge Richard Posner's, and Ronald Dworkin's jurisprudential views, expressed in their respective writings, each have both many strong adherents and equally strong critics. The three-cornered dispute among these preeminent figures in American jurisprudence has yielded many important insights that have illuminated and deepened understanding of moral questions at the core of the judicial role. It is unlikely however a consensus judgment ever will emerge as to the winner of the dispute. In this regard, the dispute turns ultimately upon disagreements over matters that preclude a decisive resolution.

As noted above, Scalia's, Judge Posner's, and Dworkin's differing views about reconciliation of a judge's lawmaking function relative to statutory interpretation with the judicial duty of fidelity to the rule of law presuppose different core values. For Scalia, Judge Posner, and Dworkin, respectively, those values are order, means–end rationality, and law as integrity. Ultimately, a person's commitment to any one of these values over the others depends largely upon her/his views on issues that cannot be settled conclusively concerning human nature, the nature of society, and ranking of harms and benefits.[23]

To fulfill her/his moral responsibility apropos interpreting American K–12 special education law a judge must bring to bear upon the interpretive task an intellectually credible theory about the relationship between statutory interpretation in the judicial process and a judge's duty of fidelity to the rule of law. The controversy over the jurisprudential views of Scalia, Judge Posner, and Dworkin makes it apparent, however, that there is more than only one such theory upon which a morally conscientious judge could draw.

K–12 Public School Educators (School Administrators, Teachers, and Other Educational Staff Members [e.g., School Psychologists and School Social Workers])

The basic moral responsibility of K–12 public school educators concerning special education is to develop and to implement educational programs for American children with disabilities that are appropriate from a moral standpoint (contrasted with a solely legal standpoint).

Chapter 2 sets forth an analysis justifying the view that a morally appropriate K–12 education for any American child, whether nondisabled or a child with a disability, with the exception of children with severe or profound intellectual disabilities, must be reasonably calculated to help the child acquire knowledge and develop abilities essential for the following:

(a) exercising rights, fulfilling responsibilities, and exemplifying ideals of membership in the American democratic body politic and
(b) having a reasonable chance for success in seeking the basic human good of self-fulfillment.[24]

According to the analysis set forth in chapter 3, a morally appropriate K–12 education for a child with severe or profound intellectual disabilities must be reasonably calculated to foster significant development of essential human capabilities relevant in the child's case given the particular aspects of his or her disability condition.[25]

Implementation of policies to assure every child with a disability in a school district receives an education reasonably calculated to fulfill the objectives set forth respectively in chapters 2 and 3 is a shared responsibility of educational administrators, teachers, and other educational staff members, such as school psychologists or social workers.

Often this shared responsibility calls for a plan requiring implementation by many different school personnel and also intricate arrangements in terms of logistics and scheduling. In every case, however, each personnel member involved has a moral responsibility to do her/his job in a manner reasonably calculated to support achievement of the result that every child with a disability in the school district is provided the kind of K–12 education to which he/she has a moral right.

The phrase "reasonably calculated," in the context of the moral right of American children with disabilities to receive an appropriate K–12 education, as noted in chapter 2, denotes a standard stronger than mere nonarbitrariness and weaker than the strong standard of justification beyond a reasonable doubt.[26] An educational program reasonably calculated to help a child acquire knowledge and develop abilities essential to the basic objectives of an appropriate K–12 education for American children, as analyzed in chapters 2 and 3, has a plausible rationale.[27]

In this regard, such a plausible rationale shifts the onus of justification to those who reject the program as inadequate, at least to the extent of deserving a considered response. If an educational program is reasonably calculated to provide a child with a disability an appropriate K–12 education, in the moral sense, then some, although not necessarily all, rational qualified, impartial persons would consider the program educationally adequate.

Since the moral responsibility to provide such a program is shared among school administrators, teachers, and other school district staff members, disagreement between these co-responsibility bearers can arise over the educational adequacy of programs developed for particular children.

K–12 Public School Administrators

For any K–12 public school district the effort to provide every child with a disability in the district the kind of education to which he/she has a moral right is a complex collaborative undertaking. The following two modes of collaboration below have special importance in this regard:

(1) working relationships between special education and regular education teachers that facilitate educational progress of children with disabilities in a regular education environment and
(2) ongoing, productive, mutually valuable communication between parents of children with disabilities and teachers, other educational staff members, and school district administrators.

Formidable difficulties often stand in the way of establishing and maintaining the above modes of collaboration for reasons such as the following:

(i) insufficient preparation and experience of both special education and regular education teachers in collaborating to address pedagogical challenges of teaching particular children with disabilities in regular education classrooms;
(ii) problems apropos balancing adequate attention to children with disabilities in a regular classroom with meeting highly stringent mandatory coverage requirements apropos diverse academic subjects;

(iii) inadequate staffing and access to other necessary educational resources caused by acute budgetary constraints; and
(iv) insufficient preparation and training of K–12 educators relative to fostering productive, mutually beneficial communication with parents of children with disabilities;
(v) ingrained resistant attitudes on the part of some regular education teachers to the presence of children with disabilities in their classrooms.

As a practical matter efforts to address the above kinds of difficulties in a school district cannot succeed without strong support, encouragement, and, when needed, initiation of effort from the district's administrators. Such support, encouragement, and effort, accordingly, are required of them correlatively with the moral right of children with disabilities in the school district to receive an appropriate K–12 education.

Insofar as every nondisabled child in the district likewise has the same moral right, school district administrators often face difficult issues that require making hard choices. In their deliberations however, concerns about how the impact of a possible choice would affect nondisabled students and of how it would affect children with disabilities must have equal importance.

Teachers and Other Educational Staff Members

Under the IDEA, as, noted in chapter 1, both substantive content and arrangements for implementation of an IEP for a child with a disability are decided by consensus judgment of an IEP team, with required members, as specified in the IDEA.[28] Suppose a school district staff member on an IEP team—for instance, a teacher, school psychologist, or school social worker—concludes that a program for a child decided upon by consensus judgment of the team is educationally inadequate. What then should she consider her moral responsibility?

To address this question two points must be kept in mind. First, the members of an IEP team, both collectively and individually, bear a moral responsibility of immense importance—to decide upon an educational plan for a child with a disability reasonably calculated to provide the child the kind of K–12 education to which he/she has a moral right. Deliberations about appropriate components of such a plan can give rise to serious disagreements among team members. For educational development of children with disabilities, however, decisions, in this regard, must be made expeditiously.

The second point concerns a morally significant distinction between two different attitudes a dissenting member of an IEP team could take toward the team's consensus judgment in regard to the appropriate educational placement for a child. First, although she may disagree with the consensus judgment, she acknowledges nonetheless that the judgment is one that reasonable and responsible educators could make. In contrast the dissenter holds the second attitude if she believes that *no* rational qualified impartial person could consider the judgment of the IEP team as morally justified.[29]

If the dissenter held the first of the above two attitudes toward the consensus judgment of the IEP team then, consistent with such an attitude, she should consider herself to have the following moral responsibilities:

(a) to articulate unmistakably to the other IEP team members that she disagrees with the team's consensus judgment;
(b) to communicate clearly to the other team members the reasons for her disagreement;
(c) despite her disagreement, to lend her best efforts to helping achieve an educationally successful implementation of the student's IEP, as decided upon by the IEP team; and
(d) as a separate, but closely, and importantly, related point, to (c) above, other members of the IEP team have a moral responsibility of willingness to listen to the dissenter: such includes both careful consideration of her dissenting viewpoint and readiness to reconsider it seriously in the future if it becomes apparent that modifications and revisions in the child's IEP are needed to provide an appropriate K–12 education for the child.

Suppose, however, the dissenter held the second of the above attitudes—that is to say, she believed that no rational qualified impartial person could regard the IEP team's consensus judgment as morally justified. She would then face the same kind of emotionally wrenching choice situation, discussed in chapter 6, that might have confronted the special education due process hearing officer in the *James M.* case if key facts concerning the case had been different.[30]

In this regard, all her possible courses of action, whether exemplifying "exit," "voice," or "loyalty," as identified and characterized in chapter 6, or a hybrid of two or more of these categories, would pose significant risk of gravely harmful consequences. Such would parallel in many respects those that would have confronted the hearing officer in the *James M.* case if there been no valid legal justification for concluding the school district had knowledge that James M. was a child with a disability at the time he was expelled.[31]

Cases in which a school district staff member disagrees with the consensus judgment of an IEP team in the strong sense that she believes no rational qualified impartial person could regard the judgment as morally justified surely (one hopes) are infrequent. Such cases, however, can, and do, occur in American K–12 public schools.[32]

Parents of Children with Disabilities

The moral responsibilities of parents of children with disabilities in regard to their children's K–12 education are similar essentially to those of parents of nondisabled children. In both cases the responsibilities concern supporting their children's educational development to the extent the parents can be reasonably expected to do so. Accordingly, such responsibilities include the following:

(a) making thoughtful, informed decisions in regard both to selection of schools and to other matters concerning K–12 education of their children that require parental authorization;
(b) monitoring conscientiously their children's academic performance and social development;
(c) providing educationally beneficial assistance with schoolwork to their children;
(d) offering encouragement and support to their children conducive to promoting their academic progress; and
(e) if necessary, assuming the role of advocate on behalf of their children to assure the children receive the kind of K–12 education to which they have a moral right.

Apropos the above moral responsibilities two further points must be made. The first concerns the qualifying condition that the responsibilities apply to the extent parents reasonably can be expected to fulfill them. It bears emphasizing that the qualification applies with respect to parents of children with disabilities and to parents of nondisabled children alike.

Every parent of K–12 school-aged children at times faces situations that require making difficult choices relative to the child's K–12 education (e.g., regarding allocation of time or money, setting and enforcing limits, etc.). For parents of K–12 children with disabilities, however, the difficult choices very often induce stress, psychological exhaustion, and/or emotional anguish at extreme levels far beyond those most parents of a nondisabled child would be likely to face in connection with the child's K–12 education.[33]

Second, some critics of special education under the IDEA appear not to agree with the last item on the above list—assuming the role of advocate for one's children, if one considers that doing so is needed to assure the children receive the kind of K–12 education to which they have a moral right. In this regard, Miriam Kurtzig Freedman, one of the severe critics quoted in chapter 1, writes,

> [The IDEA] forces parents to "advocate" for their child against their schools! Often litigation, or the threat of litigation, fractures the relationship between school and home. Among its unintended consequences is that it undermines the need for and importance of deference to the expertise of professional educators. . . . In response to the argument that parents are the best advocates for their child, often this is not so. First, it erodes the natural advocacy of teachers. Second, many parents have neither the resources nor the ability to be effective advocates.[34]

Unarguably, sometimes parents are not the best educational advocates for their children. Such is beside the point, however. The crucial issue concerns whether or not parents have a moral responsibility to assume a role of educational advocacy when they believe reasonably that doing so is needed to assure their children receive the kind of K–12 education to which they have a moral right.

The notion that regarding parents to have such a moral responsibility "erodes the natural advocacy of teachers" implies an unacceptably narrow and rigid conception of K–12 educational authority, and of the moral responsibility correlative with such authority. To the contrary (a) both K–12 educational authority and its correlative moral responsibilities are shared among lawmakers, educators, and parents and (b) the morally appropriate apportionment of such authority and responsibility are matters of significant interpretive debate and discussion.

Far from "[fracturing] the relationship between school and home," parental advocacy, when well-informed and reflective of due respect for (contrasted with deference to) the educational expertise and experience of school district personnel, is most conducive to educationally beneficial collaboration in the long run. K–12 education flourishes when:

(a) lawmakers are concerned and supportive;
(b) K–12 public school educators are competent and committed; and
(c) parents are both well informed and deeply engaged.

In regard to (c) above, deep parental engagement entails having both the resources and the abilities needed to advocate effectively on behalf of one's children if necessary to assure that they receive the kind of K–12 education to which they have a moral right. Freedman objects that many parents "lack the resources and/or abilities to be effective advocates for their children."

Such a viewpoint, even if accurate does not support the opinion Freedman appears to hold that, except (perhaps) in cases of gross malfeasance, parents should defer to the judgments of professional educators on matters concerning development and/or implementation of the children's K–12 public school educational programs. Rather, it suggests that more must be done than at present, however challenging this may be, to provide parents the resources and to help them acquire the abilities needed for well-informed, effective educational advocacy on behalf of their children.

THE DISAGREEMENT BETWEEN SEVERE CRITICS AND ADVOCATES OF K–12 SPECIAL EDUCATION UNDER THE IDEA REVISITED

The point of departure in chapter 1 was a summary of opposing views held by members of two groups, referred to respectively as the severe critics of special education in America under the IDEA (the severe critics) and advocates for children with disabilities and their families (the advocates). The discussion then proceeded to identify six morally basic questions in relation to the disagreement between the two groups but which seldom are articulated, let alone analyzed at a level of depth needed for adequate exploration.

This section revisits the disagreements to consider how the discussions and analyses in the chapters 2 through 7 bear upon the principal issues over which the severe critics and the advocates differ. Those issues, as noted in chapter 1, concern the following three issues: Is K–12 special education under the IDEA (a) unfair to nondisabled students; (b) educationally ineffective; and (c) a major source of dysfunctional conflict between parents of children with disabilities and K–12 public school districts?

In regard to (a), the severe critics' answer emphatically is "yes," pointing to the following:

(i) much greater expenditures, in some cases, devoted to education of children with disabilities than to education of nondisabled children with significant educational needs and
(ii) mandatory procedural safeguards, under the IDEA, relative to school discipline, applying exclusively to children with disabilities.

Concerning (i) above severe critics focus attention upon the diverse, often highly resource-intensive, aspects of programs to educate children with disabilities. Severe critics believe, accordingly, that K–12 public school expenditures should be redistributed. Much of the portion now devoted to special education, in their view, should go instead to help economically disadvantaged low-achieving regular education children.

As one severe critic opines, "[A]nyone who spends time in an inner city classroom can tell you that the challenges the average poor kid faces are often hard to distinguish from those you'll find in special education."[35]

The viewpoint of the severe critics summarized above overlooks the following important points. Every American child, whether she or he is nondisabled or a child with a disability, has a moral right to receive an appropriate K–12 education. Such, at any rate, is the conclusion analyzed in depth and justified in chapters 2 and 3. While it is true that "the challenges the average poor kid faces are often hard to distinguish from those you'll find in special education," the converse of this statement is no less true. The statement below by Andrew Solomon expresses the above points eloquently:

> At the far end of the disability spectrum is a zone that corresponds to poverty, a place of severe deprivation. . . . The disability poverty line varies from one community to another, but it does exist. Many disabled people experience debilitating pain, struggle with intellectual incapacities and live in permanent proximity to death.[36]

Reducing the funds allotted for K–12 special education to provide additional support for programs that address the educational needs of children in poverty, at most, would simply redistribute conditions that exacerbate suffering from one deprived group to another deprived group. The relevant moral imperative is to address the needs of *both* groups, in the respect of providing members of each the kind of K–12 education to which they have a moral right.[37]

The second principal reason the severe critics consider special education in America under the IDEA unfair to nondisabled students concerns the IDEA's extensive procedural safeguards regarding long-term suspensions (more than ten days cumulatively in a school year) and long-term expulsions. While such safeguards, as noted earlier, in effect preclude long-term suspensions and expulsions of children with disabilities, nondisabled children, in contrast, have no remotely comparable protections under the law.[38]

Chapter 5 focused upon a troubling moral issue raised by long-term suspensions or expulsions, whether of children with disabilities or nondisabled students. Both kinds of disciplinary measures deprive students of educational opportunity. The analyses and arguments set forth in chapters 2 and 3, however, elucidate and justify the idea that every American child has a moral right to receive an appropriate K–12 education.

There is a prima facie conflict, accordingly, between long-term K–12 public school suspensions and expulsions, on the one hand, and the moral right of American children to receive an appropriate K–12 education, on the other hand. For this reason, simply to repeal, or to limit substantially, the IDEA's procedural safeguards apropos discipline in K–12 public schools of children with disabilities would make an unfair situation even worse.

Contrary to the view of the severe critics, fairness in this context calls for leveling up instead of leveling down. Chapter 5 identifies and discusses five conditions for deciding in specific cases whether or not a K–12 public school long-term suspension or expulsion violates a student's moral right to receive an appropriate K–12 education. When these conditions are met, any reasonable concerns regarding fairness to nondisabled students of the IDEA's procedural safeguards relative to long-term suspensions or expulsions of children with disabilities are addressed adequately.

In regard to (b) above, the complaint that the IDEA has promoted frequent use of ineffective methods for educating children with disabilities, severe critic Miriam Kurtzig Freedman writes the following: "IDEA promotes inclusion as a civil right in spite of weak data supporting it as a 'best practice' for many [students with disabilities] for improved educational results in many situations."[39] Regular classroom inclusion, Freedman objects, is implemented often despite "scant or nonexistent evidence" that it will actually improve learning.

Data, both quantitative and qualitative, apropos efforts of K–12 educators to improve educational outcomes of children with disabilities surely bears upon disagreements over regular K–12 classroom inclusion of children with disabilities. Freedman's severely critical words, summarized above, however, fail to grasp a key issue at the *moral* crux of such disagreements.

If educational goals and objectives are agreed to by all parties relative to a placement decision, then any disagreements that arise concern solely choice of educational methods about which data assessment could be decisive. It is a serious mistake, however, to assume that such agreement is always the case in disputes concerning K–12 regular education classroom inclusion, either of a particular child with a disability or of children with disabilities in general.

To the contrary, the discussion in chapter 4 both identified and sought to elucidate two closely related major issues that often hover in the background of such disputes. First, how should one understand what it means for an American K–12 public school district to approach the ideal of an inclusive educational community? That is, to ask what moral virtues are intrinsic to such a community, and why? Second, do American K–12 public school districts have a moral responsibility to undertake significant efforts aimed at exemplifying these virtues (i.e., in addition to upholding the principle of equal educational respect and concern for all children)?

Rather than calling solely for collection and analysis of quantitative and qualitative data, the above two issues require deep interpretive reflection and careful, thoughtful moral judgment. Chapter 4 developed in detail an analysis of the first issue and also, after extensive discussion, concluded, apropos the second issue, that there are credible arguments on both sides.

Complaint (c) noted above of the severe critics is that the special education due process review system, mandated by the IDEA, has created a dysfunctional, conflict-ridden environment, which impedes severely the development of educationally beneficial cooperative relationships between parents of children with disabilities and K–12 public school educators.

The American Association of School Administrators (AASA) agrees with this complaint emphatically. An AASA report has called for putting an end to the special education due process system and replacing it with a new method, under the IDEA, to resolve disputes between parents of children with disabilities and K–12 public school districts. According to the AASA report, due process hearings often

> take a great toll on parties' personal and professional lives. For instance, families may harbor feelings of distrust and anger toward the school before, during, and after the hearing, while educational professionals may have negative and cautious attitudes toward the student and his or her family going forward. These sentiments can lead to less collaboration between the parties after the hearing and a less cooperative relationship between the parent and the school can cause subsequent problems with development of IEPs and conflict resolution with respect to changing educational placement.[40]

The position taken and the recommendations put forward in the AASA identify real problems and, accordingly, cannot be dismissed out of hand. Efforts to develop morally justified alternative conflict resolution methods to the due process system should be encouraged strongly.[41] As stated in chapter 6, however, it is a mistake to believe such efforts could succeed entirely in eliminating the need for the system of special education due process review.

The AASA proposal seeks to do so essentially through innovations that would place decision-making authority in the hands of independent educational experts, rather than due process hearing officers.[42] Such experts, it is envisioned, would base their decisions solely upon pertinent educational considerations rather than legal analysis that, in the opinion of the school administrators, often reflect inadequate knowledge and understanding of best K–12 educational practice and theory.

The above proposal, however, is deeply problematic in two respects. First, it appears to ignore the obvious. In special education due process hearings each side often calls one or more expert witnesses to offer testimony supporting its position. One is hard pressed to think of a procedure reasonably calculated to enable parties in a dispute over the appropriateness of an educational program for a child with a disability to reach agreement upon an appropriate "neutral" expert, contrasted with a mutually acceptable due process hearing officer.

Second the AASA proposal overlooks completely two key points which, hopefully, the analysis and discussion throughout this book have made apparent. The first of these points is that philosophically deep moral questions underlie many, if not most, of the issues that give rise to the deepest- and hardest-to-resolve disputes between parents of children with disabilities and K–12 public school districts. Such questions concern issues of how to understand and to apply philosophical concepts such as happiness/unhappiness, fairness, human dignity, and freedom relative to educational programs for children with disabilities.

The second point is that these difficult-to-resolve kinds of issues are complex, controversial, and pertain to matters of utmost importance both for parents and K–12 public school educators. As I noted in chapter 6, they can only be settled (at least temporarily) by decisions with the force of law behind them.

The experience and knowledge of K–12 public school educators, although essential, is insufficient, in and of itself, to resolve issues often at the core of disputes over appropriate educational programs for diverse individual children with disabilities between parents and K–12 public school districts. The discussions presented concerning the cases of *Timothy W.*, *Beth B.*, and *James M.* respectively in chapters 3, 4, and 5 suffice to make this point apparent.

CONCLUDING THOUGHTS

Much academic writing in the area of disability studies has focused upon two different ways of conceptualizing the phenomenon of disability, referred to respectively as the medical and the social models of disability. Relative to K–12 special education the medical model conceives of educational disability conditions on analogy with physical maladies, and, accordingly, adopts a general approach to address the educational needs of children who present such conditions that is modeled upon appropriate treatment interventions in a medical context.

The social model views judgments of educational disability in many cases to reflect ways in which a child is regarded and treated by society, given ingrained social attitudes, practices, and behaviors. Proponents of the social model believe the prevailing ways in which judgments of educational disability are made more often pose problems that call for social transformation rather than for case-by-case interventions based upon children's perceived educational deficits, which the proponents view as prone to reflect oppressive social biases.

The medical and the social model each has been advanced, at times, in ways that either minimize, ignore, or, in extreme cases, deny the relevance of the other model altogether. A reasonable conceptualization of educational disability, however, surely must accord significant places to both models.

Although such an integration would be necessary it could not be sufficient. An adequate account of educational disability also must incorporate important concepts from moral, political, legal, and educational philosophy to help in focusing upon basic moral questions and in thinking them through carefully.

The philosophical approach utilized throughout this book, however, is not a decision procedure capable of identifying every important moral issue of special education, let alone of providing unique (correct) positions on each of them. In this regard some immensely important questions which were raised explicitly at the time the IDEA was enacted in 1975, or shortly afterward, remain unresolved. (Appendices I and II that follow this chapter concern respectively two prime examples in this regard.)

The primary objective of this book has not been to win converts to the positions set forth in chapters 1 through 7 but instead to convey awareness and appreciation of the following three points. First, efforts to consider these issues, when undertaken carefully and thoughtfully, lead to philosophically deep and highly interpretive basic moral questions.

Second, such basic moral questions seldom are even mentioned, let alone addressed, in the context of intensely contentious and often emotionally laden debates and discussions between the severe critics of K–12 special education in America under the IDEA and the advocates for children with disabilities and their families. Third, and finally, although an analysis of basic moral questions, informed by major writings in moral, political, legal, and educational philosophy, cannot alone settle these disputes it can increase the possibility of reasonable, responsible, and principled compromise.

Hopefully the analyses and arguments set forth in this book will help all readers in the ways indicated above but especially the three co-bearers identified in this concluding chapter of the moral responsibility to assure every American child with a disability is provided the kind of K–12 education to which he/she has a moral right. If so, then even if readers disagree with some, or even most of the conclusions on specific issues set forth in the preceding seven chapters, the primary objectives of this book will have been more than amply fulfilled.

CHAPTER 7 APPENDIX I

Is K–12 Special Education Discriminatory?

Analysis of statistical data set forth in research studies conducted since the late 1960s have indicated a significantly higher percentage of African American children, as well as of Hispanic and Native American children, than of nonminority children classified as eligible for special education under the categories of specific learning disability and serious emotional disturbance.[43]

The data analyzed in these studies is information provided state by state of the total number of children in K–12 special education programs, broken down by percentages of students in various racial/ethnic categories (e.g., "African American," "White," "Hispanic," "Native American," and "Asian American/Pacific Islander").

Such statistical data alone does not suffice as a basis for definitive answers to four questions, indicated below, which are crucial from a moral standpoint regarding the percentage differential the studies indicate relative to K–12 special education placements of African American, Hispanic, and Native American children, on the one hand, and nonminority children, on the other hand:

(1) Have disproportionately large numbers of African American, Hispanic American, and Native American children been placed in special education to the children's educational detriment?
(2) If so, then is racial discrimination the predominant, or a significant, factor to explain why this has happened?
(3) Apart from questions (1) and (2), has a disproportionately large number of other African American children been denied access to special education which they needed, and as a result not received the kind of K–12 education to which they had a moral right?
(4) If so, was racial discrimination the principal, or a significant, factor to account for their inappropriate placements?

The above four questions have been addressed in both qualitative and quantitative research studies. One influential study that utilized a qualitative approach was conducted by Beth Harry and Janette Klingner, who observed classes, interviewed both teachers and administrators, and reviewed documents related to the provision of K–12 special education in an inner-city school district in Florida.[44]

Harry and Klingner found that at many schools in the district there was a large number of inexperienced new teachers and insufficient resources to provide the new teachers adequate support and mentoring (e.g., not enough teachers on the instructional staff with long-term experience teaching children at the school). Referrals for evaluation as to specific learning disability and serious emotional disturbance conditions tended to be made much more often by the new teachers than by the experienced teachers.

Furthermore, upon reviewing eligibility determinations, apropos serious emotional disturbance, Harry and Klingner concluded that, not infrequently, decisions reflected preconceptions of school psychologists, school social workers, teachers, and school administrators rather than familiarity with, and understanding of, the particular family dynamics relevant to diverse evaluated children.

The quantitative research study approach is exemplified by a widely discussed recent statistical analysis led by Paul R. Morgan. Morgan and his colleagues (hereinafter Morgan et al.) compared the relative risk for placement in K–12 special education across five disability categories, including specific learning disability and serious emotional disturbance, of African American and white children.[45]

The children were similar in the following two respects: (a) socioeconomic status (SES) and (b) score on one academic achievement test. ("Relative risk" is defined in this context as the ratio of the percentages of children in two different racial/ethnic categories classified as eligible to receive K–12 special education.)

The study yielded interesting and possibly important findings. In contrast to the results obtained from analyses of aggregate data collected state by state, when Morgan et al. disaggregated the data to compare African American children and white children who are similar in terms of SES and achievement test scores it turned out that African American children are underrepresented, rather than overrepresented in K–12 special education.

Writing about their research in a *New York Times* Op-Ed article, Morgan and his principal collaborator George L. Farkas suggested the following hypothesis to explain the high relative risk figures apropos specific learning disability and serious emotional disturbance that were obtained in prior studies that analyzed aggregate data reported state by state.[46]

A disproportionately large percentage of these children live in impoverished urban areas, Morgan and Farkas noted, that are subject to environmental conditions such as high lead concentrations and proximity to toxic wastes known to have adverse effects upon the human nervous system and brain.

The Harry and Klingner research study focuses upon different morally crucial questions than do the Morgan et al. research studies. Harry and Klingner focus upon question (1) above, while Morgan et al. focus upon question (3). The findings of each study are interesting and possibly important. Neither study, however, is definitive in the senses of having been established conclusively or of pointing clearly toward the direction in which educational and social policy should move at this time.

The phenomenon of racial discrimination in the United States directed at African Americans not only is factually complex and multidimensional but also a subject of intense ongoing controversy. A person's viewpoint on each of the four morally crucial questions identified above implicates unavoidably her or his outlooks on two much broader questions—(1) is racial discrimination an important aspect of life in America?; (2) what are the important ways it comes into play?

John Stuart Mill remarked in *On Liberty* that "[v]ery few facts tell their own story."[47] This remark has special force in regard to the complex, multidimensional, and controversial topic of racial discrimination directed at African Americans in the United States. It seems inevitable that different interpreters of both qualitative observational data and of quantitative statistical data generated by studies attempting to answer questions (1) through (4) would tell different stories.

Furthermore, the different stories, in all likelihood, would embody differing preconceptions about the nature and extent of racial discrimination affecting African Americans. Accordingly, although both the Harry Klingner qualitative study and the Morgan et al. quantitative study are valuable, neither study suffices, in and of itself, to answer the morally basic questions concerning the impact of racial discrimination against African Americans upon K–12 special education.

CHAPTER 7 APPENDIX II

Specific Learning Disabilities: Three Difficult Questions

What Is a "Specific Learning Disability" under the IDEA?

The following statutory definition of "specific learning disability" has been in place since the IDEA was enacted in 1975 (under its original title, the Education for All Handicapped Children Education Act [EAHCA]):

> The term "children with specific learning disability conditions" means those children who have a disorder in one or more of the basic psychological processes involved in understanding or in using language spoken or written, which disorder may manifest itself in imperfect ability to listen, think, speak, read, write, spell, or do mathematical calculations. Such disorders include such conditions as perceptual handicaps, brain injury, minimal brain dysfunction, dyslexia, and developmental aphasia. Such term does not include children who have learning problems which are primarily the result of visual, hearing, or motor handicaps, or mental retardation, or emotional disturbance, or environmental, cultural, or economic disadvantage.[48]

At the time of the EAHCA's enactment in 1975 there was concern that the number of children receiving special education under the specific learning disability category potentially was so large as to preclude adequate allocation of resources for K–12 special education of children under other eligibility categories. Congress thus agreed to direct the U.S. Commissioner of Education to develop "diagnostic procedures [to be used] in determining whether a particular child has a disorder or condition which places that child in the category of specific learning disabilities."[49]

As of 2015–2016, with the definition unchanged, 34 per cent of the 6.7 million children receiving special education in American K–12 public schools were classified as eligible under the category of specific learning disability.

How Can the Eligibility Condition of Specific Learning Disability Be Identified Diagnostically?

Two methodological approaches, referred to respectively as the significant discrepancy and the response to intervention (RTI) models loom large in connection with K–12 public school districts' efforts to determine whether or not a child is eligible to receive special education under the IDEA category of specific learning disability. The significant discrepancy model involves comparing the results of a child's score on an IQ test with her scores on various academic achievement tests. If, for example, a child scored 100 on the IQ test (50th percentile), one would expect, in terms of the significant discrepancy model, that her achievement test scores would be at least near the 50th percentile as well.

If her achievement scores were much lower, however, and if qualified evaluators concluded that the discrepancy could not be explained adequately in terms of other factors, then one would conclude, under the significant discrepancy model, that the child had a specific learning disability condition as defined in the IDEA.

The significant discrepancy model has been criticized strongly because in many situations a child must exhibit poor academic performance in school over a long period of time before she or he is referred for, and the school district agrees to conduct, a full-scale case study evaluation. In effect, say the critics, utilizing the significant discrepancy model thus requires a school district to wait for a child to fail before taking even the first steps needed for providing her an appropriate K–12 education.

The above criticism was an important consideration that led to two major changes regarding eligibility for special education under the category of specific learning disability Congress made when it enacted the 2004 Reauthorization of the IDEA.

First, the 2004 Reauthorization mandated that states no longer could *require* K–12 public school districts to employ the significant discrepancy model. Second, Congress included a new provision which stated the following: "[In] determining whether a child has a specific learning disability a local educational agency [i.e., a school district] may use a procedure that determines if the child responds to scientific research based intervention as a part of the evaluation procedures described . . . [elsewhere in the IDEA]."⁵⁰

The phrase "scientific research based intervention" in the 2004 Reauthorization refers to the RTI model—the second of the two principal approaches mentioned above for determining whether a child is eligible to receive special education under the category of specific leaning disability. As summarized concisely by disability law scholar Ruth Colker, under RTI,

> [W]hen a student falls behind her or his peers, a school district is supposed to employ scientifically based interventions to see if the child can meet peer-level expectations without receiving special education and related services. The intervention is "tiered" with schools trying more intense interventions before concluding that the intervention is unsuccessful. A student is classified as learning disabled only if he or she performs below his or her peers even after scientifically based intervention is attempted through the tiered process. This process can take between six months and several years. A student's IQ is not supposed to be a factor in determining the effectiveness of the intervention.⁵¹

More than 70 per cent of K–12 public school districts in the United States now incorporate the RTI model in at least some classrooms.⁵² Many critics, nonetheless, have expressed doubt as to whether the model has succeeded in accomplishing its principal objectives relative to identification of children eligible to receive special education under the category of specific learning disability. These purposes are as follows:

(1) identification, *in a timely manner*, of children with specific learning disability conditions—that is to say, to solve the "wait to fail" problem of the significant discrepancy model and
(2) (a) identification of those children who may not be eligible to receive K–12 special education under the IDEA's definition of "specific learning disability," but who, nonetheless, have serious academic problems in the primary grades and
  (b) provision to such children of education appropriate for bringing their academic up to grade level.

In regard to (1) above, as noted by Ruth Colker, in the case of some students the RTI process can extend over several years. Responding to complaints in this regard, the Office of Special Education Programs (OSEP) of the U.S. Department of Education issued in 2011 a memorandum to state directors of special education stating,

> It has come to the attention of the Office of Special Education programs (OSEP) that, in some instances local educational agencies (LEAs) may be using

Response to Intervention (RTI) strategies to delay or deny a timely evaluation for children suspected of having a disability. States and LEAs have an obligation to ensure that evaluations of children suspected of having a disability are not delayed or denied because of an RTI strategy.[53]

There is no evidence that the 2011 OSEP memorandum has had significant effects in addressing concerns about delays that may result from RTI procedures relative to undertaking evaluations of children who may be eligible for special education under the category of specific learning disability.[54]

As for (2) (a) and (2) (b), a research project involving more than 20,000 children in 13 states, sponsored by the National Center for Educational Evaluation and Regional Assistance, was undertaken in which researchers employed the following strategy, as reported in *Education Week*:[55]

> For RTI, or any other system that uses a cut score to screen students, those who perform 1 point above or below the cut score are statistically indistinguishable. A student who scores 19 on a reading level test will look very similar to a student who scores 21, but may have different learning opportunities because he missed the benchmark. . . . [The researchers] tracked the reading performance of 24,000 1st, 2nd, and 3rd grade students who barely made or barely missed the cutoff for tier 2 interventions in schools.
>
> From fall to winter of the 2011–2012 school year 1st graders who had been identified for tier 2 interventions in the fall performed 11% lower, significantly worse, on a test of overall reading ability used by the Early Childhood Longitudinal Study that winter in comparison to students who barely missed being identified for interventions in the fall.

Second- and third-grade students who had been identified for tier 2 interventions made no significant gains, although, unlike the first graders, they had no significant negative effects from the RTI intervention. Researchers not involved in the study have suggested that the study's findings may point to problems with implementation of the RTI model. Some possible problems they mentioned were inadequate screening procedures to identify students for tier 2 interventions, shortcomings in the kinds of interventions that were provided, and inadequate teacher preparation and training.

How Is the Condition of Specific Learning Disability Addressed Best Educationally?

Development and implementation of an educationally beneficial program for a child with a disability requires as a prerequisite, completion of a full, competently prepared case study evaluation. The relevant information and opinion of qualified professionals contained in the evaluation report, however, although indispensable, seldom points unambiguously toward definite detailed conclusions about how a child's program should be configured or how it should be implemented. In the words of Marleen C. Pugach,

> What students may need as a result of a disability will be influenced not only by their disability, but also by their unique intellectual ability, personality, style, likes and dislikes, ethnicity, culture, language, and life experience. . . . It also does not tell you how students learn and how the classroom or curriculum may have to be modified to help them learn. Furthermore, within each category of disability, the degree of a student's difficulties related to the disability differs for every child.[56]

An IEP team, consisting of diverse educators in a school district and a child's parents, must develop and implement collaboratively a plan adequate to address the kinds of considerations Pugach identifies in the above quotation. Many such efforts are successful but also as well there are many far less than successful efforts.[57] The entire process (i.e., child find, case study evaluation, IEP meetings, and IEP implementation) involves considerable expense.

In some cases lawmakers fail to authorize adequate funding for a school district to provide every *nondisabled* child in a school district an educational program that is appropriate in a moral sense, even from the standpoint of the minimum content interpretation proposed in chapter 2.[58] Such a circumstance results in an irresolvable conflict between the other two principal co-bearers of the moral responsibility to provide children with disabilities a morally appropriate K–12 education—that is, between public school educators and parents of children with disabilities.

NOTES

1. See chapter 6, pp. 129–54.
2. See Brian Schrag, *Civility and Community Audio Book*, eds. John Lachs and Mike Hassel, Produced by Pat Childs.
3. See Dworkin, *Law's Empire*, 46–86.
4. See chapter 2, pp. 19–48.
5. Rawls, *A Theory of Justice*, 61.
6. See, chapter 2, n.
7. An issue is highly viewpoint-dependent when positions that people take on the issue unavoidably implicate in crucial ways their respective views on questions that cannot be resolved conclusively in regard to human nature, the nature of society, and/or the comparative rankings of diverse benefits and harms.
8. For purposes of this discussion the term "judge" refers to anyone authorized to perform a judicial role—that is, to be the decision maker in a procedure for adjudicating disputes with the force of law behind it. In this regard, see chapter 6, pp. 129–54.

9. See chapter 6, pp. 129–54.
10. 458 U.S. 176 (1982).
11. See pp. 4–5.
12. Benjamin N. Cardozo, *The Nature of the Judicial Process* (Yale University Press: New Haven, 1921), 10.
13. See chapter 6, pp. 129–54.
14. Reference to discussion in chapter 6 of the moral limits of the judicial duty of fidelity to the rule of law.
15. Antonin Scalia (1936–2016) was an associate judge of the U.S. Supreme Court (1986–2016). Richard Posner served as a judge on the U.S. Court of Appeals for the Seventh Circuit from 1981 to 2017. Before becoming a judge he was the Lee and Brena Freeman Professor of Law at the University of Chicago Law School. Ronald Dworkin (1931–2013) was the Frank Henry Sommer Professor of Law and Philosophy at New York University and Professor of Jurisprudence at University College, London.
16. An attempt to probe underneath the language, so understood, in order to discern the intent of the legislature that enacted the statute, Scalia noted, leads to an irresolvable issue—how to understand the concept of intention when applied to a collective body such as a legislature?

A judge who sought to avoid this issue by hypothesizing how a "typical" or "reasonable" legislator would have understood the language, in Scalia's view, unavoidably would arrive at conclusions that reflected his or her own moral judgments concerning social policy. Were such an approach to become widespread, Scalia warned, it would undermine the separation of powers essential to American constitutional democracy by creating uncertainty and confusion about the nature and extent of congressional lawmaking authority.

17. Antonin Scalia, *A Matter of Interpretation* (Princeton University Press: Princeton, NJ, 1997), 25.
18. Comparison and contrast of Judge Posner's jurisprudential outlook with the philosophical ideas and/or sensibilities, of William James and John Dewey the two most well-known American philosophers who identified themselves as "Pragmatists," is an interesting but also a large subject, unfortunately far beyond the scope of this book.
19. Richard Posner, *The Problematics of Moral and Legal Theory* (Harvard University Press: Cambridge, MA, 1999), 211.
20. As for reconciling Pragmatism, as Judge Posner conceives of it, with the judicial duty of fidelity to the rule of law, Posner appears to regard this as unnecessary. He acknowledges the importance of the concept of precedent for judicial decision but solely for a practical purpose it serves—specifically, enabling lawyers to predict outcomes of cases (Posner, *The Problematics of Moral and Legal Theory* [cited at n. 19], 208).

In contrast, for Judge Posner, the notion that judges are bound by a judicial duty of fidelity to the rule of law, as most often elucidated, presupposes one or the other of both of two conceptions he rejects unequivocally. The first conception is doctrinal legal analysis, as taught in most law schools, which Judge Posner refers to as "legalism" (see Posner, *How Judges Think*, (Harvard University Press: Cambridge, MA, 2008), 7–9.

The second conception is moral philosophy, including both classical and contemporary works, which Judge Posner refers to as "academic moralism" (Posner, *The Problems of Moral and Legal Theory* [cited at n. 19], 5). Judge Posner regards "legalism" as confusing and obfuscating, and he considers academic moral philosophy as irrelevant to the real issues calling for resolution in legal disputes.

21. Dworkin, *Law's Empire*, 211.

22. Law as integrity then, under Dworkin's view, requires that a judge "test his interpretation of any part of the great network of political structures and legal decisions of his community by asking whether it could form part of a coherent theory justifying the network as a whole" (p. 245). Dworkin makes it apparent that the kind of justification he has in mind here is an account that provides the best reconciliation of relevant statutory language and case law with the core moral principles and aspirations of American democratic government.

23. On moral disagreements that cannot be resolved alone by reaching agreement about relevant facts see Gert, *Common Morality*, 13–25.

24. See chapter 2, pp. 19–48.

25. See chapter 3, pp. 49–80.

26. See p. 38.

27. See chapter 2, pp. 19–48.

28. 20 U.S.C. 1414 (d) (1) (B).

29. On the distinction between the two possible attitudes a dissenter could take see chapter 6 at pp. 129–54.

30. See chapter 6, pp. 129–54.

31. See chapter 6, pp. 129–54.

32. See, e.g., Ruth Colker, "Disabled Education," *Rethinking Schools* 28, no. 1 (Fall, 2013): 26–27.

33. See Solomon, *Far From the Tree*.

34. See chapter 1, pp. 1–18.

35. Worth, "The Scandal of Special Education," 280.

36. See Solomon, *Far From the Tree* (cited at), 32. In regard to Solomon's point, the following observation is pertinent. The kind of suffering a person is liable to experience when aware of herself as impoverished and the kind of suffering that can occur when a person perceives himself as intellectually disabled may be similar not only quantitatively but also qualitatively. Consider, for example, the devastating effect upon both self-esteem and the sense of social identity that either perception of oneself as impoverished or of being intellectually disabled can have.

37. As a separate, yet important, point, the topic of special education placement decisions for African American inner-city children relative to the two IDEA categories of specific learning disability and serious emotional disturbance is a large, troubling, and complex subject. See Chapter 7 Appendix I.

38. See chapter 5, n.10.

39. See chapter 1, pp. 1–18.

40. AASA report, *Rethinking Special Education Due Process*, Sasha Pudelski AASA Assistant Director, Policy and Advocacy (April 2016).

41. See chapter 6, pp. 129–54.

42. The crux of the AASA proposal is to replace the IDEA's right of parents of a child with a disability to file for a due process hearing with a procedure under which in cases of disputes the parties would select jointly a neutral special education expert consultant. (Attorneys would not be allowed to serve in this role.)

The consultant would make a placement recommendation for the child whose program was in dispute within twenty-one days of his/her initial meeting with the disputants. The disputants then would be required to agree to implement the recommendation and allow it to continue for a mutually agreed-upon time period. If at the end of this time period the parents considered their child's educational placement educationally inappropriate they could then file a lawsuit (pp. 17–20).

43. See, e.g., *Racial Equality in Special Education*, eds. Daniel J. Losen and Gary Orfield (Harvard Education Press: Cambridge, MA, 2002).

44. Beth Harry and Janette Klingner, *Why are so Many Minority Students in Special Education?* (Teachers College Press: New York, 2006).

45. Paul R. Morgan et al., "Are Black Children Disproportionately Overrepresented in Special Education," *Exceptional Children* 83 (2017): 181–98.

46. Paul L. Morgan and George Farkas, "Is Special Education Racist?" *New York Times*, September 20, 2015.

47. John Stuart Mill, *Three Essays by John Stuart Mill* (Oxford University Press: London, UK, 1969), 27.

48. 20 U.S.C. 1401 (30) (A) (B) (C).

49. Ruth Colker, *Disabled Education* (New York University Press: New York, 2013), 217.

50. 20 U.S.C. 1414 (b) (6) (B). The IDEA, however, does not include a statutory guidance concerning the kinds of approaches that qualify as "scientific research based intervention."

51. Colker, *Disabled Education*, 226.

52. Sarah D. Sparks, "Study: RTI Practice Falls Short of Promise," *Education Week*, November 6, 2015, https://www.edweek.org/ew//articles/2015/11/11/study-rti-practice-falls-short-of-promise.html.

53. OSEP memorandum to State Directors of Special Education, January 25, 2011 (OSEP 11-07).

54. Colker, *Disabled Education*, 227.

55. See note 53.

56. Marleen C. Pugach, *Because Teaching Matters* (John Wiley & Sons:Hoboken, NJ, 2009), 264.

57. Ruth Colker, who not only is a disability law scholar but also an attorney for parents in IDEA due process cases, writes:

> Having attended IEP meetings for many years . . . I can report that virtually no parent can be an effective advocate at such meetings alone. I have attended meetings with 15 or 20 school personnel and one parent. The parent is lucky if he or she can even identify who was present, let alone describe the issues considered at the meeting. (*Disabled Education*, 26).

58. See chapter 2, pp. 19–48.

Acknowledgments

Earlier versions of chapters 3, 4, 5, and 6 appeared respectively in the following publications:

"The Zero-Reject Policy in Special Education-A Moral Analysis," *Theory and Research in Education* Vol. 3(3), 2005 pp. 273–98 (chapter 3).
"Inclusion and Justice in Special Education," in *A Companion to the Philosophy of Education*, ed. Randall Curren (Malden, MA. Blackwell Publishing Co. 2003) pp. 525–39 (chapter 4).
"Limitations Upon Legitimate Authority to Suspend and Expel K–12 Public School Students: A Moral Analysis," *Theory and Research in Education* Vol. 9(3) 2011 pp. 265–81 (chapter 5).
"The Judicial Duty of Fidelity to Law: A Gertian Analysis," *Teaching Ethics* Vol. 14(1) 2013 pp. 21–50 (chapter 6).

As stated in the Preface, this book aims to "achieve a successful combination of experience and theory." Such an aim never could have been pursued seriously without the guidance, support, assistance, and encouragement of many people, which as the dates of the above mentioned publications may suggest, extended over many years.

Each person identified in the following list read and commented, upon an earlier version of one or, in the case of quite a few of these individuals, several of the book's seven chapters: Harry Brighouse, Randall Curren, Michael Davis, Scott Dick, Richard Eldridge, Asia Ferren, Matthew Fisher, Charles Fox, Tobias Fuchs, Brett Fulkerson-Smith, Bernard Gert, Heather Gert, Joshua Gert, Roger Gilman, Kevin Harrington, Stephen Harris, Elizabeth Hildt, Roberta Israeloff, Kelly Laas, Joanne Steiner Ladenson, Alasdair Mac Intyre, Martin Malin, Mohammed Mehdi, Deborah Mower,

StephenNathanson, Martha Nussbaum, Christian Perring, Andrew Rehfeld, Ginger Rhoads, Warren Schmaus, Brian Schrag, George Sherman, Anita Silvers, Aaron Snyder, Mark Weber, Vivian Weil, Lois Weinberg, Matthew Williams, and David Wasserman.

The intellectual acuteness, knowledge, and generosity of each of the above-listed individuals were invaluable. None of them, however, is responsible for any deficiencies this book may still have. As with anyone presenting himself/herself as the author of a published work, the final responsibility rests with me alone.

Major philosophical theories of social justice play a large role throughout this book as conceptual resources for identifying and analyzing controversial and difficult-to-resolve moral issues, such as those basic to K–12 special education.

Among the strongest factors reinforcing my belief, in the value of such an approach, has been the stellar performances of competing undergraduate student teams at the National Championship Competition of the Association for Practical and Professional Ethics Intercollegiate Ethics Bowl (APPE-IEB). Participating teams, for many years now consistently have utilized major philosophical theories of social justice to analyze a wide range of difficult issues of practical and professional ethics in ways that exemplify clarity, thoughtfulness, and moral insight.

Participating as an ethics bowl judge or match moderator in many APPE-IEB competitions has strengthened my belief that major philosophical theories of social justice can be valuable tools of analysis in moral deliberation concerning important issues about which, ultimately, decisions must be made.

I am immensely grateful to Professor Martin A. Cohen (1916–2000), who was a distinguished labor arbitrator who taught at the Stuart School of Business of the Illinois Institute of Technology. I sought the advice of Professor Cohen ("Marty" to everyone who knew him well) about putting my educational background in law to use, beyond teaching and academic writing, by becoming a labor arbitrator and/or an administrative hearing officer.

Marty generously offered to take me on as his apprentice, which involved accompanying him to hearings he conducted, taking notes, and writing practice case summaries, which we then discussed. Over the two-year apprenticeship I learned the rudiments of conducting a hearing, and also was introduced to important complexities, and subtleties of the hearing process.

The apprenticeship turned out to be one of the essential background conditions that made possible the most personally fulfilling years in my academic/professional life. During the years I served as a special education due process hearing officer, I also originated the ethics bowl and then took the lead in organizing and developing the APPE-IEB.

In this period two activities—special education due process review and the ethics bowl—both of which, albeit in different ways, seek to promote the interrelated social goods of justice and moral understanding, were each extremely important parts of my professional life. I was able to make meaningful and distinctive contributions in each activity given the particular combination of my interests, abilities, temperament, and educational background, the latter of which included indispensably the two-year apprenticeship with Marty Cohen.

The immediately preceding expression of acknowledgment applies likewise to the following of my colleagues as Illinois special education due process hearing officers: Marie Bracki, Ann Breen Greco, Alan Cook, Julia Dempsey, Vivian Gordon, Marian McElroy, Francis Nowak, Stacey Stutzman, and James Wolter. Each of these fine people, in diverse ways, provided valuable examples of high-level competence, commitment, and integrity in relation to the position of a special education due process hearing officer.

Over many years now, both my awareness and understanding of difficult issues that teachers and administrators in K–12 public schools face on a continuous basis have been increased substantially as a result of conversations with Carol Steiner, who is a now retired outstanding teacher and school principal in Kalamazoo, Michigan. I benefited from hearing the viewpoints of a thoughtful and articulate fifth-grade public school student about diverse issues concerning school discipline and inclusion from discussions with Penelope Jo Stern. (Disclosure: Penelope is my granddaughter.)

The presentation of crucial arguments and analyses in this book is much more readily accessible than it otherwise would have been thanks to the expert editorial assistance of Zoe Spirra, a longtime friend, who is an experienced editor and also studied philosophy on the graduate level.

As indicated above, Kelly Laas is a colleague who read and prepared comments upon chapters of this book. She also, however, extended herself to provide assistance that was crucial in connection with moving forward on completion of the book within a reasonable time frame. Specifically, she helped me learn how to use the latest version of Microsoft Word. Thank you for this again, Kelly!

In my book's cover image by artist Eileen Meindl O'Hagan two pears appear in varying shades of light and darkness. This shaded image of a fruit symbolizing justice in some cultural traditions, and fulfillment in others, evoked for me the ambiguities, complexities, and depth, both intellectual and emotional, of basic moral issues in K–12 special education.

Finally, my greatest and deepest debt of thanks is owed to Joanne Steiner Ladenson, my wife, soul mate, best friend, child-rearing partner, valued professional colleague, and inseparable companion in confronting adversities and challenges, pursuing adventures, and sharing incomparably memorable moments in life. This book is dedicated lovingly to her.

Index

AASA. *See* American Association of School Administrators
ADHD. *See* Attention Deficit Hyperactivity Disorder
Agassi, Alex, 20
Alito, Justice Samuel, 128n26
All's Well that Ends Well, 46n16
alternative education, duty to provide for expelled students, 114–15
American Association of School Administrators, proposal concerning special education due process review, 171–72
American democratic body politic: ideals of membership in, 25; membership defined, 22; rights and responsibilities of members, 23–25
anger management counselling, duty to provide for at-risk students, 113
appropriate K–12 education: elements of for Group A children, 22–27; elements of for Group B children, 50–52; justification of moral right to for Group A children, 28–37; justification of moral right to for Group B children, 52–72; minimum content interpretation of, 37–42
Aquinas, Saint Thomas. *See* natural law theory

Aristotle: definition of virtue, 67; human beings as social and political animals, 67; *Nicomachean Ethics*, 67, 79n47
assistive technology, 81
at-risk students, duty of heightened attention to, 113–14
attention deficit hyperactivity disorder (ADHD), 119, 132
Austin, John. *See* legal positivism

Berube, Michael, 17n17
Beth B. *See Beth B. v. Van Clay*
Beth B. v. Van Clay (*Beth B.*), 81–85, 97, 98, 103n3, 172
Billy Budd, 152n48
Blackmun, Justice Harry, 124n2
Board of Education of the Hendrik Hudson School District v. Rowley, 4, 5, 16n14, 83, 90, 159

capabilities theory of social justice: core ideas of, 32, 33, 67; as moral basis of right to an appropriate K–12 education for Group A children, 33–34; as moral basis of the zero-reject policy, 67–69
Cardozo, Justice Benjamin, 159
child with a disability. *See* Individuals with Disabilities Education Act

(IDEA), statutory definition of 'child with a disability,'
civic identity, 60, 77n16
Civil Rights Act of 1964, 2
claim rights, moral rights as examples of, 20–21
Coady, C.A.J., 145
Colker, Ruth, 178
common morality: defined, 135; essential components of, 135–36; grounding in human nature of, 136–37; incompleteness and informality of, 137
community: community of principle, 95; moral ideal of, 87. *See also* inclusive educational community, ideal of
constitutional democratic government, essential elements of, 100–101
cost-benefit comparisons: between education of Group B children and deprived Group A children, 23, 54–56, 168–69. *See also* justice, distributive
Cover, Robert, 23, 146

Davies, Robertson. *See What's Bred in the Bone*
Decatur, Illinois six, 109–10, 120–24
deference, 110–11, 126n9
democratic deliberation: abilities necessary for, 25–26; attitude intrinsic to, 23–25
deprivation: educational deprivation, 28; meaning (general), 28
Dewey, John, 45n12, 87, 101. *See also* community, moral ideal of
discipline and punishment, internal morality of, 115–18
Down syndrome, 59
due process: basic moral justification of, 131–33; statutory rights under the IDEA concerning, 3–4. *See also* internal morality of discipline and punishment
due process hearings. *See* special education due process review system

duties: attached to roles, positions, and statuses, 156; moral rule concerning, 136
Dworkin, Ronald, 160–62, 181n15, 182n22. *See also* community, community of principle
dyslexia, 94

elected legislators: basic responsibilities of apropos K–12 special education, 159–62; defined, 159
eligibility for K–12 special education: IDEA mandated process for determination of, 3. *See also* Individuals with Disabilities Education Act (IDEA), statutory definition of 'child with a disability,'
Endrew F. v. Douglas County S.D. RE 1, 16n14
equal educational respect and concern, principle of, 38; contrasted with ideal of an inclusive educational community, 95–98; responsibilities of school districts apropos, 92–95
equal protection clause (14th Amendment of U.S. Constitution), 4, 76n7
ethics of care, 90
evaluation. *See* eligibility for K–12 special education, IDEA mandated process for determination of
evils, basic evils according to Bernard Gert, 136
expulsions from K–12 public schools. *See* James M. case

fairness. *See* Rawlsian justice as fairness
families. *See* moderate libertarianism, significance of family relationships for
Farkas, George L., 175, 176
Feinberg, Joel, 26, 27
fidelity to the rule of law (judicial duty of): moral justification and limits, 139–42; relationship to moral rule 'Obey the law', 139

free appropriate public education (FAPE), 1, 3, 5. *See also Board of Education of the Hendrik Hudson School District v. Rowley*
Freedman, Miriam Kurtzig, 7, 170
freedom: moral rule regarding deprivation of, 21, 136; of speech, 31. *See also* freedom of choice
freedom of choice: core concept of libertarianism, 34, 71–72; relationship to self-fulfillment, 27, 71–72
Friedman, David, 47
Fugitive Slave Act of 1850, 149
Fuller, Lon L., 116
full inclusion. *See* inclusion, full inclusion contrasted with strong inclusion

general education diploma (GED), 115
Gert, Bernard. *See* common morality
Gettysburg Address, 25
Gewirth, Alan, 22, 23, 28, 40, 70
Goss v. Lopez, 116, 124n2
Group A children: capabilities account basis of right to an appropriate K–12 education for, 32–34; defined, 12; moderate libertarian basis of right to an appropriate K–12 education for, 34–36; Rawlsian justice as fairness basis of right to an appropriate K–12 education for, 31–32; utilitarian basis of right to an appropriate K–12 education for, 29–31
Group B children: capabilities account basis of right to an appropriate K–12 education for, 67–69; defined, 13; moderate libertarian basis of right to an appropriate K–12 education for, 69–72; Rawlsian justice as fairness basis of right to an appropriate K–12 education for, 61–67; utilitarian basis of right to an appropriate K–12 education for, 53–61
Gun-Free Schools Act, 119

Gutmann, Amy, 23

happiness, 29, 30, 37, 53, 59, 67, 133, 172. *See also* utilitarianism
harms. *See* evils, basic evils according to Bernard Gert
Harry, Beth, 174, 175, 176
Hirschman, Albert, 144
Hobbes, Thomas, 136, 151n22
Huckleberry Finn, 138
human dignity. *See* capabilities theory of social justice, core ideas; Kant, Immanuel

IDEA. *See* Individuals with Disabilities Education Act
IEP. *See* individual educational plan
impartiality, 115, 116, 128n21
inclusion: criticisms and responses to criticism of, 7–8, 170–71; full inclusion contrasted with strong inclusion, 86–92. *See also* inclusive educational community, ideal of
inclusive educational community: contrasted with principle of equal educational respect and concern, 95–98; ideal of, 86–92
individual educational plan, 3, 5, 16n4, 58, 59, 164, 165, 180
Individuals with Disabilities Education Act (IDEA): criticisms and responses to criticisms of, 6–9, 167, 168–72; statutory definition of 'child with a disability,' 76n9; summary of key provisions, 3–5
infanticide of infants with severe disabilities. *See* Plato; Singer, Peter
Ingraham v. Wright, 126n10
institutional/organizational dissent. *See* Hirschman, Albert
intellectual disabilities: mild or moderate, 42–43; severe or profound, 43–44. *See also* zero reject policy
internal morality of discipline and punishment, 115–18

Jackson, Jesse, 110, 122
James, William, 181n18
James M. case, 108, 109, 118–20, 143–48
judges: law making role in statutory interpretation, 159–62. *See also* fidelity to the rule of law (judicial duty of)
justice: basic purpose of law according to natural law theory, 134; distributive. *See* equal educational respect and concern, principle of; Rawlsian justice as fairness; discipline and punishment. *See* internal morality of discipline and punishment

K–12 public school administrators. *See* K–12 public school educators
K–12 public school educators: defined, 162; moral responsibilities of, 162–66. *See also* equal educational respect and concern, principle of
K–12 public school teachers. *See* K–12 public school educators
Kant, Immanuel, 61, 62, 64
Kelman, Mark, 6
King Solomon, 140
Kittay, Eva Feder, 68, 91
Klingner, Janette, 174, 175, 176
Kropotkin, Peter, 97

law: duty of obedience to: moral grounding and limits of, 135–39; relationship to morality. *See* legal positivism; natural law theory
least restrictive environment (LRE), 1, 3, 5, 82, 83, 99. *See also* Beth B. v. Van Clay
legal positivism, 134, 135
libertarianism: core ideas of, 29, 47n32; distinction between moderate and radical libertarianism. *See* moderate libertarianism
liberty. *See* freedom

Lincoln, Abraham. *See* Gettysburg Address
Lomasky, Loren. *See* moderate libertarianism

mainstreaming of children with disabilities, 84, 94
manifestation determination, 126–27n12
Maslow, Abraham, 79n47
mediation, 133, 150n8
medical model of disability, 172–73
Mencius, 144
Mill, John Stuart, 27, 29, 40, 53, 104n13, 176. *See also* On Liberty
Mills. *See* Mills v. Board of Education of the District of Columbia
Mills v. Board of Education of the District of Columbia, 4, 66
moderate libertarianism: distinction between moderate and radical libertarianism, 34–35; as moral basis of the right to an appropriate K–12 education for Group A Children, 34–36; as moral basis of the zero reject policy, 69–71; significance of family relationships for, 71–72
Mooney, Jonathan, 8
moral ideals: defined, 136; democratic deliberation: attitude intrinsic to. *See also* inclusive educational community, ideal of
moral reasoning. *See* moral rule violations, decision procedure concerning justified violations
moral responsibilities: understood as morally required role-related duties, 155–56
moral rights: correlativity with moral responsibilities, 155–56. *See also* claim-rights
moral rules. *See* common morality, essential components of
moral rule violations: decision procedure concerning justified violations, 136, 141–42; distinction

between weak and strong justification of, 138; morally relevant features of, 136, 141–42
Morgan, Paul R., 175, 176
Morse v. Frederick, 128n26

Narveson, Jan, 47nn32, 37
natural law theory, 134, 183n57
New Jersey v. T.L.O, 126n10
Nussbaum, Martha. *See* capabilities account of social justice

obedience to law: moral rule concerning. justification of, 135, 139. *See also* presumptive moral force. of the moral rule 'obey the law'
On Liberty, 27, 40
opportunity, 62, 114–15. *See also* deprivation
order, 135, 138, 139

PARC. *See Pennsylvania Assn. for Retarded Children v. Commonwealth of Pennsylvania*
parents of children with disabilities: advocacy role, 167–68; responsibilities of apropos K–12 education of their children; rights under the IDEA, 3, 166
peer buddies (student helper programs), 69
Pennsylvania Assn. for Retarded Children v. Commonwealth of Pennsylvania, 4, 66
permanent vegetative state. *See* zero-reject policy, limits of
Plato, 91, 101
Posner, Richard, 153n50, 160–62, 181n15. *See also* Pragmatism
postmodernism, 101
Pragmatism, 160, 181n18
presumptive moral force: defined: 130; of judicial duty of fidelity to the rule of law, 139–40, 143; of moral rule 'Obey the law, 138–39

proportionality. *See* discipline and punishment, internal morality of
Pugach, Marleen, 180
punishment. *See* school discipline and punishment

racial/ethnic minority discrimination in K–12 special education, 174–76
rationality (rational persons): attitude toward common morality when considered impartially, 137; essential elements of, 137
Rawls, John. *See* Rawlsian justice as fairness
Rawlsian justice as fairness: difference principle, 32, 62; greatest basic liberty principle, 31, 61; as moral basis of right to an appropriate K–12 education for Group A children, 31–32; as moral basis of the zero-reject policy, 61–67; veil of ignorance, 62
response to intervention (RTI), 177–79
restorative justice programs, 113
Rett Syndrome, 81
Rothbard, Murray, 47
Rowley. See Board of Education of the Hendrik Hudson School District v. Rowley
Rowley, Amy, 90, 91
RTI. *See* response to intervention

San Antonio Independent School District v. Rodriquez, 76n10, 78n32
Scalia, Justice Antonin, 160, 161, 181nn15, 17. *See also* textualism
Scanlon, Thomas, 132
school discipline. *See* school discipline and punishment
school discipline and punishment: mandated IDEA requirements apropos children with disabilities, 3–4. *See also* internal morality of discipline and punishment
self-fulfillment: aspiration fulfillment, 26; capacity fulfillment, 26–27;

essential elements of, 23, 26. *See also* appropriate K–12 education
serious emotional disturbance, 76n9, 112, 127n12, 134
significant discrepancy criterion, 177
Silvers, Anita, 104n27
Singer, Peter, 58–61
social identity, 60, 77n16
social model of disability, 172–73
Solomon, Andrew, 132
special education due process review system: brief description of, 3; positions concerning of critics and responses of defenders, 7, 9, 171–72
specific learning disabilities, 76n9, 94, 176–79, 182n37
strong inclusion. *See* inclusion, full inclusion contrasted with strong inclusion
Swan, Joseph, 147

Taney, Roger, 147
textualism, 160
A Theory of Justice, 31, 63. *See also* Rawlsian justice as fairness
Thomas, Justice Clarence, 128n26
Thompson, Dennis, 23
Timothy W. v. Rochester NH School District 875, 4, 49, 66, 68, 72–75
Tolstoy, Leo, 124n2

unhappiness. *See* utilitarianism, criterion of justice
United Nations Declaration of Human Rights, 65
United States Department of Education, 16n1, 178
United States Office of Civil Rights, 133
United States Office of Special Education Programs (OSEP), 178–79
utilitarianism: criterion of justice, 53; as moral basis of right to an appropriate K–12 education for Group A children, 29–31; as moral basis of the zero reject policy, 53–61

Villegas, Tim, 87
violations of moral rules. *See* moral rule violations

What's Bred in the Bone, 56, 57, 58, 72
Worth, Robert, 7

zero reject policy: capabilities account of social justice, as moral basis of; limits of, 72–73; moderate libertarianism, as moral basis of; Rawlsian justice as fairness, as moral basis of; utilitarianism, as moral basis of

About the Author

Robert F. Ladenson served for over twenty years as a special education due process hearing officer adjudicating disputes between parents of children with disabilities and public school districts under federal and state special education laws. He is emeritus professor of philosophy at the Illinois Institute of Technology where he taught and did scholarly work specializing in moral, political, legal, and educational philosophy. He originated and, for fifteen years, was the principal organizer and developer of the Association for Practical and Professional Ethics Intercollegiate Ethics Bowl (APPE-IEB), which is an academic competition in which now more than 150 colleges and universities take part.

www.ingramcontent.com/pod-product-compliance
Lightning Source LLC
Chambersburg PA
CBHW022013300426
44117CB00005B/159